To the front-line social workers who daily stand in harm's
way to protect our children

Contents

Acknowledgements

My thanks are due to Karen Bowler, commissioning editor at The Policy Press, for believing in the potential for this book and to her first-class editorial team. I am much indebted to colleagues at the Centre for Social Work at the University of Nottingham, who have been supportive of my study leave to complete this project during an exceptionally busy period for the Centre. My gratitude also to my mother, Dorcas, who once more took time away from family and friends to correct my rough drafts and offer invaluable advice on improving the initial manuscript. Thanks go to Andrew for, yet again, converting photocopies into electronic files for me. Finally, I wish to express appreciation to my partner Gill for pardoning my absences and creating such scrumptious feasts as to make dining out time misspent.

CHAPTER ONE

Introduction

Aggression and social work internationally

Findings from research conducted not only in the UK, but also in Australia, Canada and the US reveal that social workers generally and child protection social workers particularly are the subject of aggressive behaviour from some service-users and parents. Horejsi et al (1994), surveying child protection social workers in the US, found that 10% of them had experienced physical violence, and 97% of them verbal abuse, from parents or their partners. In another American study conducted by Newhill (2003, p 46) who surveyed over 1,000 qualified practitioners, 24% reported being the victim of a physical assault and 50% had been threatened by a service-user. In a further study by Ringstad (2005) of a similar sample size, 15% of social workers reported being physically attacked, while 62% reported experiencing a psychological assault, such as being shouted at or insulted, by a service-user. In Australia, Koritsas et al (2010) discovered that out of over 200 social workers, 9% had been physically assaulted, 47% threatened and 57% verbally abused. These compare with the higher figures of 18%, 64% and 94% respectively for child protection social workers as surveyed by Stanley and Goddard (2002). In Canada, Macdonald and Sirotich (2001) found that among their sample of almost 200 social workers 88% reported having been verbally harassed, 29% sexually harassed and 64% threatened with physical harm. Conversely, Ringstad's (2005) survey of over 1,000 American social workers revealed that 12% of them had psychologically assaulted a service-user, mainly by shouting at or insulting them or by acting out of spite. Around 4% of practitioners admitted to physically attacking a service-user, usually by grabbing or pushing them. Taken altogether, these research studies indicate that the experience both of being the victim of aggression and of being an aggressor is not particular to British practitioners, whose experiences are the subject of this book, but confront social workers in many different countries.

Failures in practice and training

A series of scandals involving the deaths of children at the hands of their carers have revealed failures to protect children from neglect and abuse. Many of the subsequent public inquiries and serious case reviews exposed the highly conflicted situations in which social workers are expected to discharge their statutory duties and the sometimes intense hostility directed towards them by parents or their partners. The social worker for Richard Fraser, killed by his father in 1977 aged five years old, felt so threatened by the aggressive attitudes of Richard's father and step-mother that she asked to be removed from work with the family (London Borough of Lambeth, 1982, para 62). The commission set up to investigate the circumstances of Kimberley Carlile's death aged four years old, who was murdered by her mother's partner in 1986, concluded that professionals had almost certainly been intimidated by both mother and partner (London Borough of Greenwich, 1987, p 198). Newham Area Child Protection Committee (2002, p 7), when inquiring into the death of Ainlee Labonte aged two years old, described her mother as 'manipulative' and 'aggressive'. The report roundly criticised social work practice, observing that 'the fear with which the family are regarded leads to almost paralysis in terms of action' (2002, p 18).

The public inquiry conducted by Laming (2003) into the death of Victoria Climbié aged eight years old at the hands of Ms Kouao, her great aunt, found that the poor practice of some social workers was exacerbated by the 'difficult' and 'manipulative' behaviour of Ms Kouao. Haringey Local Safeguarding Children Board's (2009) *Serious case review: Baby Peter* into the death of an infant discovered that social workers had been intimidated by the baby's mother and failed to sufficiently challenge her version of events or the standards of care she provided to her children. The serious case review into the events surrounding the starving to death of Khyra Ishaq in May 2008, a child known to Birmingham City's Children's Services, likewise concluded that professionals were intimidated by both Khyra's mother and step-father. Consequently, they failed to insist on interviewing Khyra in the months leading up to her death

Graham Badman, the author of *Serious case review: Baby Peter*, called for 'authoritative social work practice' leading to 'effective challenging of uncooperative or violent clients' (Butler, 2010, p 4). This perspective was endorsed by Ofsted (2010, para 94), which evaluated 150 serious case reviews during the period April 2009–March 2010 and found that 'a recurring theme in the reviews is that there had been insufficient challenge by those involved in the case'. Ofsted (2010, para 94) particularly highlighted the importance of 'not accepting at face value what the parents or others in the family said' and 'questioning by individual professionals and agencies of their own and others' views, decisions and actions'. The Social Work Task Force (2009, p18) concluded that weaknesses in child protection practice reflected deficits in social work training for 'managing conflict and hostility'. Notably, the inquiry into Ainlee's death, reporting in 2002, called for better training for social workers dealing with aggressive parents, while that into the death of Khyra Ishaq made exactly the same recommendation in 2010; indicating that training had improved little during the intervening eight-year period. This conclusion was substantiated by a survey conducted in 2011 of over 600 front-line child protection social workers in which 90% reported that they had received no qualifying training and 49% had received no training at all to deal with hostile and aggressive behaviour by parents or their partners (*Community Care*, 2011a, p 4).

Littlechild (2008, p 671), in his review of the literature on risk and child protection, indicates that a substantial body of research now exists that reveals the degree to which fear of violence from service-users can adversely affect assessment and decision-making in child protection. However, many inquiries also reveal the extent to which the difficulties of working with threatening and abusive caregivers are aggravated by conflict between colleagues and, on occasion, blatant hostility. Wakefield City Council's (2007) inquiry into sexual abuse by foster carers discovered that disagreement between the social work teams responsible for fostering and child protection had impaired the ability of Children's Services to respond effectively to child abuse concerns. Similarly, Laming (2003) discovered multiple conflicts between professionals leading up to Victoria Climbié's death, which are enumerated in Box 1.1.

Box 1.1: The Victoria Climbié inquiry (Laming, 2003)

Laming (2003) discovered the following multiple conflicts between professionals leading up to Victoria Climbié's death:

- arguments between social workers in different teams as to who was responsible for Victoria on her discharge from hospital;
- disagreement between doctors over the cause of Victoria's injuries;
- tensions between medical staff and social workers regarding the risk of harm;
- mutual hostility between the police and social workers;
- grievances of social workers over the standards of supervision provided by team leaders; and
- animosity felt by social workers towards managers who failed to address their concerns.

Inquiries into the deaths or serious abuse of children frequently highlight the inability to effectively address conflict with caregivers, children or colleagues as a major source of child protection failures. Social workers face unique demands created by conflict, hostility and aggression in child protection contexts. These can be pervasive in relationships with colleagues, parents, partners and children alike, as can mutual support, cooperation and partnership. Sometimes, practitioners will have a solid foundation of mutual respect and liking from which to deal with interpersonal conflicts or challenge abusive behaviour directed towards them. At other times, professionals will be working with disobliging or angry people who resent the demands of child protection interventions. Both contexts demand advanced skills to negotiate differences and resolve conflicts.

Using case studies to explore child protection practice

Case studies have played a prominent role in public administration research as it is a widely employed method to examine and improve decision-making in local and central government (McNabb, 2010). Yin (1994, p 13) promoted single-case and multi-case studies as a means of investigating social phenomenon in circumstances where 'the boundaries between phenomenon and context are not clearly evident'. Such case studies interrogate the interactions between individuals in groups, alongside the processes that occur within organisations. Critical case research utilises this approach to focus on situations of crisis within an organisation. Arguably, they are atypical instances as critical cases by definition examine acute and often exceptional situations. However, their usefulness lies in how these extreme instances foreground the underlying dynamics of routine child protection practice. Critical case research can reveal the complex interplay of personal encounters between the practitioner and caregivers, colleagues and front-line managers, shaped by the structures and processes of the organisation and framed by the legal imperatives of safeguarding children.

This book utilises the reports of independent and public inquiries into the severe maltreatment of children by their caregivers, which are commissioned periodically by local and central government. Also examined are a number of serious case reviews conducted by Local Safeguarding Children Boards whenever a child already known to children's services dies or suffers serious injury due to abuse or neglect. These inquiries and serious case reviews are essentially studies of crisis situations and they can assist to investigate how aggression affects social work practice in child protection. McNabb (2010, p 36) insists that 'the primary objective of critical research is to help people change their beliefs and actions as part of a process of helping them become more aware of the unconscious basis for the way they act'. Therefore, the critical case studies comprising this book consider the social and psychological influences operating upon practitioners that impede good practice in the area of child protection and offer guidance on developing their capability. Serious case reviews where parental aggression constituted a prime influence on the practice of social workers were identified, and case studies drawn from this selection to highlight common issues in relation to parental aggression. These recurrent themes were checked against the findings of Brandon et al (2009) and Ofsted (2010) in their biannual analyses of serious case reviews to ensure that they actually reflected common occurrences.

Child protection and safeguarding

The modern child protection system in Britain evolved during the 20th century. For many decades, it focused on protecting children from maltreatment and intervening in families where children were 'at risk of significant harm'. However, the introduction of the Children Act 1989 in England and Wales, together with similar legislation elsewhere in the UK, augmented the categories of children for which social workers held a remit. By the 1990s, government-commissioned reports and government-issued guidance were introducing the concept of 'safeguarding', a term that referred to a much broader agenda (Frost and Parton, 2009, pp 63–4). 'Safeguarding' requires social workers, in cooperation with professionals from other agencies, to prevent impairment to children's health and development alongside the promotion of their welfare. Legislation places duties on a range of agencies to instrument this expanded set of responsibilities. Nevertheless, child protection remains a core activity within this wider professional remit. Indeed, the financial constraints faced by social work agencies over subsequent years have inhibited effective preventive practice with families in need of practical and therapeutic support, as evidenced in this book. Consequently, the interventions of social workers concerned with children's welfare still remain concentrated around abuse or neglect. The inquiries and serious case reviews examined in later chapters focus on the child protection responsibilities of social workers. However, these should be understood within the wider context of 'safeguarding' that frames the activities of social workers and the professionals with whom they collaborate to protect children.

Structure of the book

The rest of this chapter examines evidence regarding the nature and incidence of aggression in child protection social work in the UK. Chapter Two draws extensively on theory and research from the field of social psychology to examine aggression and explain its occurrence. Chapters Three through Nine each explore two case studies derived from either an official inquiry or a serious case review. Theory drawn predominantly, though not exclusively, from the social psychology of aggression is employed to analyse the interactions between individuals and examine decision-making in relation to child protection activities. The challenges faced by practitioners in each of these case studies are highlighted. The social and psychological dynamics encountered by social workers in situations characterised by conflict and aggression are shown to be prevalent in child protection contexts. Finally, each of these chapters considers the common personal inhibitions of many social workers in child protection and sets out guidance to address skills deficits for working with conflict, hostility and aggression.

Throughout, there are various references to social workers, social care workers, practitioners and professionals. Many of the case studies examined involved not only social workers, but also a myriad of workers from other disciplines and agencies. Where comments relate to social workers as well as to unqualified care workers, these are referred to collectively as 'social care workers'. References to 'professionals' include social workers alongside professionally qualified personnel from other disciplines. While the Harvard system is used to indicate in-text references, where information contained in the case studies derives only from the official reports of the related inquiry or serious case review, this has been shorted to denote just page or paragraph numbers.

Tensions in child protection practice

Taken together, the Children Act 1989, the Children (Scotland) Act 1995 and the Children (Northern Ireland) Order 1995 enshrine similar child protection legislation for all the countries of the UK. Each statute requires the state to support parents to bring up children within their home environment and to work in partnership with parents or guardians unless this is inconsistent with safeguarding the child. This overarching principle is reiterated in government-issued policy and practice guidance. Box 1.2 elaborates the principle of partnership-working, which is fundamental to good practice with families, quoting from the Department of Health's (2000) *Framework for the assessment of children in need and their families.* This definition, contained in the English guidance for assessing children's needs, reflects that adopted elsewhere in the UK.

Box 1.2: Principles underpinning assessment of children in need

The Department of Health's (2000, pp 12–13) *Framework for the assessment of children in need and their families* makes a number of explicit statements requiring social workers to develop positive working relationships with family members:

- 'Partnership between the State and the family, in situations where families are in need of assistance in bringing up their children, lies at the heart of child care legislation.'
- 'In the process of what is happening to a child, it will be critical to develop a co-operative working relationship, so that parents or caregivers feel respected and informed, that staff are being open and honest with them, and that they in turn are confident about providing vital information about their child, themselves and their circumstances.'
- 'Developing a working relationship with children and family members will not always be easy to achieve and can be difficult especially when there have been concerns about significant harm to the child. However resistant the family or difficult the circumstances, it remains important to continue to try to find ways of engaging the family in the assessment process.'

Partnership-working is reiterated in the standards of professional proficiency set out in the Health & Care Professions Council's *Standards of proficiency – social workers in England* (HCPC, 2012), which reflects similar codes of conduct for social workers elsewhere in the UK and encapsulate a central practice dilemma. These standards require practitioners to simultaneously: 'respect and uphold the rights, dignity, values and autonomy of every service user and carer'; 'address practices which present a risk to or from service users and carers or others'; and 'maintain the safety of service users, carers and colleagues' (paras 2.7, 2.4 and 15.1, respectively). Achieving this exacting balance pervades child protection work and can magnify the challenges of managing conflict with family members. Consequently, even where social workers are adept at confronting non-compliance or dealing with aggression, they must still act to preserve partnership-working with family members. Such an injunction imposes additional demands upon practitioners already operating in circumstances of considerable complexity and conflict and where children are at constant risk. The requirement to work in partnership with caregivers and children alongside respect for their views, rights and autonomy presents exceptional challenges when they direct abuse or violence at practitioners. Littlechild (2005a, p 72) concludes from his research into violence against child protection social workers that 'the responsibility and stress of trying to balance their own safety, the protection of children and working in partnership with very vulnerable, and sometimes defensive, aggressive and threatening parents, can cause major stress for some workers'.

Incidence of conflict in child protection

Resistance to social work interventions in situations where a child is suspected or known to be *at risk of significant harm* can take a number of forms along a continuum of behaviours. These range from passive non-compliance with agency interventions to threats or acts of physical violence by family members against practitioners. Different family members can engage in a fluctuating assortment of these behaviours at different points during: initial assessment; a child in need assessment; a child protection investigation; the implementation of a child protection plan; or legal proceedings. It is therefore essential to comprehend the nature and incidence of resistant behaviours to social work intervention. Sources offering insight into these dynamics are independent or public inquiries or serious case reviews. It is important to note that these constitute very small numbers, with only around 150 conducted annually, compared to the total number of children subject to a Child Protection Plan, which is currently at around 45,000 each year for the whole of the UK (*Community Care Online*, 2012c).

Brandon et al (2009, p 15) stress that 'a study of serious case reviews is not a study of typical safeguarding practice' as they are concerned with the gravest instances of child abuse or neglect. Even allowing for this proviso, taken together, independent inquiries, public inquires and serious case reviews do nevertheless highlight the challenges confronting social workers in some of the most intractable instances of child maltreatment. Every two years, serious case reviews completed in England are analysed to inform policy and practice in child protection. Brandon et al (2009, pp 3, 112), in their detailed *Biennial analysis of serious case reviews 2005–07*, which centred on a stratified sample of 40 serious case reviews drawn from a total of 189, found that:

> Three quarters of the 40 families did not co-operate with services. Patterns of hostility and lack of compliance included: deliberate deception, disguised compliance and 'telling workers what they want to hear', selective engagement, and sporadic, passive or desultory compliance. Reluctant parental co-operation and multiple moves

meant that many children went off the radar of professionals.... Some of the reviews showed, in retrospect, that apparent co-operation was feigned, and that parents and carers withheld the truth and were not willing or able to protect the child. Each family member may have their own version of the truth and pretence in order to placate a violent partner or conceal substance misuse. This behaviour/way of looking at the world can become habitual.

Brandon et al (2009, p 63) broadly define 'co-operation' as a 'willingness to engage with agencies and persistent help seeking' and 'lack of co-operation' as 'hostility, avoidance of contact, many missed appointments, disguised or partial compliance, and ambivalent or selective co-operation'. The study also provides a taxonomy of cooperation, as detailed in the Box 1.3.

Box 1.3: Taxonomy of child and family cooperation

Brandon et al (2009, p 63) identify five different levels of engagement and cooperation with children's services and aligned agencies involved in child welfare and safeguarding, as follows:

1. *Not cooperative, actively avoiding involvement/hostile* – Refusal to engage with services or actively hostile/violent. Actively avoiding or eluding agencies or moving frequently, going missing. Many or most missed appointments with most services. May include disguised compliance.
2. *Low cooperation* – Reluctance to engage, some missed appointments/generally not good at keeping appointments. May avoid/elude some agencies, not others. May withdraw and disappear (developing into not cooperative).
3. *Neutral/some cooperation* – Take it or leave it view about services, or patchy engagement. Not avoiding or refusing services, but professionals may need to work to engage family. May be passive cooperation.
4. *Cooperation* – Good engagement, keeps all or most appointments, seeks and uses help easily. May self-refer.
5. *Highly cooperative or persistently seeking help* – Pattern of a high level of, possibly, panicky help-seeking from many different agencies. Needing constant reassurance.

Brandon et al (2009, p 64) also caution that:

it was difficult to assign children or their parents to any one of the 5 single categories of cooperation as parents' behaviour was changeable and many often showed different behaviours with different professionals. Also, the child's mother might be cooperative while the father was hostile, or (less often) vice versa.... It is, therefore, *not* helpful to consider the different types of co-operation as a continuum representing increasing or diminishing levels of co-operation … but rather as fluid, overlapping categories which can change very quickly.

At the same time, Brandon et al (2009, p 64) highlight how 'poor co-operation and hostility can be minimised and overlooked' when front-line professionals or their managers fail to analyse emergent patterns of behaviour or sufficiently analyse the dynamics of a situation. While non-cooperation tends to be associated with inherently hostile parents, it can also be a response to poor practice. As Brandon et al (2009, p 64) note, drawing on evidence compiled by HM Treasury and Department for Education and Skills (2007, p 85), parental non-engagement can be due to:

- professionals who provoke hostility with their own behaviour;
- negative experiences of services;
- being in denial about their problems;
- fearing children will be removed if problems are admitted;
- getting no support for non-acute problems; and
- an overwhelming amount of support when problems become so bad that they meet service thresholds.

Brandon et al (2009) clearly highlight non-cooperation by caregivers as a major impediment to safeguarding children. It could be argued that the conclusions of Brandon and her colleagues, which are based on a selection of the gravest instances of child abuse, cannot be generalised to other child protection cases. However, Bell (1999) found that one third of respondents undertaking child protection investigations claimed that they were unable to complete these thoroughly due to non-cooperation by caregivers. This would indicate that non-cooperation by parents and their partners or relatives with assessment or care planning is a major source of conflict between practitioners and caregivers right across the spectrum of child protection cases.

Incidence of aggression against social workers

Based on an analysis of national British Crime Surveys produced by the Home Office, Budd (1999) discovered that social workers are eight times more likely to be physically assaulted than the average employee. In a subsequent analysis of the 2002/03 survey, Upson (2004) estimated that 3.3% of health and social welfare professionals (which includes social workers) had suffered one or more assaults during the past year compared to 2.6% of those in protective services, which comprises prison officers and doormen. These figures illustrate the extent to which social workers are exposed to violence as compared to other occupational groups. More detailed studies focusing specifically on the experiences of social care workers, which includes social workers, have also been conducted. Balloch and McLean (1999) administered questionnaires in England, Scotland and

Table 1.1: Experience of physical attack, threats and verbal abuse during the past year

Category of abuse	Managers	Field social work staff	Home care workers	Residential workers
Physical attack				
England	16%	10%	2%	29%
Scotland	18%	19%	1%	58%
Threats of violence				
England	19%	29%	5%	29%
Scotland	29%	32%	2%	49%
Shouted at/insulted				
England	49%	61%	28%	57%
Scotland	56%	65%	25%	60%
None of the above				
England	44%	36%	72%	38%
Scotland	42%	28%	73%	26%

Source: Reproduced from Pahl (1999, Table 5.3).

Northern Ireland to 2,000 social care workers in community and residential settings, enquiring about their experiences of violence and abuse from users and their relatives. Tables 1.1 and 1.2 set out the key findings.

As revealed by Table 1.1, verbal abuse is the most common form of aggressive behaviour, followed by threats of violence and then actual bodily harm. It is worth noting that about a third of social workers in community and residential settings had not experienced any form of abuse or violence. These figures also indicate that while community-based social workers are less likely to be physically attacked than residential social care workers, they are almost as likely to be verbally abused or threatened with violence. Among field social workers in England who experienced violence or abuse, 30% of these incidents occurred in their offices while 34% took place in the service-user's home (Pahl, 1999, p 95). Usually, it happened during routine tasks, such as interviewing, assessment or giving advice. The survey also found gender differences in the degree of violence or abuse experienced by workers. Table 1.2 indicates that male social care workers, including social workers, are at greater risk of threats or assaults from service-users than are their female counterparts. Accounting for this gendered variation, Pahl (1999, p 98) speculates that this may be attributable to the following reasons: that male workers may be 'more likely to be asked to intervene in potentially dangerous situations'; that 'service users may perceive male staff as more challenging and provocative'; or that 'female members of staff may be more skilled at deflecting and defusing violence'.

Table 1.2: Attacks, threats and abuse against social care staff in the year prior to the survey in England

Type of incident	Percentage of male staff	Percentage of female staff
Physical attack	21%	11%
Threats of violence	30%	16%
Shouted at or insulted	59%	42%

Source: Reproduced from Pahl (1999, Table 5.5)

The findings of Balloch and McLean (1999) are consistent with previous smaller-scale surveys conducted during the 1980s and 1990s (Brockman and McLean, 2000, pp 9–11). These findings are broadly in line with a more recent survey conducted by Unison (2009) of 3,500 local government employees, which included 233 social workers, of whom: 65% reported being verbally abused; 26% experienced physical threats; and 9% endured physical violence, with 0.5% requiring medical treatment. All of these surveys investigated the experiences of social workers in both adults' and children's services. By contrast, *Community Care* (2011a, pp 4–5) published the results of a survey conducted in 2011 of 600 front-line child protection social workers, over 40% of whom had more than 10 years' experience in practice. Key findings from this research are presented in Table 1.3.

Table 1.3: Threats to children's social workers by parents

Type of incident	Percentage of social workers affected
Deal with hostile and intimidating parents every week	50%
Threatened by parent in last six months	61%
Multiple threats over the last six months	77%
Threats to their person	68%
Threats to their family	26%
Threats to make a complaint	77%

Source: Community Care (2011a, pp 4–5).

These figures reveal very high levels of threatening behaviour by parents towards social workers. The vast majority of these consist of parents attempting to threaten practitioners through intimating that they will make a complaint against them. Many others, however, seek to frighten social workers by suggesting that they will be physically assaulted by the parent or another family member. Approximately half of practitioners working in child protection reported that they dealt with hostile and intimidating parents every week. It is not only caregivers who sometimes intimidate social workers. Sinclair and Gibbs (1998) sent questionnaires to around 500 residential care staff and interviewed approximately 200 children in almost 50 children's homes. They found violent behaviour by children prior to admission to residential care, with: 8% persistently violent to other children; 43% occasionally violent to other children; and 40% violent to adults. Once accommodated in residential care, almost half of the children participating in the study reported regular confrontations with social care workers. While a number of inquiries and serious case reviews describe the intimidating behaviour of caregivers and examine its impact on safeguarding activities, few to date have given consideration to the aggression and non-cooperation of children and young people.

Nature of abuse and violence against social workers

The ways in which some parents and other caregivers frighten practitioners bears closer scrutiny. Turning to fieldwork, Littlechild (2005a, 2005b) reports on research conducted with 70 child protection social workers and their managers in one local authority in England, which questioned them about their experiences of aggression and violence from service-users. A key finding of this study was that while incidences of actual violence against field social workers in child protection were comparatively rare, other forms of aggression, such as threats and verbal abuse, were fairly common. Of those reporting experiences of violence or aggression, these included:

- kneed in the body;
- attacked with a knife;
- threatened with violence;
- threats relating to the social worker's family;
- verbally abused;
- set upon by a dog;
- held hostage by user;
- followed by men in a car or on the street;
- the worker's car vandalised;
- telephone calls to social worker's home;
- user stating they knew where the social worker lived; and
- complaints against the worker.

Littlechild (2005a, p 66) emphasises the difference between direct violence, which tended to be one-off incidents, and indirect forms of violence such as threats, which were 'part of a set of dynamics that built up over time'. Indirect violence sometimes came to characterise the relationship between practitioners and users, as opposed to a behaviour occasionally resorted to by a user. A survey of 600 child protection social workers reported by *Community Care* (2011a, p 20) reproduced a number of graphic accounts of extreme forms of intimidation by parents or family members. British social workers recounted incidents in which they: were threatened by dogs; were held at knifepoint; were held hostage in a family home; had had their parked car damaged; had had their car rammed while driving; had received death threats by letter or telephone; and had been surrounded by a hostile crowd. One social worker responding to the *Community Care* (2011a, p 20) survey described the escalating range of abusive behaviour from parents:

> After having applied for care proceedings I had to move out of my home for a period and get safety alarms fitted. I suffered harassment for many months, threats of violence, [parents] taking photos of me and my car and both parents turned up outside my work with a baseball bat and waited by my car in the dark. Fortunately they were stopped by police. They also made numerous complaints about my practice. Although none of them were upheld it was the constant barrage of letters as well as threats of physical harm which affected me.

Practitioners from minority communities are often confronted with additional forms of abusive behaviour. There is evidence to show that social care workers in general, and child protection social workers in particular, from black and minority ethnic communities are regularly subject to racial abuse by some caregivers and children (Littlechild, 2005b, p 394). Managers of child protection social workers responding to interview questions put by Littlechild (2005b, p 394) admitted that racist abuse directed at front-line workers from minority ethnic backgrounds was commonplace. Davey (1999, p 117), in an analysis of the Balloch and McLean (1999) survey of 2,000 social care workers, suggested that black and minority ethnic social care workers were no more likely to be subject to violence or abuse than their white counterparts, but that the nature of abuse by users and their relatives could take a racist form. Davey (1999, p 117) found that 41% of black and Asian workers reported being racially abused by a service-user or their relative within the past year. One in eight of them stated that this happened 'very often' or 'fairly often'. Nearly all of the perpetrators of the abuse were white. These incidents included:

- racist abuse;
- racist swear words;
- insults or comments;
- inappropriately questioning the authority of the worker;
- not wanting to be touched by the worker; and
- requesting a white worker.

Under-reporting of aggression against social workers

The National Task Force on Violence against Social Care Staff (2001, para 1.2) concluded that 'violent incidents are under-reported in social care organisations'. Brockman and McLean (2000, pp 4–6), in their review of the literature on violence and abuse against social care workers, argue that the widespread under-reporting of incidents has concealed the true extent of this problem. While physical violence is often reported, instances of threats or verbal abuse usually are not. This is reflected in the survey of child protection workers conducted by *Community Care* (2011a, p 4), which reported that only 22% of threats made by parents to physically harm them or their families were reported to the police. Brockman and McLean (2000, p 5), drawing on evidence from two decades of research, attribute the low rate of reporting by social care workers to 'lack of management support, fear of an unfavourable response, and the belief that verbal abuse and threats are part of the job'. This unsympathetic work culture commonly leads social workers to blame themselves for violent incidents, which in turn influences their decision not to report it. These findings are echoed in the survey reported by *Community Care* (2011a, pp 4–5), with around 66% of social workers claiming that intimidation by parents was not taken sufficiently seriously either by local or national government. Moreover, 33% stated that when they had been subjected to threats from parents, support from their agency had been 'poor' or 'very poor'. One practitioner's response to the survey question about management support epitomised the perspective of many, stating that 'there is an unspoken expectation that social workers should tolerate aggressive behaviour from service-users and that somehow it is our fault if threats spill over into actual physical violence or if we feel affected by such behaviour' (*Community Care*, 2011a, p 4). In a number of studies, female social care workers and those from minority ethnic backgrounds complain that they are often not taken seriously by management when reporting sexual or racial harassment (Brockman and McLean, 2000, p 5). This is likely to account for the very low reporting of these particular types of abusive behaviours directed at front-line practitioners by children and their carers.

In research undertaken by Littlechild (2005b, p 392), child protection social workers stated that while they were likely to report violent incidents and felt reasonably confident of receiving support from their agency, they were much less likely to report threats or other forms of intimidation. Social workers in the study explained that normally they did not report non-violent incidents because they lacked the tangibility of a physical assault. Front-line practitioners largely attributed this difference to the absence of clear agency procedures or definitions around non-violent aggressive behaviour by parents, partners or children as opposed to physical assault. Paradoxically, the same social workers indicated that they were subject to a much higher incidence of non-violent aggressive behaviour than physical attacks, which they deemed 'comparatively rare'. Although many child protection workers described feeling supported and protected by the agency, this was often attributed to the actions of other front-line colleagues and supervisors, rather than management.

Social workers generally regarded senior managers and councillors as lacking an understanding of the difficulties confronting them in this area (Littlechild, 2005b, p 392). All of the child protection managers participating in the same study agreed that 'violence and aggression' pervaded the work, but admitted that verbal abuse and threats 'were rarely reported or recorded unless clear threats were attached to them' (Littlechild, 2005b, p 394). These managers also admitted that parental aggression meant that there was a 'tension involved in balancing the safety of the worker against the protection of the child in such situations'. Given this background, it is notable that in the survey published by *Community Care* (2011a, p 4), just over half of child protection social workers reported that either they did not know of, or their organisation did not have, protocols for working with hostile and intimidating parents.

The National Task Force on Violence against Social Care Staff (2001, para 9.1) concluded that while residential workers with teenagers experienced the majority of violent incidents, they also had access to the most developed formal support systems. By comparison, social workers who suffered fewer physically aggressive encounters with service-users relied on less adequate formal and informal systems for assistance. Moreover, the National Task Force on Violence against Social Care Staff (2001, para 9.1) opined that 'field workers suffered violence less frequently, but the threat and impact of it can be very severe because they are often alone and a long way from support when it happens and it is often totally unexpected'. Box 1.4 outlines the reasons identified in Macdonald and Sirotich's (2001) Canadian study of social workers as to why they failed to report incidents of aggressive behaviour by service-users. These responses shed more light on the reasons for under-reporting in the UK.

Box 1.4: Reasons for failure to report users' aggressive behaviour

Macdonald and Sirotich (2001) surveyed 171 Canadian social workers and asked them about their reasons for not reporting a violent or threatening incident perpetrated against them by service-users. The following list reveals the different factors that influence many social workers in their decision whether or not to report such an incident to their manager:

- 69% thought the incident was not sufficiently serious;
- 66% perceived violence to be 'part of the job';
- 55% decided that there was nothing to be gained from reporting the incident;
- 45% believed that there would be negative consequences for the user;
- 31% thought that it might appear as if they could not cope in the job;
- 24% were convinced that their employing agency would be unsupportive; and
- 14% believed that they would be blamed for the incident.

Macdonald and Sirotich (2001) surmised that the under-reporting of aggressive behaviour perpetrated by service-users against practitioners was due to 'the professional socialisation of social workers'. This emphasises person-centredness and views users as essentially disadvantaged people whose difficulties will be yet greater if their aggressive behaviour is officially reported.

Conflict and aggression in the workplace

The behaviour by some parents, partners and children is not the only source of aggression towards social workers. While it is highly unlikely that a manager or fellow worker would physically attack a front-line worker, colleagues can express aggression in much more subtle ways, which can cause considerable distress. Staff dealing routinely with child abuse in a context of budgetary constraint, high media attention and a blame culture can experience high levels of stress, which in turn can have an impact on their own relationships with one another. Low tolerance thresholds due to chronic stress, combined with elevated levels of anxiety in an area of great complexity and uncertainty, can increase the incidences of conflict: among fieldworkers; between front-line staff and their managers; and between social workers and professionals in other agencies.

Conflicts, particularly in situations of unequal power between management and workers, or between colleagues of different seniority, can take the form of bullying. The Trades Union Congress (TUC, 2007), which draws on empirical research from several large-scale surveys of workers across occupational groups, reveals that 10% had been bullied at work within the previous six-month period, rising to 25% within the last five years. The TUC (2007) has produced a list of behaviours associated with workplace bullying:

- competent staff being constantly criticised, having responsibilities removed or being given trivial tasks to do;
- shouting at staff;
- persistently picking on people in front of others or in private;
- blocking promotion;
- regularly and deliberately ignoring or excluding individuals from work activities;
- setting a person up to fail by overloading them with work or setting impossible deadlines;
- consistently attacking a member of staff in terms of their professional or personal standing; and
- regularly making the same person the butt of jokes.

Aside from incidents of discrimination by colleagues or managers, an increasing number of social care workers experience some form of bullying, which tends to be more pronounced in circumstances of funding shortfalls or service cutbacks (*Community Care*, 2011b, p 13). Bullying by a colleague or manager for purely personal reasons happens to a significant number of staff, with detrimental consequences for them in terms of their health and working relationships. Unison (2002, pp 2–3) defines bullying as 'offensive, intimidating malicious, insulting or humiliating behaviour, abuse of power or authority which attempts to undermine an individual or group of employees and which may cause them to suffer stress'. According to Unison (2002, p 3), bullying can take a number of different forms:

- withholding information that can affect the worker's performance;
- ignoring views and opinions;
- setting unreasonable/impossible deadlines;
- setting unmanageable workloads;
- humiliating staff in front of others; and
- being shouted at or being the target of spontaneous rage.

For any of these occurrences to constitute bullying, the behaviour on the part of a colleague or manager must be persistent over a period of time. A single incident or occasional incidents, while distressing, do not constitute bullying. However, if such incidents are sufficiently serious, a front-line social worker may well wish to pursue a complaint against the offending member of staff. Nevertheless, the first resort should always be to negotiate a dispute rather than prematurely resorting to rights-based threats or complaints procedures.

Health impacts on social workers

Studies conducted by Smith and Nursten (1998) and Pahl (1999) both indicate that violence and threats of violence to social workers generally, but those in child protection more particularly, are a major cause of work-related stress. Littlechild (2005a, p 71) identified the effects on child protection social workers of violent and non-violent behaviour towards them by users. These included feelings of: shock; anxiety; fear; anger towards the user; depression; and physical pain. In turn, this resulted in social workers being: exceptionally wary of the user; reluctant to make home visits; and an undermining of confidence in their own professional abilities. Many practitioners admitted that their experience of aggression by caregivers had detrimentally affected their practice with the family involved. Around 50% of child protection social workers responding to the questionnaire administered by *Community Care* (2011a, p 4) described detrimental impacts on their health, which included 'an inability to sleep, panic attacks, fears about the safety of their own children, lack of self-confidence, mental exhaustion and fears they were taking the stress and anxiety it caused them out on other family members at home'. A number of practitioners gave personal accounts of the impact on their lives of working with intimidating parents, some of which are reproduced here:

> I often dream about them at night and I cannot switch off when I get home. I'm worried when out in the local area with my own family in case I bump into some of these families. I worry about picking up the telephone at work, because I always expect it to be hostile parents.

> Most of the time I can handle the situation. When other situations are arising with my other cases I feel overloaded and less able to remain unaffected by the hostility.

> It raises anxiety about doing simple things such as home visits, core group meetings and making phone calls.

> Felt undermined, scared of repercussions, powerless and bullied into not being able to speak openly with the parent about my concerns for his children and that he was emotionally abusing and intimidating them.

In addition to the adverse effects on practice, the National Task Force on Violence against Social Care Staff (National Task Force, 2001, para 5.4) directly links incidences of violence to:

- lost working days due to illness caused by injury or stress;
- increased staff turnover;
- individuals or organisations paralysed by fear; and
- damage to buildings and furnishings.

In terms of bullying by colleagues and managers in the workplace, the TUC (2011) identified this as a factor in work-related stress. Significantly, the Health and Safety Executive (2011, p 16) revealed that over 2.5% of health care professionals and social workers reported work-related illnesses during the previous 12-month period compared to a national average for all employees in Britain of 1.75%. Indeed, it is higher than the reported illness rates of around 1.75% for employees in the education, construction, manufacturing and business sectors. Lloyd et al (2002), in their literature review, concluded that social workers tend to experience higher levels of work-related stress than comparable occupational groups. Employers plainly have a vested interest in securing the safety of social workers and preserving their health if they are to retain their workforce and enable workers to achieve good practice. But employers also have wide-ranging legal responsibilities to look after their social care staff.

Protecting social workers from aggression

In Britain, the health and safety of social workers, whether in residential, day care or fieldwork settings, is protected by the Health and Safety at Work etc Act 1974, which places legal duties on all employers towards their employees. These duties are elaborated in the Health and Safety Executive's (2000) 'Approved code of practice and guidance', which provides practical instruction to employers on assessing the dangers posed to the health and safety of their employees and obliges them to design procedures and practices that prevent or reduce these risks. Under the common law duty of care, employers must also avoid acts or omissions that they could reasonably have foreseen would cause harm to an employee. In addition to the protections afforded by statute and common law, in England the Social Work Reform Board's *Standards for employers of social workers in England and supervision framework* (SWRB, 2011) further specifies the obligations of employers towards social care staff. Section Four of the standards for employers deals specifically with dangerous behaviour and is reproduced in Box 1.5.

> **Box 1.5: *Standards for employers of social workers in England and supervison framework* (SWRB, 2011)**
>
> The standards place responsibility on employers as follows:
>
> - A social worker's working environment, resources and access to practical tools and support should be designed to deliver safe and effective personal practice. Employers should meet the safety and welfare needs of social workers.
> - Make a quiet space available for formal supervision, informal confidential professional discussions between colleagues, and team meetings. There should be a suitable space for confidential interviews and adequate safety measures to protect practitioners.

- Foster a culture of openness and equality in the organisation that empowers social workers to make appropriate professional judgements within a supportive environment.
- Enable social workers and managers to raise concerns about inadequate resources, operational difficulties, workload issues or their own skills and capacity for work without fear of recrimination.
- Have in place effective systems for reporting and responding to concerns raised by social workers and managers so that risks are assessed and preventative and protective measures are taken.
- Ensure that the risks of violence, harassment and bullying are assessed, minimised and prevented. Where such instances do occur, there should be clear procedures in place to address, monitor and review the situation.

Similar provisions are contained in codes of practice for employers of social workers elsewhere in the UK. Yet, despite legal protections and codes of practice, the evidence from surveys dating back to the 1980s reveals relatively high levels of aggression directed at social workers. Evidence derived from inquiries and serious case reviews presented in this book also indicate inadequate policies, procedures and precautions instituted by employers, or where satisfactory ones do exist, they are ineffectively implemented by front-line managers. Consequently, many child protection social workers have felt professionally unsupported when confronted by hostility and aggression from parents, their partners or children. As both the research and critical case studies testify, practitioners themselves have sometimes been reluctant to seek the advice and support they need when faced with uncooperative and aggressive behaviour by caregivers. In a profession that prides itself on therapeutic encounter, practical assistance and partnership-working, acknowledging the excessive aggression directed at social workers and the detrimental impact it has upon their practice challenges orthodox notions of social work. Training on how to manage the hostility of people reluctant to engage with children's social care services (also referred to as involuntary clients) is focused on the use of empathy, transparency, contracting, problem-solving and role-modelling by the practitioner to the exclusion of a well-grounded theoretical knowledge of aggression and the acquisition of a wider repertoire of skills.

Points for practice

- Public inquiries and serious case reviews reveal conflicts between professionals that can exacerbate those between social workers and parents or guardians.
- Research indicates that child protection social workers are confronted by non-cooperation and hostility from a number of parents, which can escalate into aggressive behaviour.
- The requirement to work in partnership with parents to protect their children while also managing hostile or aggressive behaviour can cause stress to social workers and make additional professional demands upon them.

- Social workers may be faced with a range of intimidating behaviours by parents or other family members, which are most likely to occur in the practitioner's office or the family's home.
- All employers are subject to legal requirements to ensure the health and safety of their workforce, which includes employers of social workers whether in the public or independent sectors.

CHAPTER TWO

Theories of conflict and aggression

Theory for conflict and aggression

Disputes with colleagues, managers, parents and children are inevitable in child protection work, which involves differences of opinion over professional judgements and the interference in family life. Sometimes, these disputes are characterised by verbally abusive, threatening or occasionally violent behaviour. Definitions of conflict and aggression, together with the theories that explain these social phenomena, provide vital insights into how interpersonal encounters arouse hostility, ignite anger and, ultimately, produce aggressive behaviour. Comprehending the roots of aggression, its triggers and the personal factors that inhibit or enhance its expression enables practitioners to examine their own aggressive predispositions as well as guiding their management of other people's aggressive behaviour. This chapter commences with key definitions before detailing theories that explain the causes of anger, belligerence and, sometimes, violent behaviour.

Definition of conflict

There are various definitions of conflict, which, according to Kool (2008, p 137), coalesce around a set of four key characteristics:

* Conflicts consist of opposing interests between individuals, which are perceived to be mutually exclusive.
* The individuals concerned are aware of these opposing interests.
* Each person believes that others involved in the conflict aim to thwart his or her interests.
* Conflict arises from past and present interactions.

Sell (2011, p 57) claims that 'most human conflicts of interest do not involve tangible material resources but instead involve conflicts over course of action (retrospective and prospective), exchanges of information, social alliances, and other abstract cost–benefit tradeoffs between individuals'. Isenhart and Spangle (2000, pp 14–5) attempt to capture the various sources of conflict, which are enumerated in Box 2.1.

Box 2.1: Sources of conflict

- *Data* – People may disagree over the best sources of information, its reliability or interpretation.
- *Interests* – Different people's wants or perceived needs may result in disputes with others.
- *Procedures* – People may disagree over how to resolve a problem or make a decision, they may believe that the process is unfair or unclear.
- *Values* – People may have differences of opinion over what is important or should be prioritised.
- *Relationships* – People may lack trust in one another or feel that they are not respected or listened to, resulting in non-cooperation with each other.
- *Roles* – There may be differences of view between people as to the expectations of different social or professional roles.
- *Communication* – Failure to share information, misinterpretation of verbal or non-verbal communication, or differences of opinion as to what has been said or its meaning often cause conflict.

Carpenter and Kennedy (1988) describe a *conflict spiral*, comprising sequential sets of interactions that move from initial disagreement, through increasing levels of escalation, towards intractability. However, Carpenter and Kennedy (1988, p 17) are quick to point out that 'the lesson of the conflict spiral is not that the progress is inevitable but that it is predictable when nothing is done to manage the conflict'. The conflict spiral is described as follows:

1. Problem emerges.
2. Sides form as controversy grows.
3. Positions harden as parties become narrower and more rigid in their perspectives.
4. Communication stops and parties become adversarial.
5. Conflict goes outside of the immediate context as parties look for support and power.
6. Perceptions become distorted and parties lose objectivity.
7. A sense of crisis emerges as community divides into factions and coalitions.
8. Uncertainty arises about outcomes as options for parties become fewer.

Conventional wisdom suggests that conflict is generally detrimental to those involved and often dysfunctional in child protection work, for example, when professionals from different disciplinary backgrounds disagree with each other at a strategy meeting on the gravity of the risk to a child. This can be especially so if such controversies then pull in colleagues or managers from outside the strategy meeting, as suggested by the conflict spiral. Box 2.2 enumerates the commonly recognised harmful effects of interpersonal conflict.

Box 2.2: Detrimental impacts of interpersonal conflict

Lewicki et al (2010, p 19) examined the literature to identify the detrimental effects that are usually associated with conflict. These are quoted as follows:

Competitive, win–lose goals – Parties compete against each other because they believe that their interdependence is such that goals are in opposition and both cannot simultaneously achieve their objectives.

Misperception and bias – As conflict intensifies, perceptions become distorted. People come to view things consistently with their own perspective of the conflict. Hence they tend to interpret people and events as being either with them or against them.

Emotionality – Conflicts tend to become emotionally charged as the parties become anxious, irritated, annoyed, angry, or frustrated. Emotions overwhelm clear thinking, and the parties may become increasingly irrational as the conflict escalates.

Decreased communication – Productive communication declines with conflict. Parties communicate less with those who disagree with them and more with those who agree.

Blurred issues – The central issues in the dispute become blurred and less well defined. Generalizations abound. The conflict becomes a vortex that sucks in unrelated issues and innocent bystanders.

Rigid communications – The parties become locked into positions. As the other side challenges them, parties become more committed to their points of view and less willing to back down from them for fear of losing face and looking foolish.

Magnified differences, minimized similarities – Factors that distinguish and separate [the parties] from each other become highlighted and emphasized, while similarities that they share become oversimplified and minimized.

Escalation of the conflict – As the conflict progresses, each side becomes more entrenched in its own view, less tolerant and accepting of the other, more defensive and less communicative, and more emotional.

While acknowledging the potentially damaging consequences of conflict, Lewicki et al (2010, p 20) also argue that it can be highly productive when people engage in negotiation to resolve conflict. This process can: improve problem-solving skills; increase adaptation; highlight strengths; promote self-awareness; increase awareness of others; enhance personal development; energise; and act as a stimulus for new approaches. However, the beneficial aspects of conflict are dependent on the willingness of those involved to enter into meaningful negotiation with each other to address the dispute. This, of course, is not always the case and the conflict may escalate, resulting in those at loggerheads resorting to ever more excessive means in order to achieve their goals.

Definition of aggression

Based on earlier work by social psychologists, Geen (2001, p 2) argues that any definition of aggression must include a recognition that the aggressor intends to harm another person in some way. This conceptualisation of aggression excludes the notion that the injury caused to another individual is somehow accidental or, indeed, that the other person wants the harm done to them as a result of aggressive behaviour. In order to capture these elements of aggression, Geen (2001, p 3) formulates a broad definition: 'Aggression is the delivery of an aversive stimulus from one person to another, with intent to harm and with an expectation of causing such harm, when the other person is motivated to escape or avoid the stimulus'.

This definition has the advantage of moving beyond conventional lay ideas about aggression, which tend to concentrate on overt acts of violence. Instead, Geen (2001, p 3) suggests that aggression encompasses a range of conduct through which one person seeks to harm another. Underwood (2003) identifies four distinctive types of aggression: physical aggression; property damage; verbal aggression (including threats of violence); and social aggression (including spreading rumours and manipulating or directly damaging relationships). Hence, a variety of behaviours can be categorised as forms of aggression, including:

- physical assault;
- threats of assault;
- the destruction of property;
- intimidation;
- harassment;

- shouting;
- insults;
- malicious gossip; and
- social snubs.

People engage in these types of behaviours for many different reasons and to gain an assortment of advantages, but the main motivations behind aggression can be divided into two groupings. The first concerns what is commonly termed *reactive aggression*. This is behaviour caused by some form of provocation, for example, a threat, an insult or a direct physical attack by another person. The aggressive behaviour is essentially a reaction to someone else's aggression and is usually attended by anger. For this reason, *reactive aggression* is also referred to as *affective aggression*. It is retaliatory in nature, but there can be considerable delay between the act of *reactive aggression* and the original behaviour that provoked it. Rather than reacting immediately to a provocation, an aggressor may 'hold a grudge' and await an opportune moment to retaliate against the person who has harmed the aggressor in the first instance. It is also important to note that defining aggression in this way means that acts of self-defence in the face of aggressive behaviour can themselves constitute acts of *reactive aggression*. This has clear implications for social workers reacting to aggressive behaviour by colleagues, caregivers or children, which will be explored later.

Conversely, *proactive aggression* is a form of unprovoked aggression. It is often not associated with or driven by anger and is simply a means of gaining sought-after benefits. The aggressive child in school may seek increased social status through bullying a fellow pupil or a coveted mobile phone through threatening another child with physical injury. Since *proactive aggression* is a means of obtaining a desired end for the aggressor, it is also described in the social psychology literature as *instrumental aggression*. *Proactive aggression* can also be used to achieve coercive power over someone else. For instance, if a front-line manager uses the threat of redundancy to pressure a social worker into accepting yet more cases despite an already high workload, this constitutes a form of *proactive aggression*. However, the distinction between *reactive* and *proactive* aggression is often indiscernible. In situations of domestic violence, an abusive male partner may physically assault a mother or her child to gain power over them, but also due to some perceived provocation by them. Similarly, caregivers confronted by practitioners intervening in their lives to safeguard children may simultaneously react aggressively against what they view as unwarranted intrusion while engaging in *proactive aggression* to gain other services such as rehousing.

Passive-aggressive behaviour

Geen's (2001, p 3) definition of aggression captures a broad range of verbal and physical acts intended to cause harm to others. This definition is unsatisfactory in relation to a group of behaviours that are not overtly aggressive, but which nevertheless are expressions of anger, umbrage or resentment and are often designed to obstruct the actions or goals of another person. Conduct of this nature is referred to as *passive-aggressive* behaviour. For example, a mother who resents a child protection plan stipulation to attend a parenting programme to improve her ability to set boundaries for an under-age daughter engaging in unprotected sex with multiple partners may not openly express her outrage at being required to attend, but may instead consistently join the sessions halfway through. In doing so, she will effectively sabotage the utility of the parenting programme.

Research into *passive-aggressive* behaviour indicates that where it has become a character trait, this probably derives from a childhood distinguished by caregivers who imposed punitive punishments for: expressions of anger; failure to submit to instruction; or efforts by the child to assert autonomy. The culmination of this is a heightened sensitivity to interpersonal dynamics of power and control during childhood and into later life (Benjamin, 1993). In adulthood such an individual tends to become preoccupied by power relationships and control by others. They can experience themselves as vulnerable to control by others and perceive reasonable requests as interfering demands. Because that adult suffered disproportionate punishment for expressions of anger or autonomy during childhood, he or she has learnt to articulate anger and autonomy in a muted form that does not attract notice or penalty. Indeed, so subtle may be the expression of aggression that it is virtually indiscernible as antagonism.

Accounting for *passive-aggressive* behaviour in adulthood, psychologists agree that it 'results from a disruption in learning how to navigate hierarchical relationships during childhood. This disruption leads to ineffective self-assertion and, thereby, negativistic mood states and cognitions' (Hopwood et al, 2009, p 257). Consequently, people whose conduct is characterised by passive-aggressive behaviour often also suffer from depression. Other indications of *passive-aggressive* tendencies are persistently 'feeling underappreciated, resenting others, complaining of misfortune, and alternating between defiance and obedience' (Hopwood et al, 2009, p 263). Such behaviour as 'purposefully ineffective work, unjustified protests, avoiding obligations by forgetting, believing that the person does a better job than is objectively being done, resenting suggestions for improvement, and obstructing others' efforts' have also been associated with *passive-aggressive* traits (Hopwood et al, 2009, p 263).

While some individuals may be predisposed to react in *passive-aggressive* ways in order to resist the expectations, requests or demands of others, engagement in this type of behaviour is highly context-dependent. This means that it is the situation rather than someone's personality that is most influential in eliciting *passive-aggressive* responses. To illustrate, as part of a child protection plan, a social worker supervises a father's attendance with his son at a series of speech therapist appointments. The father exhibits *passive-aggressive* behaviour by not objecting to the imposition of regular attendance with the speech therapist, but missing many appointments without any substantive reason. This could be attributable to the fact that the social worker actually is controlling, because protecting the child from harm necessarily involves instructing the father (ie situational), or it could be due to the father's long-standing antagonism to any form of external control (ie personality). This distinction between situational factors and personality traits can be important if practitioners are to develop effective strategies to protect children with a caregiver exhibiting *passive-aggressive* behaviours.

Likewise, social work colleagues, front-line managers and professionals from other agencies can also engage in *passive-aggressive* behaviours when, for example, they resent instruction from a line manager or case conference to perform a specified task. Within the workplace, *passive-aggressive* conduct may be acted out through: repeated non-attendance by the same professionals at multi-agency meetings; persistent late arrival for work; non-performance of a designated professional task; or excessive argumentation with colleagues and managers over task performance. Crucially, *passive-aggressive* responses are characterised by repetition of the same or similar behaviour, as opposed to occasional episodes of, for instance, non-attendance, lateness or argumentativeness. It is also possible that colleagues, like caregivers or, indeed, children, may not themselves be entirely aware of the *passive-aggressive* nature of their behaviour. In short, social workers, like caregivers or children, can resist aspects of control by others, even when that control may be exercised by a legitimate authority and in a manner that is both reasonable and appropriate.

Biology and aggression

While the earlier definitions assist to identify the phenomenon of aggression, they fail to explain why some people confronted by provocative behaviour react aggressively and others do not. Nor do they offer insights as to why some individuals engage in violence rather than other less destructive forms of aggression. Research in the fields of biology, neurology and social psychology have produced equivocal findings, which indicate that while genetic, hormonal and neurological factors are implicated in aggressive behaviour, they are interdependent with situational ones (Geen, 2001, pp 8–16). Consequently, the causal antecedents of a person's aggression are difficult to trace back to biological variables because the occurrence of aggression is so intricately bound up with the social situation in which the aggressive act takes place. In other words, even when a person is predisposed to behave aggressively, it is ultimately the factors in a social situation that elicit the aggressive act. This has led social psychologists such as Bandura (1983) to argue that while an individual's physiology may predispose them towards aggression (eg higher levels of the hormone testosterone and lower levels of the neurotransmitter serotonin are correlated with increased aggression), this is only latent. Whether a person actually behaves aggressively also depends on the social influences to which he or she has been subject over their lifetime, but most particularly during childhood.

Social learning theory and aggression

Social learning theory developed by Bandura (Bandura et al, 1963; Bandura, 1983) postulates that individuals learn behaviours through observing those of others, particularly parents or caregivers, but also peers, during childhood and adolescence. This type of social learning is known as *modelling*. Thus, a child who grows up witnessing his father hitting his mother is more likely to acquire aggressive responses to social situations than a child not exposed to domestic violence. This is because the child assimilates what he or she sees into a set of basic rules about conduct, whereby a 'repertoire of aggressive behaviours is built' (Geen, 2001, p 17). Such behaviours are maintained and reinforced through a system of rewards and punishments, referred to as *instrumental conditioning* and based on behavioural theory. Therefore, if a young person observes a peer achieving greater social status (reward) as a consequence of assaulting another youth, then this behaviour may become part of that young person's repertoire. Such acts of aggression will be reinforced if that young person on assaulting others also gains social status and coercive power. Conversely, were the same young person to experience hostility from peers or adults for assaulting another child, this would constitute social punishment and lead to the extinction of aggression in this form. Ultimately, the more successful the witnessed aggressive act appears to be at attaining rewards, the more likely it will be adopted by the observer.

According to Bandura (1983), the form that aggressive behaviour takes, its occurrence and the sorts of social situations that evoke it are learned responses, not innate biological reactions. Therefore, the aggressive behaviour that social workers encounter from caregivers or children is a product of their previous experiences of aggression, as witnesses, perpetrators or victims of aggression. The social processes of *modelling* and *instrumental learning* culminate in the acquisition of *aggressive scripts*. These scripts are generalised cognitive schemata that guide the performance of aggressive behaviour. They comprise a set of normative beliefs about when to engage in aggressive acts. A father exposed to domestic violence as a child may have developed an *aggressive script* that endorses shouting at and insulting a woman during a conflict, but not a man. Hence, a female social worker is more likely to be exposed to this kind of verbal aggression by that particular father compared to her male counterpart.

Social learning is also implicated in the development of pro-social skills, which children hone in peer relationships as they grow older. Although research is limited, it does indicate that children who utilise pro-social coping skills are less reliant on aggressive strategies in dealing with conflict and challenge (Wright and Craig, 2010, p 50). Dumas et al (1994, p 349) concluded that 'children who cope pro-socially tend to use information exchange, behaviour management, and problem solving'. On the other hand, 'aggressive children had a more limited repertoire of communication skills, were less able to communicate effectively, and were more likely to engage in disruptive communication' (Wright and Craig, 2010, p 50). They also relied on 'overt and covert aggression and on blaming others' (Dumas et al, 1994, p 349). This theoretical perspective, known as the *Skills Deficiency Model*, construes aggression as a skills deficit that develops in childhood and can become entrenched over the individual's lifespan.

The *Skills Deficiency Model* has a number of practice implications. If children, or caregivers when they were children, did not acquire sufficient opportunity to develop skills in problem management and information exchange, then they are more likely to resort to aggressive strategies as the only means of dealing with perceived provocation. Likewise, some practitioners may also have skills deficiencies derived from early life experiences and may be unable to engage effectively in constructive argumentation with caregivers or children. As a result, the social workers might turn to covert aggressive strategies such as labelling parents as non-compliant and jeopardising their working relationship with other professionals, rather than explicitly challenging caregivers' or children's problematic attitudes or behaviour. To take another example, within the office environment, a social worker may encounter a team leader who relies on verbal aggression rather than measured discussion to push through his or her decisions, due to skills deficits in managing disputes deriving from their childhood experiences.

Engaging in aggression also depends on how the social situation is interpreted by an individual. Behaviour that constitutes a provocation for one person does not necessarily do so for another. One front-line social worker may interpret the advice of their supervisor as helpful, while another perceives it to be a criticism of their professional judgement and based on personal dislike. The first social worker is unlikely to take offence as they detect no hostile intent on the part of the supervisor, while the second practitioner does and will consequently feel attacked. Interpretation of a social situation necessitates observing and synthesising verbal and non-verbal cues to give it social meaning. During childhood and adolescence, each person develops a characteristic way of taking in and interpreting their social world. Aggressive individuals may process social information quite differently from those who are usually non-aggressive. Typically, aggressive individuals tend to interpret other people's behaviour as being motivated by hostile intentions even when most other observers would describe such behaviour as non-aggressive or ambiguous. Someone who commonly ascribes malevolent intent to others will assume he or she is being attacked and respond aggressively in turn. This characteristic form of *social information processing*, which often ignores the conciliatory verbal and non-verbal cues in a social situation, is referred to as *hostile attribution bias* (Geen, 2001; Krahé, 2001). This attribution bias can be exacerbated by anger, which 'tends to disrupt and disorganise cognitive processes' as angry people are apt 'to simplify information processing and to make judgements that are more black and white' than those who are composed (Tedeschi and Nesler, 1993, p 29).

Social workers may be confronted with angry parents or children who, because of their own childhood experiences of maltreatment, actually have difficulty perceiving the genuinely non-hostile actions of professionals. However, practitioners must be careful not to use the notion of *hostile attribution bias* as a pretext for ignoring the justified fear and resentment that family members often express when faced with unwanted social work interventions. Poor professional practice, limited provision or substandard services can provoke annoyance leading to aggressive responses by caregivers and children alike. Indeed, social workers are no more immune from developing *hostile attribution biases* than are those they seek to help. Colleagues, be they managers, supervisors or front-line workers, can also enact *aggressive scripts* derived from their own experiences of poor parenting or discrimination during adolescence and in later life. Practitioners can be equally guilty of ascribing malicious intent to the confusing behaviour of family members. A practitioner's aggressive response to a parent or child may take the form of increased intervention or denial of service. Equally, the inappropriate use of authority can be used to disguise essentially aggressive reactions to practice situations. For this reason, social workers need to be alert to their own motivations for a safeguarding decision. In summary, the *perception* of being attacked either physically, verbally or non-verbally (eg a threatening posture) constitutes the prime motivator for aggressive behaviour.

Violation of social norms

In every society and situation there are social expectations as to how different people should behave. The failure of some individuals to comply with these expectations can lead to aggressive reprisal by others. Inadvertent norm violation may be forgiven where the offender apologises. Conversely, intended norm violations are likely to attract retaliatory responses by others. For instance, a teenage girl who shouts at a teacher during a lesson attended by other pupils is most probably perpetrating a deliberate act of provocation. It is therefore a calculated violation of the norms that regulate behaviour in a classroom context. What is perceived to be an aggressive act is understood as being so in the light of social norms. To take another example, boys engaging in horseplay are likely to think that pushing and shoving is acceptable. But if one boy uses excessive physical force, he will be deemed to be aggressive. This is because he is overstepping the normative boundaries concerning physical contact in this social context.

Different communities within society can be subject to distinct cultural influences or a mix of influences from diverse sources due to multiculturalism or the impact of global mass media. Nicotera and Robinson (2010, p 114), in their overview of the literature on this topic, concluded that 'cultural factors very likely mediate or moderate the relationship between aggressive predispositions and aggressive behaviour'. However, they refuted the popularly held notion that some cultures are more passive or aggressive than others, an assumption not supported by the research evidence. In other words, culture is just one variable among many others that influences understandings of social norms, what constitutes their violation and what counts as an acceptable response to a contravention. Organisations and informal social groups can also establish their own culture in terms of important values, cherished goals and norms of behaviour. These can range from fairly straightforward conventions about time-keeping to more rigorous demands of conformity to a rigid set of behavioural expectations. Those of a higher status or possessing more power within an organisation or group may well be able to defy its norms without incurring any penalty. Conversely, less powerful individuals in the organisation or group are likely to be subject to sanctions designed to enforce their compliance with social norms.

Specific social situations are also affected by the differing expectations of the individuals who are a party to them. To elaborate on the earlier example, if the boys engaging in horseplay have different cultural heritages, or are simply from diverse family backgrounds, they may hold divergent norms regarding the use of physical force in this social context. Consequently, one boy can assume that there has been a violation of the norm based on the family and peer influences on his own development, while another boy perceives no norm violation. Plainly, this sort of misunderstanding has considerable potential for cycles of aggression and retaliation, as individuals misinterpret one another's motives in social situations. Arguably, a grosser violation of social norms occurs when social workers intervene in families, with parents taking exception to interference in their normative rights as parents to bring up their children as they choose. The perception of norm violation in the social contexts created by safeguarding can be a contributory factor in aggression against social workers by caregivers and children alike.

Frustration–aggression hypothesis

While either experiencing an attack or believing that one is about to take place are the main sources of aggression, frustration is also widely implicated in acts of aggression. Frustration can be defined as the interruption of an 'effortless flow of activity' or the 'blocking of progress towards a goal' (Geen, 2001, pp 22, 26). Dollard et al (1939) were the first to postulate that frustration could lead to aggressive behaviour. Since then, a number of studies in social psychology have revealed that frustration can result from a variety of sources, as listed by Geen (2001, p 22):

- disappointment;
- irritation at punitive intervention;
- annoyance;
- helplessness; and
- curtailment of freedom.

This is a very broad definition of frustration and, consequently, an exceedingly wide range of events can frustrate goal-directed activity. This is as true of practitioners as it is of parents or children. Everyone is subject to some degree of frustration in their daily lives, yet not everyone reacts aggressively to the obstruction of their activity. Therefore, frustration is not a direct cause of aggression, but a contributory factor. A person who experiences numerous frustrations in the course of a day, or cumulatively over a period of time, is more likely to engage in an aggressive response as a result. For example, a social worker who has been passed over for promotion to senior practitioner earlier in the year, has been denied a place on a three-day training course they wanted to attend that week and has spent the morning driving round three different addresses to find no one answering the door is plainly enduring an expanding set of disappointments. These have the potential to culminate in an aggressive response to yet another source of frustration, be it from a caregiver, child or colleague.

Turning to the backgrounds of families involved in the child protection system, Baldwin and Carruthers (1998) discovered that approximately 25% of children on the child protection register in Coventry lived in one of the city's most deprived wards, where only 12% of Coventry's child population lived. Similarly, Baldwin and Spencer (1993) found that the three poorest wards in Glasgow accounted for four times the number of children on the child protection register than any other area of the city. Research undertaken by Gibbons et al (1995) revealed that 57% of the families involved in the child protection system had no wage-earner, while 54% of them were claiming Income Support, a means-tested benefit only available to the poorest people. Poverty is pervasive among families coming to the attention of child protection social workers and the repeated frustrations arising from deprivation or chronic debt precipitate aggression among a proportion of caregivers, their partners and children.

Displaced and safety-valve aggression

The cause of frustration may not necessarily be from an identifiable person or even another person at all. Catalano et al (1993) discovered that being made redundant can result in elevated levels of physical aggression towards members of the community, partners and children. Not only can parents or caregivers who have lost their job become more predisposed to aggressive behaviour towards other family members, but they can also displace their aggression onto social workers. *Displaced aggression* usually occurs when there is no identifiable target for a retaliatory aggressive response. Similarly, when reductions in central government grants to local government result in redundancies among front-line social workers, leaving a much-reduced staff complement to carry the same workload, anger among practitioners has no clear target. In these circumstances, it will probably be expressed towards those in close proximity, such as other colleagues, family members or, indeed, users of children's services.

Conversely, *displaced aggression* also occurs when a person can identify the source of their frustration, but is inhibited from acting against the person causing it. A father afraid of more stringent social work interventions may actually become more aggressive towards his 'at-risk' child. In this instance, an aggressive response is deflected away from the practitioner, who is perceived as the source of provocation, and towards another target, the child who had done nothing to provoke the father. Equally, a child subject to frequent verbal tirades by a caregiver may direct *displaced aggression* towards a social worker in order to avoid a punitive retaliatory response by a caregiver upon whom the child is dependent. Such behaviours are sometimes termed *safety-valve aggression* and are a common response to fear of retribution by the person who constitutes the real source of frustration. Social workers frustrated by supervisors, managers or agency requirements may themselves engage in *safety-valve aggression* against service-users, colleagues or their family, as they can vent their anger while avoiding retaliation that might occur were they to direct it at their superiors.

Frustration, and hence aggression as a correlate, can also occur when individuals are unable to achieve a desired end or accomplish a task that they wish to complete (Geen, 2001, p 26). Invariably, everyone faces these common vexations from time to time. But, for a number of people, they may be a daily occurrence, leading to feelings of helplessness and disappointment, for example, the unemployed parent rejected time and again by employers or the social worker unable to finish paperwork within normal office hours. These experiences of repeated failure culminating in frustration can lead to forms of *displaced* and *safety-valve aggression* likely to be perpetrated against people who have no causal connection with the original source of aggravation. Parents, children and practitioners alike can strike out at others without provocation if they suffer successive frustrations in their day-to-day lives.

Stress

Conceptualising aggression as stemming from frustration implicates a vast assortment of incidents that comprise of the mundane hassles of life, such as missing a bus or the local shop being out of milk. But these can be much more serious and pervasive. The NSPCC (2008) highlights the link established by prevalence studies between poverty on the one hand and elevated levels of child neglect, emotional abuse and physical maltreatment on the other. The research does not prove that poverty causes child abuse; most poor parents do not maltreat their children. But it does indicate that stress factors associated with social deprivation, such as debt, ill-health, unemployment, substandard housing and being a victim of crime, increase the risk of harm to children. Therefore, the majority of caregivers who come to the attention of the child protection system are experiencing a wide range of profound frustrations. Geen (2001, p 26) hypothesises that 'any significant change for the worse in a person's situation may be sufficiently aversive to cause increased stress and arousal, and that the arousal thus engendered may activate and energize aggressive responses'. In this instance, arousal refers to a set of physiological changes in the body in response to a stressor, particularly an increased heart and respiratory rate.

Any phenomenon that causes a person to feel stress (experienced as physical or mental tension) can be defined as a *stressor*. The *stress response* is an attempt by the body to counter the stressor and return itself to a state of equilibrium (Lovallo, 2005, pp 29–30). Stress is primarily a physiological reaction that prepares the body for a 'fight or flight' response, that is, to deal with the stressor through fighting it or to avoid it by running away. Most stressors experienced in everyday life are not a threat to the life or physical integrity of the individual, but nevertheless stimulate a *stress response*. Living with chronic debt, the challenging behaviour of a child or a heavy workload are all potential stressors, but neither a 'fight' nor 'flight' response would be adaptive here. Yet, despite this, the parents or workers exposed to these stressors will still experience the physiological symptoms of a *stress response*. Chronic stress manifests in a number of well-documented symptoms, which are listed by MIND (2005, p 12) in its report on workplace stress and reproduced in Table 2.1.

Table 2.1: Symptoms of stress

Physical symptoms	Psychological symptoms	Group-level stress
Insomnia and sleep disturbances	Inability to focus and concentrate	Disputes and disaffection
Fatigue	Loss of sense of humour	Increased staff turnover
Muscle tension and pain	High levels of anxiety and worry	Increased grievances and
Heart palpitations	Constant irritability towards others	complaints
Stomach upset	Withdrawal from social contact	
Gastrointestinal problems		
Breathlessness without exertion		
Headaches		

Source: Adapted from MIND (2005, p 12).

Whether a person experiences an event or situation as a stressor depends on their perception of it. One social worker might consider 15 active child protection cases as excessive and stressful, while another may regard it as an average workload that they feel able to manage. Lazarus and Folkman (1984) developed a model of stress that involves the individual making a *primary appraisal* of the event to determine whether it is a threat to him or her followed by a *secondary appraisal* as to the resources available to him or her to cope with that threat. It is this two-dimensional appraisal process that shapes a person's physiological, psychological, affective and behavioural responses to potentially threatening events or situations. A mother who has a young child with challenging behaviour, perceived as a stressor, will have fewer resources to call upon if she is in debt, is a single parent with a limited social network or has poor parenting skills due to neglect during her own upbringing. This is in contrast to a middle-income two-parent family with good parenting skills and a wide kinship network who are faced with the same stressor in terms of challenging behaviour. The latter have greater personal, social and financial resources that they can mobilise to manage the cause of their stress. This could include a greater repertoire of effective coping strategies, care by a relative and the ability to buy toys or leisure activities for their child. While both mothers may experience care of their child as stressful, the single indebted mother will plainly be subject to a more intense stress response and is more likely to reach the *stage of exhaustion* than the middle-income mother.

As negative emotions such as irritability, anger and hostility are positively correlated with stress, social workers, children and parents or carers can equally find themselves subject to ongoing sources of stress that lead them to behave in aggressive ways in day-to-day interactions with one another (Lloyd et al, 2002; Lovallo, 2005). Since a stressor constitutes a form of threat to the individual, it also often evokes feelings of fear. Fear and anger are closely interwoven in situations characterised by stress. Lindenfield (2000, p 76) argues that individuals can experience confusion as the presence of both emotions together interferes with the expression of each. A social worker worried by the allocation of yet another complex child protection case may be too afraid to vent her anger towards a team leader. Alternatively, a mother accused of mistreating her infant daughter may express intense anger in the presence of the social worker when she is actually feeling extremely frightened at the prospect of her child being taken away into state care. The *stress response* is also of importance for another reason. Individuals who deal with an act of aggression (a stressor) by choosing to 'fight' are likely to respond with a retaliatory act of verbal or physical aggression. Those who take 'flight' will usually seek to avoid a confrontation with the aggressor either by literally running away or by engaging in other avoidance strategies such as missing a scheduled meeting or behaving deferentially with the perceived aggressor. Practitioners, social work managers, parents and children are all predisposed to deal with stressors through 'fight' or 'flight' responses.

Environmental stressors and aggression

Research indicates that individuals are not only provoked to aggression by the behaviour of others, but they can also become aggressive as a reaction to impersonal factors. Environmental factors such as high or low temperatures, noise pollution, or overcrowding may be experienced as uncontrollable and inescapable. Secondary analysis of historical data from a number of countries shows a positive correlation between higher temperatures and crime, with a disproportionate increase in violent offences (Anderson and Anderson, 1984, 1996; Anderson et al, 1995, 1997). Long hot summers precipitating irritability among the general population and culminating in aggressive behaviour is now a well recognised phenomenon. Specifically, hotter years or seasons are positively correlated with increased homicides, rapes, assaults, riots and domestic violence. Anderson et al (1996), in a laboratory experiment, found that research subjects exposed to uncomfortably low temperatures or uncomfortably high ones both exhibited increased hostility in terms of cognition and emotion compared to those working in conditions of moderate temperature. This finding has implications for social workers occupying unpleasantly hot or cold open-plan offices and their background levels of stress. These environmental stressors may also affect impoverished families unable to afford the repair of faulty heating systems or reluctant to adequately heat their homes during cold weather because of high utility costs relative to household income.

Like temperature, the stress-related effects of noise have also been well researched (Geen, 2001, p 36). Noise pollution has become a pervasive problem in many urban areas due to building construction and traffic. While noise has been found not to be a direct cause of aggression, it does appear to be an intervening factor that can increase the intensity of a person's aggression once they have been provoked. Conversely, in terms of the frustration–aggression hypothesis, high noise levels can lower an individual's ability to tolerate frustration. As a result, people frequently exposed to high noise levels are more likely to react aggressively to an interpersonal provocation than those who are not so exposed (Geen, 2001, p 36). Modern forms of entertainment such as televisions, computers, music centres and personal stereos can also be a source of noise pollution, albeit that these are likely to be linked to identifiable individuals. When people live in high-density occupation, such as tower blocks or large multiple-occupied terraced houses, numerous centres of loud noise can feel uncontrollable and inescapable, leading to elevated and persistent stress.

Overcrowding itself is yet another environmental factor that can increase the likelihood of interpersonal aggression. Crowded family accommodation and the violation of personal space have both been found to induce higher levels of aggressive behaviour (Krahé, 2001). As the majority of families subject to child protection interventions are from low-income groups, they are much more likely than other sections of the population to experience overcrowded accommodation in disadvantaged areas (NSPCC, 2008). Brandon et al (2009, p 3), in their study of

40 serious case reviews, found that 'almost half (45%) of the families were highly mobile and were living in poor conditions'.

Stress and the social work role

A review of the literature into the causes of workplace stress among social workers conducted by Lloyd et al (2002) in conjunction with work by Thompson et al (1994, p 19) and Wilmot (1998) identifies another set of important factors. This concerns *role stress*, which is now widely recognised across different occupational groups and consists of three key dimensions. Thompson et al (1994, p 19) suggest that *role ambiguity* occurs if there is a lack of clarity concerning the scope of the practitioner's responsibility. A social worker can have multiple roles when intervening with a family, ranging from therapeutic work with parents and children, to offering practical support, to arranging services. This is a wide portfolio of professional activities, which can become bewildering where a child is at risk of significant harm and the practitioner is not clear as to what role they should be performing in relation to different family members. *Role overload* is also identified by Thompson et al (1994, p 19) as problematic and ensues when practitioners are obliged to perform too many roles at once within a limited time span; for example, being required to work therapeutically with parents, befriend the child, complete a core assessment of the family and make an application to the Family Court for a Supervision Order to oversee the child's welfare at home within relatively short timescales.

In more extreme circumstances, *role incompatibility* can occur when the expectations or requirements of different stakeholders are contradictory. Social workers caught in this dilemma are subject to the additional stress of trying to work with conflicting demands; for instance, the expectation of *looked-after* children that they have some choice over a foster placement as opposed to the funding priorities of management which dictate that social workers obtain value for money in such placement decisions, which may preclude children's choices. Both these imperatives are actually formalised in government-issued guidance to social workers and their agencies, making the *role incompatibility* they produce all the more acute for practitioners. *Role incompatibility* also tends to be amplified by the care and control functions social workers normally exercise when safeguarding children, which can leave them unsure as to how these should be balanced against one another in a given situation. To illustrate: *role incompatibility* can easily be created when a social worker intervenes in a family to assist a father to improve his care of a neglected child while simultaneously endeavouring to protect that same child from neglect.

Gender and aggression

Men are popularly believed to be more aggressive than women, with their greater aggression being attributed to the hormone testosterone. Research studies reveal a much more complex picture than this conventional wisdom allows. Wright and Craig (2010, p 49), in their review of the evidence, aver that whether or not gender differences are identified in aggressiveness depends largely on the definition of aggression adopted. Often, aggression is interpreted narrowly by researchers in terms of physical violence. The research evidence appears to show little gender difference in the expression of aggression if it is conceptualised along the lines of Geen's (2001, p 3) definition to include any behaviour designed to harm. Notably, Bettencourt and Miller (1996), in their analysis of previous studies on sex differences, concluded that when physical aggression was the aggressive strategy available to both men and women, men were rated more aggressive. On the other hand, when the aggressive strategy was verbal or written, these sex differences disappeared, with both genders exhibiting much the same level of aggression. Nevertheless, studies of aggression do consistently demonstrate gendered forms of expression. To directly quote Wright and Craig (2010, p 49), who summarise the research findings in this area:

- Boys exhibit frustration and anger in very physical and direct ways.
- Girls use more subtle and indirect forms of social aggression focused on relational and social characteristics.
- Girls appear more likely to hurt others by damaging relationships with peers than boys.
- Girls rate social aggression as more hurtful than physical aggression.
- Boys rate physical aggression as more hurtful than social aggression.

Gendered differences appear to be explicable in terms of *role theory*, which conceptualises social behaviour as performance and to a large extent socially prescribed, as opposed to being instinctive or based on human biology. Thus, a person learns to become masculine or feminine through learning a social role rather than expressing an essential nature. *Social learning theory* (discussed earlier) means that males learn sex-appropriate behaviour through observing other males and the administration of punishment and rewards for their behaviours. A boy who cries when pushed in the playground is punished by other children by being called a 'sissy' or 'gay'. Conversely, a boy who is pushed and responds to this provocation by shoving the other child in return is likely to be approved of by parents and peers alike. Masculinity is socially constructed as assertiveness, competitiveness, physical strength and rationality. Behaviours that demonstrate these traits tend to be socially rewarded. The masculine role is thus internalised because, from infancy onwards, boys are rewarded for performing the behaviours associated with it.

Similar social learning processes shape the behaviour of girls as they observe other females and emulate their behaviour. Like boys, these behaviours are then reinforced through a system of rewards and punishments. This reinforcement maintains behaviours associated with femininity, typically those expressing caring, emotionality and domesticity. Girls exhibiting competitiveness or physical aggression are much more likely than boys to be socially punished by being labelled a 'tomboy' or 'rough'. Hence, girls grow up learning to constrain their physically aggressive impulses in a way that is much less common among boys. This does not mean that they stop being aggressive. As the research evidence compiled by Wright and Craig (2010, p 49) reveals, girls adopt different aggressive strategies from boys. On the basis of previous studies, Geen (2001, p 62) notes that 'women were more likely than men to consider aggression inappropriate, to repress aggression and to experience guilt or anxiety in connection with aggressive actions'. A number of other significant sex differences to emerge from the research record are highlighted by Geen (2001, pp 62–3) and are summarised as follows:

- Women are more angered than men by condescending behaviour or verbal abuse from a man or woman.
- Men are more angered than women by a physical attack from another man.
- Threats to the self-esteem of women have little impact on their aggressiveness, in contrast to insults or physical attacks, which provoke aggressiveness.
- Threats to the self-esteem of men are as likely to provoke an aggressive response as is a physical attack.

Gendered expressions of anger, frustration and hostility and gendered reactions to different types of provocation have implications for social work practice with parents, their partners and children. Boys' and men's more overt, direct and physically threatening expressions of aggression may attract attention, while the more covert, indirect and less physically aggressive behaviours of girls and mothers or female partners may go unnoticed or unanalysed. Appreciating the gendered nature of aggressive expression is crucial to recognising and working effectively with the hostility of different family members. An awareness of the gendered aspects of reactive aggression in mothers, fathers, their partners, sons and daughters is also essential to avoiding unnecessary provocation or de-escalating an aggressive response once it has occurred. A social worker who realises early in an encounter with a teenaged father that perceived threats to his self-esteem can trigger a violent response is much better placed to manage the interaction in a manner that reduces the likelihood of an attack.

Alcohol and aggression

Brandon et al (2009, Table 19) found that out of 189 serious case reviews for the period 2005–07 where a child was killed or seriously injured, there were a set of common parental characteristics, which included alcohol or drug misuse often in conjunction with domestic violence. These findings are summarised in Table 2.2. Brandon et al's (2009, p 3) more detailed analysis of 40 of these serious case reviews revealed that 'Nearly three quarters of the children lived with past or present domestic violence and/or past or present parental mental ill health, and/

or past or present parental substance misuse. These three parental characteristics often co-existed'.

Ofsted's (2010, para 20) examination of serious case reviews for the year 2009/10 found similar results, noting that:

> common characteristics of the families were similar to those identified in Ofsted's previous reports. The most common issues were domestic violence, mental ill-health, and drug and alcohol misuse. Frequently, more than one of these characteristics were present. Overall, domestic violence was a factor in cases involving 61 children, mental ill-health for 44 children, drug misuse for 36 children and alcohol abuse for 27 children.

While domestic violence rather than alcohol abuse was most pervasive in the backgrounds of families where a child died or was seriously injured, alcohol remains a common factor in both serious case reviews and in public inquiries. Wiehe (1998), in an overview of the literature, identified high alcohol consumption as a contributory factor in physical and sexual violence against children and female partners. Since many of the graver family situations confronting social workers involve alcohol abuse, it is important to examine its relationship with aggression.

Table 2.2: Parental characteristics in serous case reviews, 2005–07

Parent characteristic	Number of cases
Domestic violence	49
Mental health problems – parent	32
Drug misuse – parent	28
Alcohol misuse – parent	19
Child of teenage pregnancy	18
Parent is a care-leaver	5
Parent in care	4

Source: Adapted from Brandon et al (2009, Table 19).

As both Krahé (2001) and Geen (2001) highlight in their overviews of the research on alcohol and aggression, the relationship between the two is not one of direct cause and effect. The consumption of alcohol creates both physiological and psychological changes associated with aggressive behaviour. When consumed, alcohol is rapidly absorbed into the bloodstream and circulated round the body, acting to depress the central nervous system. Initially, it creates mild euphoria followed by reduction in attention and sensory-motor control accompanied by impaired judgement, mental confusion and longer reaction times. Intoxication produces a number of psychological changes. People who are inebriated are less capable of accurately interpreting social cues and tend to over-focus on cues associated with aggression – such as a raised voice – in any given situation (Gantner and Taylor, 1992). In other words, social information processing is adversely affected by alcohol, with non-intoxicated individuals able to accurately read a much greater variety of social cues while those who are intoxicated misconstrue social situations.

Ito et al (1996), in their review of the research, found that people under the influence of alcohol are less inhibited by normal social constraints on aggressive behaviour than those who are sober. A major inhibitor of aggression is the social opprobrium directed at those who engage in unprovoked aggressive behaviour, whereas a proportionate aggressive reaction to provocation is considered justified and is not usually censured. An intoxicated person is disinhibited from these sorts of social constraints and is more likely to either engage in unprovoked aggression or to react more aggressively to mild provocation than is someone who is sober. Social workers are therefore at greater risk of verbal abuse or physical aggression from caregivers or young people who are drunk.

In relation to the frustration–aggression hypothesis, intoxicated individuals also respond more aggressively when frustrated in their goal attainment than do non-intoxicated individuals (Ito et al, 1996). This is linked to the exaggerated emotional states observed in people who are intoxicated. Furthermore, those under the influence of alcohol are less self-aware than individuals who are sober. Drunkenness reduces a person's ability to monitor their own behaviour and, hence, impairs the self-consciousness that normally acts to inhibit aggression. Research findings indicate that men and women are equally aggressive under the influence of alcohol, with little evidence of gender differences (Krahé, 2001, p 77). Yet, not everyone who consumes alcohol becomes aggressive, which means that there are also situational variables in play that mediate the link between alcohol consumption and aggressive behaviour.

Drug misuse and aggression

As already indicated earlier, Brandon et al (2009, Table 19) discovered that a large proportion of parents whose children were seriously injured or killed while in their care took illicit drugs. Many of these families were also characterised by high levels of domestic violence. Chermack et al (2008) found that the abuse of cannabis, cocaine and illicit opiates were positively correlated with psychological and physical violence between intimate partners. Rates of physical aggression exhibited by men and women undergoing treatment for substance misuse are known to be two or three times higher than among a random sample of the population (Chermack et al, 2008, p 40). While there is an established link between drug abuse and aggression, as Chermack et al (2008, p 42) observe, this relationship is not entirely clear. Aggression associated with drug use may be attributable to a variety of causes, including: the aggression-enhancing effects of drugs; self-medication with drugs to reduce aggressive impulses; use of drugs following a violent altercation; fights over drugs; and irritability due to withdrawal symptoms.

Goldstein (1995) posited a tripartite conceptual framework to account for the elevated levels of interpersonal aggression associated with substance misuse among members of the general population. This comprises the psychopharmacological effects of drugs, such as perceptual distortions or a hostile interpretation of another person's neutral or friendly behaviour, precipitating a 'fight' response. The intoxicating effects of drugs (like those of alcohol) include the inhibition of a normal fear of incurring punishment for aggressive behaviour. This inevitably makes the expression of aggression more likely. The second dimension to Goldstein's framework contends that aggression occurs in the process of procuring drugs or for economic gain in relation to the acquisition of drugs. The third component concerns aggression related to drug misuse subcultures due to conflict over drug procurement, drug use, the exchange of favours and the payment of debts.

While the psychopharmacological effects of drugs and conflict over their procurement and use contribute to aggressive behaviour by drug users, these may be intensified by a history of childhood abuse, domestic violence or substance misuse by parents (Chermack et al, 2008). Moreover, the level of aggressive behaviour exhibited by a drug user can be significantly influenced by the type of substance he or she is abusing. Research studies indicate that intoxication with cocaine is more likely to precipitate physically aggressive behaviour than is marijuana, hallucinogens, stimulants, opiates or sedatives (Chermac et al, 2008). Heroin-dependent users are also more likely to be physically aggressive than are users of marijuana, stimulants, hallucinogens or sedatives (Bácskai et al, 2011). There is less distinction in levels of psychological aggression between different classes of drugs. Nevertheless, all classes of drugs produce increased verbal aggression among male and female users (Chermack et al, 2008). Poly-substance use is common among drug users. The combined effect of taking a number of drugs simultaneously can exacerbate the aggression-enhancing effects of any one substance (Chermack et al, 2008, p 266). But, as indicated by Goldstein (1995), much aggression may be attributable to conflict over drugs or withdrawal symptoms, as well as the effects of intoxication.

Mental health and aggression

The Brandon et al (2009) analysis of serious case reviews found that the mental health of a parent was of concern in a significant proportion of families where a child was killed or seriously harmed. Research indicates that men and women diagnosed with a range of mental disorders are more likely to be verbally or physically aggressive than their counterparts in the general population (Bǎcskai et al, 2011, pp 1333–4). This does not mean that everyone who has a mental health problem is violent or abusive; only that a proportion of those experiencing mental illness are more aggressive than those enjoying good mental health. Studies of individuals with a diagnosis of schizophrenia or bipolar disorder suggest that there is a greater chance that they will engage in aggressive behaviour than members of the general population (Garno et al, 2008; Volavka and Citrome, 2008; Látalová, 2009; Bǎcskai et al, 2011, pp 1333–4). However, such findings fail to explain why the majority of people with a diagnosis of schizophrenia or bipolar disorder are not violent.

Evidence from research suggests that aggression committed by people with a psychotic disorder is associated with other factors, such as substance misuse and non-compliance with medication (Spidel et al, 2010, pp 171–2). Alcohol or substance abuse combined with non-adherence to medication among those with severe mental illnesses was significantly associated with serious violent acts in the community (Swartz et al, 1998; Walsh et al, 2001). In this connection, it is salient that around 50% of people with a severe mental health problem abuse substances or alcohol (Linszen et al, 1997; Spidel et al, 2010). The widespread public perception that people who have a diagnosis of schizophrenia or bipolar disorder are violent is therefore grossly misleading and a form of negative stereotyping. Nevertheless, if people with schizophrenia or bipolar disorder abuse alcohol or drugs while refusing to take prescribed medication, the probability of their becoming aggressive significantly increases.

A number of personality disorders are associated with a greater tendency to engage in aggressive acts. Anti-social personality disorder and borderline personality disorder are associated with elevated levels of aggressiveness across a number of studies (Garno et al, 2008; Ostrov and Houston, 2008, p 1147; Ross and Babcock, 2009; Látalová and Praško, 2010). According to the internationally recognised Diagnostic and Statistical Manual of Mental Disorders (DSM-IV-TR) produced by the American Psychiatric Association, people with anti-social behaviour disorder exhibit impulsiveness, irritability, aggressiveness, have a reckless disregard for the safety of others and lack remorse. They often remain indifferent to, or else rationalise, their mistreatment of others. Their behaviour is characterised by non-conformity to legal or social norms. Although anti-social behaviour disorder is only diagnosed in those over the age of 18 years, it is associated with conduct disorders among children under that age.

The DSM-IV-TR criteria for the diagnosis of a borderline personality disorder notes that it is characterised by 'a pervasive pattern of instability of interpersonal relationships, self-image, and affects, and marked impulsivity beginning by early adulthood'. People with this personality disorder exhibit reactivity of mood, which results in unpredictable and sporadic expressions of irritability, anxiety and often intense uncontrollable anger. They may also experience stress-related paranoia. Reactive physical aggression and relational aggression is strongly associated with both anti-social and borderline personality disorders. Relational aggression among those with anti-social personality characteristics usually takes the form of deception, using others, hostility and suspiciousness, while among those with borderline personality traits, it is often reflected in the manipulation of others (Ostrov and Houston, 2008). Obsessive–Compulsive Disorder (OCD) and Attention Deficit Hyperactivity Disorder (ADHD), which both exhibit problems of impulse control, are also linked to elevated levels of impulsive aggressive behaviour (American Psychiatric Association, 2000; Dowson and Blackwell, 2010). This does not mean that all individuals diagnosed with OCD or ADHD are aggressive. Rather, it suggests that those with these particular mental health problems are more likely than members of the general population to become aggressive.

The DSM-IV-TR criteria for paranoid personality disorder indicate that this is also associated with elevated levels of anger and aggression. People with this disorder are distrustful of others and generally suspect them of engaging in deceit or efforts to cause harm. The loyalty, benign actions and innocent motives of close family members and friends are repeatedly questioned and doubted. Individuals with a paranoid personality disorder are liable to interpret neutral and even benevolent remarks as direct attacks upon them. Indeed, they actively search their social environment for clues to validate their entrenched suspicion of others. Those with paranoid tendencies tend to be unforgiving of real or imagined transgressions and hold grievances against others for sustained periods of time. It is their hypersensitivity to any offence and their persistent interpretation of others' behaviour as forms of personal attack that results in recurrent bouts of anger and exhibitions of aggression.

Social interaction theory

In contradistinction to the foregoing theories of aggression, which seek to explain affective aggression, a social interactionist approach focuses on *proactive* or *instrumental* aggression. It examines the nature of coercive strategies and why people choose to use them to achieve their goals. Felson and Tedeschi (1993, pp 1–2) are among the foremost proponents of this approach and the main tenets of their theory are reproduced in Box 2.3.

Box 2.3: Key principles of the social interactionist approach

1. It interprets aggression as instrumental behaviour – as a means to achieving certain values or goals.
2. It is critical of the view that aggression is 'pushed out' or 'compelled' by inner forces, such as aggressive energy, instincts, hormones, brain centres, thanatos and frustration. Instead, aggressive behaviour is viewed as a normal consequence of conflict in human relations.
3. It treats situational and interpersonal factors as critical in instigating aggression. This leads to consideration of the behaviour of antagonists and third parties as well as of the actor.
4. It emphasises the phenomenology of actors, whose values and expectations are important in the evaluations of decision alternatives. Actors often view their own aggression as legitimate and even moralistic. Thus, beliefs about justice and equity, the assignment of blame, and the accounts that people give to excuse or justify their behaviour are central.

Tedeschi and Felson (1994, p 348) argue that a person chooses a coercive strategy in order to:

• control the behaviour of others;

- restore justice; and
- assert and protect positive identities.

Felson and Tedeschi (1993, p 3) elaborate on these prime motivations, postulating that aggression primarily 'consists of punitive actions that attempt to redress some grievance or injustice', which are designed to 'prevent continuation of the undesired behaviour or to deter others from performing similar behaviour'. According to this model, aggression may also be triggered when a social rule has been violated and the offended person acts to rebuke or punish the rule-breaker. When a person is provoked, he or she is likely to view their act of retaliation as a form of justice or an act to restore justice. Finally, people retaliate to maintain valued or positive identities, which are often associated with notions of honour and the importance of saving face. In this connection, the presence of others can escalate an aggressive response, as the person engaging in retaliation is doing so to retain honour or save face in front of an audience. Within this explanatory framework, the verbal aggression of a father towards a social worker who accuses him of neglecting his child may be an expression of outrage at the violation of his rights to bring up his child as he wishes. On this reading, the aggression of the father is an attempt to restore justice. Likewise, a female practitioner who insults a male colleague in response to what she believes is his sexist comment may also be using aggression to reassert a positive identity as a professional woman. Nevertheless, as Felson and Tedeschi (1993, p 3) acknowledge, aggression can be purely predatory, involving acts of exploitation or social control such as bullying to gain a desired end.

Within the *social interactionist perspective*, Tedeschi and Nesler (1993) place great emphasis upon the nature of the grievance. They aver that the perception of having suffered an injustice is a major cause of aggression and this makes it imperative to understand how a person's sense of grievance is produced and culminates in retaliatory action. According to this theoretical perspective, there are three processes involved in the development of a grievance that is normally attended by anger:

1. *Naming* – perceiving that an injury to the person has occurred.
2. *Blaming* – attributing responsibility for the injury.
3. *Claiming* – making a demand for a remedy from the person deemed responsible.

Box 2.4: Types of events resulting in grievances

Based on previous research, Tedeschi and Nesler (1993, pp 15–16) identified the classes of events most likely to generate grievances:

    1.   Injury, pain, or unpleasant sensations produced by physical stimuli or the perception of an intent to inflict physical harm.

2. Loss or damage to existing or expected goods or resources or the perception of an intention to impose deprivation of resources.
3. Perceived damage to social identities.
4. Political harm in the form of the violation of rights, interference with opportunities or constraints on freedoms.

These sources of grievance are particularly pertinent to social work. The first class of events involving physical contact is more likely in the context of working with children, where forms of physical restraint are threatened or used, leading to grievances on the part of *looked-after* children in foster or residential placements. Social workers may themselves be subject to threats of, or actual, assault by a child or caregiver, occasioning both anger and grievance. Regarding the second category, social workers may withdraw resources from families or find their own car damaged by a parent in retaliation, leaving all parties experiencing a deep sense of grievance. In terms of social identities, the third class of events, research shows that 'people are concerned about the quality of treatment that they receive from others in social interactions' (Tedeschi and Nesler, 1993, p 15). This includes being treated with respect, honesty, politeness and matters relating to interactional justice such as fairness and punctuality. Norm-violating behaviour by another person also falls into this category. These aspects are plainly integral to professional relationships with caregivers and children. Social workers who fail to offer parents and their partners respect and integrity will create grievances. The last category regarding political harm bears directly upon the powers of social workers in child protection work and concerns all compulsory interventions in families that are either sanctioned by the court or that take place in the shadow of possible court action.

According to Tedeschi and Felson (1994), individuals have choices as to whether to engage in a coercive or non-coercive strategy to obtain desired outcomes. A non-coercive strategy would include, for example, making a request or offering a benefit for compliance, whereas a coercive strategy uses threat or punishment to achieve personal ends. According to Tedeschi and Felson (1994), a person will choose a coercive or non-coercive strategy based on a rational assessment of: the costs and benefits of a particular course of action; its ethical acceptability to the individual; and a calculation of the likelihood of success in achieving the desired goal. This decision-making process will also involve deciding which coercive strategy to adopt; that of threat, actual punishment or physical force. The use of a coercive strategy is to obtain a desired outcome rather than to harm another person per se. Tedeschi and Felson (1994) do allow that the coercive strategy chosen by someone will reflect a *coercive script*, which, like an *aggressive script*, is generated from early experiences of coercive behaviour, both as victim and perpetrator. A *coercive script* predisposes an individual to particular types of coercive behaviour in particular kinds of situations based on his or her internal schemata. It also means that a person may be more predisposed to use a coercive as opposed to a non-coercive strategy in the first instance. Consequently, social workers' own *coercive scripts* will profoundly shape how they respond to the grievances they sometimes experience in relation to colleagues, managers, caregivers and children. Similarly, parents, their partners and children who come into contact with the child protection system may well feel aggrieved by the violations of their rights, the contravention of accepted social norms or the decisions of social workers and their team leaders. Like practitioners', the individual *coercive scripts* of parents, partners and children will equally determine their reactions to the conflicts they encounter as they come into contact with the child protection system.

Self-control and aggression

Aggression scripts and *hostile attribution bias* are examples of individual differences that influence the degree to which a particular person engages in aggressive behaviour. Impulse control is also a major factor in whether or not a person exhibits aggression in a given situation. As already discussed, certain drugs and alcohol tend to disinhibit individuals and remove internal constraints, such as the fear of retribution or social opprobrium. Because of their temperament or their early life experiences, some individuals have less impulse control than others. They may also hold beliefs justifying aggression at the least provocation, while others hold more normative beliefs that greatly restrain resorting to aggressive acts except under gross provocation. For instance, an adolescent male involved in gang culture may believe that reacting to provocation with violence is an appropriate response that projects a macho image while enhancing his status among peers. Conversely, another male adolescent may hold religious convictions that prohibit the expression of anger; thus, his beliefs act to constrain aggressive behaviour. For another, sociability is a major factor in restraining them from aggression, as most people are concerned about the feelings of other people and wish to be liked and approved of by them. Ultimately, persistent resort to aggression for minor or imaginary acts of provocation can lead to social ostracism, as others seek to avoid the aggressor.

Kool (2008, pp 74–5) pulls together research findings from a number of studies to show that impulse control can be reduced when self-control has been exerted over a prolonged period of time or when individuals are required to exert impulse control in relation to several things at once. In other words, self-control requires reserves of mental and emotional energy that can be depleted over time or in the face of multiple demands for self-control. A mother caring for a child who has learning difficulties and presents with challenging behaviour may have less impulse control when interacting with a social worker perceived as provocative because of his intention to commence a child protection investigation. The result may be a verbally abusive outburst by the mother against the practitioner. Similarly, a social worker may endure a permanently high caseload and a noisy overcrowded open-plan office every day. A mother arriving half an hour late to a supervised contact session with her fostered child may be the tipping point for that social worker, which provokes her to angrily confront the mother with her unpunctuality and to threaten the termination of the contact arrangement. In the following passage, Baumeister (1999, p 263) emphasises the pivotal role of self-control in the prevention of violence, but his observations might equally apply to other forms of aggression, whether perpetrated by service-users or social workers:

> The immediate, proximal cause of violence is the collapse of these inner restraining forces. This point is crucial, because it means that many of our efforts to understand violence are looking at the questions the wrong way. To produce violence, it is not necessary to promote it actively. All that is necessary is to stop restraining or preventing it. Once the restraints are removed, there are plenty of reasons for people to strike at each other.

Points for practice

- Differences of opinion or belief over information, interests, procedures, values, relationships, roles and communication can all constitute the basis for conflict.
- Once set in motion, conflict quickly escalates to narrow perceptions, magnify differences and entrench positions.
- Social learning theory suggests that aggressive responses are learnt during childhood through family and peer interactions, which then develop into habitual ways of reacting to events and others into adulthood.
- The frustration–aggression hypothesis advances the proposition that any incident that thwarts a person from achieving their goals is liable to cause some degree of anger and potentially aggressive behaviour.
- Social interaction theory conceptualises aggression as a reaction to a perceived injustice and an attempt to correct a wrong or administer punishment.
- Stress and environmental factors such as overcrowding and noise pollution are prime causes of anger and aggression.
- Research indicates that there are no gender differences in the prevalence of aggressive behaviour, but males tend to express aggression more directly through physical confrontation, while females are more likely to use relational strategies such as malicious gossip or ostracism.
- Substance misuse is positively correlated with aggressive behaviour, as drugs and alcohol tend to impair judgement and disinhibit individuals, lowering their fear of social approbation and punishment.
- People who have certain personality disorders may be more inclined to aggression, as can those with a mental health problem who exacerbate this through drug misuse or non-compliance with treatment.

CHAPTER THREE

Managing conflict with colleagues

Conflicts in the workplace

Differences of perspective or opinion inevitably arise between social workers in their everyday working lives as colleagues disagree over the allocation of resources within the office or a course of action in relation to a child at risk. Sometimes, disagreement can arise due to misinterpretation of another's motives, a misunderstanding or misinformation about a particular aspect of the work. For social workers involved in child protection, these unavoidable sources of conflict are often exacerbated by agency context. The circumstances surrounding the deaths of Victoria Climbié and Peter Connelly offer an insight into how the state of affairs in the workplace can increase the potential for conflict between colleagues. They also illustrate how conflicts that can be experienced as extremely personal are actually manifestations of broader organisational difficulties that interfere in the working relationships between colleagues. It is notable that many of the factors that hampered good social work practice in relation to Victoria during 1999 were still significant impediments for practitioners almost a decade later when Peter died at the hands of his mother and step-father in 2007. This chapter explores the conflicts between colleagues that emerge from the public inquiry and serious case review conducted into the deaths of Victoria and Peter, respectively.

Case Study 3.1: Victoria Climbié

Summary – Laming (2003) *The Victoria Climbié inquiry*

Victoria was born on 2 November 1991 in the Ivory Coast. Her Great Aunt, Ms Kouao, then resident in France, on a visit to the Ivory Coast in 1998, offered to take Victoria back to Europe. Victoria lived in France with Ms Kouao for five months and then travelled to London on Ms Kouao's French passport as her daughter, Anna, in April 1999. Ms Kouao was provided with hostel accommodation by Ealing's Homeless Persons' Unit and regularly called at Ealing Social Services for subsistence payments. No assessment of Victoria as possibly a *child in need* was conducted. A distant relative of Ms Kouao's saw Victoria on several occasions and was so worried about her loss of weight that she made two anonymous telephone calls to Brent Social Services. Due to a combination of poor record-keeping and social work practice, no effective action was taken. In June 1999, Ms Kouao met Mr Manning for the first time and, in July, both she and Victoria moved to live with him in his small bedsit. Physical abuse of Victoria intensified at this point.

A paid carer for Victoria was so alarmed by the extent of her injuries that she took Victoria to the Central Middlesex Hospital in July 1999. On admission, Victoria was examined by a paediatric registrar who concluded that a number of Victoria's injuries were non-accidental. However, this was contradicted by a consultant paediatrician who concluded that they were due to scabies. Consequently, Victoria, who had been placed under Police Protection in hospital, was permitted to leave with Ms Kouao the next morning. A week later, Victoria was admitted to North Middlesex Hospital with a serious scald to the face and non-accidental injuries were again suspected after a medical examination. A referral was made to Haringey Social Services and a Strategy Meeting was held, resulting in the case being allocated to a social worker, who made several home visits to Mr Manning's bedsit. Nevertheless, Victoria was still discharged from North Middlesex Hospital back into Ms Kouao's care. In November 1999, Ms Kouao arrived at the North Tottenham District offices of Haringey Social Services claiming that Mr Manning had sexually molested Victoria, but retracted this allegation a day later. This matter was not investigated and no professional was to see Victoria again until her admission to North Middlesex Hospital on 24 February 2000, the day before her death.

In 2001, Ms Kouao and Mr Manning were convicted of murdering Victoria.

The impact of underfunding

The subsequent public inquiry into the events surrounding Victoria's death was to discover a series of comparable problems at Ealing, Brent and Haringey Children's Social Services caused by underfunding and understaffing. To avoid repetition, these are considered in detail only in relation to Brent Children's Social Services. The *Standard Spending Assessment* is the notional sum of money central government allocates to local authorities for expenditures on different aspects of their activities. In the financial year 1998/99, Brent was given a *Standard Spending Assessment* for Children's Social Services of £28.12 million but the actual spend was only about £14.5 million (para 5.41). The Director of Social Services at the time admitted that Brent Council's decision to allocate only half the *Standard Spending Assessment* figure 'had resulted in "severe pressures and stresses" including long-term illnesses and absences among a number of service unit directors and front-line staff' (para 5.43). This meant that all teams in Children's Social Services were carrying vacancies and that a number of child protection cases were unallocated. As a result of chronic underfunding, front-line Children's Social Services suffered reductions in personnel, with 10 posts being deleted and a further 13 vacancies frozen in 1997. Even though eight more social workers were eventually recruited in 1998, as one local councillor shamefully confessed to the Laming Inquiry, overall this meant 'down 23 and up 8' (para 5.49).

Brent Council's failure to allocate sufficient monies to Children's Social Services had a number of dire consequences for front-line child protection workers. The duty team manager during 1999, at the time when the two referrals relating to the anonymous phone calls about Victoria passed through his office, presented evidence at the public inquiry. He acknowledged that his team 'was staffed entirely by agency workers who had not qualified in England' and that 'it was not acceptable to have people on short-term contracts at the front-line of contact with very vulnerable children' (para 5.60). Moreover, he revealed that agency staff 'did not stay long enough to be trained and their induction was varied or non-existent' (para 5.61). He was told by one of the assistant directors of children's services 'that the financial cost of a week's worth of induction outweighed the financial cost of the workers being allocated cases immediately' (para 5.61). Consequently, new agency workers joining the duty team were left to rely on other front-line social workers or their supervisors for guidance (para 5.62). Inevitably, this would have added to the already high workload burden on existing staff.

During the late 1990s, Brent Children's Services was an under-resourced agency, characterised by short-term employment contracts, inexperienced social workers and a high staff turnover compounded by inadequate training, which would undoubtedly have caused stress to practitioners. Indeed, as the Director of Social Services was to acknowledge at the public inquiry, social workers were subject to 'severe pressures and stresses', which produced soaring levels of illness. Front-line practitioners engaged in child protection activity could not easily perform adaptive 'fight' or 'flight' responses and, therefore, could not alleviate the stressors they encountered. The cumulative impact of operating in such a relentless working environment was that many practitioners became exhausted as their physical and mental energy was depleted. According to the Laming (2003) inquiry, senior management were aware of this state of affairs, but did nothing to remedy it. This meant, in effect, that even when practitioners and their line managers did engage in a 'fight' response, that is, to complain to senior management, no changes occurred. In the face of this, many front-line staff turned to 'flight' as a coping mechanism and simply resigned from the agency, hence the high staff turnover. For those who remained, many would have experienced lack of concentration and irritability. As all front-line staff were subject to the same workplace stresses, irritable exchanges would have quickly entered the *conflict spiral*, deteriorating into factionalised office disputes.

Brent Children's Services suffered a particularly gross underspend, but the experience of working for an under-resourced agency is not unique to the social workers employed by Brent London Borough Council during 1999. The global financial crisis, which began in September 2008, has precipitated cutbacks across the public sector, resulting in substantial reductions to the monies available for children's social care services. The Local Government Association reported in 2010 that local authorities were experiencing cuts in their budgets of 7% each year for the next four years. The non-schools children's services budget, which incorporates children's social care, was due to suffer a total cut of 12% (*BBC News*, 2010a). *Community Care Online* (2011, 2012d) continues to report inferior child protection services due to financial cutbacks. These budgetary cuts have coincided with: soaring referrals; increased applications for Care Orders; and a steep rise in the number of children subject to Child Protection Plans in the wake of the negative media attention and blame attributed to social workers for not preventing the death of baby Peter Connelly at the hands of his carers in 2007 (*Community Care Online*, 2012c, 2012d). Consequently, some practitioners may still find themselves employed in child protection agencies coping with chronic resource shortages. For others, even when agencies are effectively staffed, lack of training opportunities (either due to work pressures preventing attendance or the limited number of courses available) can still cause work-related stress. When this occurs, a minor transgression by a colleague can elicit a disproportionate and aggressive response from another practitioner. If that colleague is also working in stressful circumstances, the scope for a series of increasingly aggressive interactions is fairly limitless.

Organisational structure and stress

Brent Children's Social Services, who were involved with Victoria, had two in-take teams that undertook initial assessments with children and families before passing these on to six Long Term Teams if they required further social work involvement. The two in-take teams consisted of the Duty Team and the Child Protection Investigation and Assessment Team, also known as the Child Protection Team. These two teams were supported by the Duty Administrative Team, which was responsible for logging all initial referrals onto a database and checking if the families or individual's concerned were already known to Brent Social Services. This organisational structure is represented diagrammatically in Figure 3.1.

There were three major problems with this organisational structure. First, the separation of the two intake teams into the Duty Team responsible for *child in need* cases and the Child Protection Team responsible for child protection cases 'meant that there was often doubt as to whether a particular case was in the right place' (para 5.173). As Lord Laming was to observe:

> At times of heavy workload and stretched resources, the temptation to reclassify a case so that responsibility for it could be transferred onto another team could result in social workers being too eager either to downgrade or play up the seriousness of a particular case. (para 5.175)

Plainly, differences of opinion over whether a case should be classified as *child in need* or *child protection* in a situation of high workloads and understaffing could be a major site of conflict between colleagues from different teams.

Figure 3.1: The organisational structure of Brent Children's Social Services

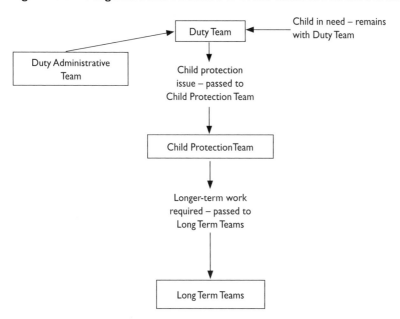

Second, due to the high numbers of referrals relative to the staff available to deal with them, the Child Protection Team was unable to pass families requiring further work onto the Long Term Teams due to lack of capacity within these teams. The Duty Team manager described to the public inquiry how:

> It had become a common theme for me to go to the allocation meeting with cases for allocation to a 'long-term' team, only to return with the same cases because there was insufficient resource availability in long-term teams to deal with the cases. (para 5.18)

This created considerable problems when children such as Victoria came to the attention of Brent London Borough Council.

Third, the high and increasing workloads of the two intake teams had ramifications for the Duty Administrative Team. Like front-line services, the Duty Administrative Team was also grossly understaffed. The manager of this team informed the inquiry that although notionally there were supposed to be four members of administrative staff, at the time, in fact, one post had been frozen and therefore not filled, while another employee was off on sick leave (para 5.31). Hence, during the period when Brent's Children's Social Services would have received the two anonymous telephone calls from a distant relative of Ms Kouao's, the Duty Administrative Team had only half its notional staff complement. A number of witnesses before the inquiry spoke of this team as being 'relentlessly overworked' and 'overburdened'. Records revealed that in June 1999, 'only 107 referrals (42 percent) were logged onto the system within one working week, and 41 (16 percent) took between four and 12 weeks' (para 5.34). In fact, the two referrals for Victoria took many weeks to be logged and were not cross-referenced.

Events at Brent Children's Social Services reveal the way in which organisational structures can themselves be a source of additional stress and the focus of dispute and disgruntlement. Social workers on the Duty, Child Protection and Long Term Teams can hardly be censored for trying to stave off increases to their already excessive workloads in circumstances where effective child protection was being overwhelmed by sheer numbers. As a result, different social work teams were liable to be in dispute with each other regarding the designation of a case as *child in need* or *child protection*. The problems experienced by the Duty Administration Team added to this source of stress. With only half its full staff complement, the Team struggled to respond to the needs and requirements of front-line social workers. This would undoubtedly have led to further dissatisfactions and arguments between staff, as practitioners found themselves unable to obtain vital information or had to complete time-consuming tasks that were more properly those of the Duty Administrative Team.

These dynamics are far from unique to Brent and have certainly not been consigned to the past. In a recent survey of 170 front-line child protection social workers, 60% reported that they had come under pressure from management to reclassify child protection cases as child in need cases in order to save money. This meant that child protection thresholds were being raised (*Community Care Online*, 2011). The British Association of Social Workers and Unison both currently report that a significant proportion of child protection social workers are being required to undertake administrative tasks as the numbers of support staff are cut back due to the reduction of central government grants to local authorities, which amounts to 28% in real terms over the period 2010/11 to 2014/15 (*Community Care*, 2011c; *Community Care Online*, 2012d).

At Brent Children's Social Services, the ongoing uncertainty created by the knowledge that new referrals were not being entered onto the system, together with the unreliability of administrative support, would have added to the stressors already acting upon social workers. The cumulative impact of these multiple sources of stress would have left practitioners feeling annoyed, occasioning verbal aggression towards colleagues in other teams, such as abrasive interactions or threats to initiate complaints. Alternatively, this may have been expressed as social aggression, with practitioners on one team sharing or spreading malicious gossip about colleagues on another one. Arguably, any social worker who found themselves in the febrile atmosphere of what Laming (2003, p 64) described as 'an under-resourced, understaffed, under-managed and dysfunctional environment' would have reacted similarly.

In any setting, organisational arrangements can create barriers to optimum working practices or generate avoidable disputes over roles, responsibilities and remits. Understaffing or poor working practices in one team can detrimentally impact on those in others, regardless of which agency. As social workers and their front-line managers usually have no direct control over problems in another team, it can be a particularly disempowering situation, confronted as they are by an irremovable stressor. Conflict between different teams or departments within an organisation can arise in any line of work and for innumerable and diverse reasons. While the stressor may be located in a different part of the organisation, workers affected elsewhere are likely to *displace* their stress-related irritability onto their immediate colleagues. This happens most commonly when *reactive aggression*, such as shouting or being abrasive, cannot be expressed against the person responsible for causing annoyance and is instead redirected at those in closer everyday proximity. Caregivers and children may also be the targets of *displaced aggression* by social workers who behave brusquely towards them when workplace stress and frustration cannot be successfully alleviated.

Physical working environment and stress

The organisational problems in Brent Children's Social Services were compounded by the lack of space at its offices. There was inadequate filing space, which meant that files were piled up on desks and in the corners of rooms without being properly categorised or organised (para 5.36). Space for employees was also severely limited, with Laming (2003) discovering that:

> The duty child protection and duty administrative teams shared an open-plan office on the ground floor of the children's social work building. I heard evidence that the building was 'overcrowded', 'grotty' and 'neglected'. The Social Services Inspectorate in 2000 said the accommodation for duty work needed to be improved to meet health and safety requirements....The seven duty social workers ... worked at one side of the room and the six child protection social workers were stationed at the opposite side of the room. (para 5.13)

Environmental stressors can also cause irritability and precipitate needless disputes between colleagues. In this case, an overcrowded open-plan office would have exacerbated the already highly stressed situation in which social workers were operating at Brent Children's Social Services. The higher noise levels created by the greater density of people in a confined area would have constituted yet another stressor. Open-plan offices are now commonplace in children's services and, in addition, social workers will often be hot-desking. Therefore, open-plan offices, if poorly laid out or congested, can contribute to the stress of practitioners. As with the stress caused by understaffing and organisational arrangements, the open-plan design, with its attendant overcrowding and higher noise levels, was a pervasive and inescapable stressor that social workers could neither 'fight' nor engage in 'flight' from. Consequently, the physical environment of the office would have contributed to illness and absence among practitioners. These conditions would have added to the workplace challenges confronting social workers dealing with referrals about Victoria and her family.

Managing stress in the workplace

Being a child protection social worker is inherently stressful and remains so even in the most positive, supportive and well-resourced of workplaces. Practitioners have a responsibility to monitor their own stress levels and the impact stress has on their behaviour towards colleagues, caregivers and children. Reducing stress, due to the irritability and low tolerance of frustration that it precipitates, requires practitioners to be mindful of their own needs for relaxation, leisure and social interaction outside the workplace. It is vital to negotiate time for these with employers, friends and family. One social worker might need to make a request to their manager for part-time or flexitime arrangements, while another needs to persuade a partner into endorsing an evening out playing five-a-side football with friends. MIND (2005, pp 13–14) identifies seven aspects of work that contribute to stress in the workplace, which are just as applicable to child protection and are reproduced in Box 3.1.

Box 3.1: Sources of stress at work

- *Factors intrinsic to the job* – This includes factors such as poor working conditions (eg noise, lighting, smells), shift work, long hours, travel, risk and danger, new technology, work overload, and work underload.
- *Role in the organisation* – Role ambiguity, role conflict and the degrees of responsibility for others can act as major sources of stress.
- *Personality and coping strategy* – The coping strategies a person uses to cope with stress and how effectively he or she uses them can also impact on the experience of stress.
- *Relationships at work* – Poor relationships can be defined as those that include low trust, low supportiveness and low interest in listening and trying to deal with problems that confront individuals.
- *Career development* – Lack of job security, fear of redundancy, obsolescence or retirement and numerous performance appraisals can cause pressure and strain.
- *Organisational structure and climate* – Lack of a sense of belonging, lack of adequate opportunities to participate, feelings of undue restrictions on behaviour and exclusion from office communications and consultations can all be sources of stress at work.
- *Home and work interface* – Long, uncertain or unsocial hours, working away from home, taking work home, high levels of responsibility, job insecurity, and job relocation may all adversely affect family responsibilities and leisure activities.

REFLECTIVE EXERCISE ON WORKPLACE STRESS

Think about an agency where you have been employed recently or are currently employed and, using the sources of workplace stress identified in Box 3.1 as a guide, identify the stressors that you have encountered. Ask yourself the following questions:

- Are these stressors specific to you or do you think they are likely to affect other workers as well? If they are specific to you, why do you think this is so?
- How do you react when you experience stress – what are your typical thoughts, emotions and behaviours when you experience stress? How might the way you react to stressors in the workplace affect those you work with?
- How do you think your stress reactions might influence how colleagues respond to you in turn?

The linkage of stress to irritability and, ultimately, expressions of aggression makes it imperative that social workers take time to consider their stress reactions and try to minimise these through a range of workplace strategies. Some of these are largely within the power of social workers, such as: asking for help; talking to colleagues about feeling stressed, frightened or upset; learning relaxation techniques; and achieving a healthy work–life balance. Reducing stress at work requires practitioners to avoid long office hours and excessive overtime or, where this is necessary on occasion, to ensure that they take regular time in lieu or annual leave. It also means being realistic about the number of families and the complexity of their circumstances that can be worked with simultaneously. These approaches to stress reduction involve negotiating leave and workloads with supervisors or team leaders. The next chapter examines the implications of high caseloads for conflict among colleagues and with managers and explores the skills needed to successfully negotiate work with supervisors or team leaders.

Case Study 3.2: Peter Connelly

Summary – Haringey Local Safeguarding Children Board (2010) *Serious case review 'Child A'*

Mr Connelly and Ms Connelly, who were of white British heritage, moved to the Haringey London Borough Council area and had three children together before the birth of Peter in March 2006. At around the time of Peter's birth, the couple separated. Ms Connelly made three visits to her GP with Peter, who had a number of bruises, in the period of September to December 2006. Ms Connelly claimed that Peter bruised easily and had fallen down stairs. During the third consultation on 11 December 2006, the GP referred Peter to Whittington Hospital for further investigation. A number of bruises were discovered on Peter's body that could not be explained by any medical condition. A Strategy Discussion was held on 12 December and the notes of that meeting recorded that the bruises might have been caused by 'pummelling'. A consultant paediatrician concluded that the bruising was 'very suggestive of non-accidental injury'. Police and social workers interviewed the older children and Ms Connelly, but received no satisfactory explanation as to Peter's bruises. Consequently, Peter, together with another of Ms Connelly's children, was placed on the Child Protection Register in December 2006.

In April 2007, Ms Connelly took Peter to the Accident and Emergency Department of North Middlesex University Hospital with swelling on the left side of his head. He was also found to have bruising on other parts of his body. Ms Connelly told medical staff that Peter had been pushed by another child. Peter was discharged home from hospital a few days later. Peter was again admitted to the same Accident and Emergency Department just over a month later, where multiple bruises were again discovered on his body. A Strategy Meeting was held on 4 June 2007 at which it was agreed to commence a child protection enquiry. There continued to be regular contact by health and social care professionals with the family, who generally reported that all appeared well. On 1 August, Ms Connelly took Peter to the Child Development Centre, where he was discovered to be grossly underweight. The doctor who saw Peter at the Centre diagnosed a viral infection. Two days later, on the morning of 3 August 2007, the London Ambulance Service responded to a 999 call from Ms Connelly and found Peter dead at his home.

In 2008, Ms Connelly, Mr Barker (Peter's step-father) and Mr Owen (Mr Barker's brother) were all convicted of causing or allowing Peter's death.

Understaffing, staff turnover and workloads

At the time of Peter's death, there were a high number of unallocated cases due to lack of capacity at Haringey's Children and Young People's Service. Even a year after Peter's death, there remained around 400 unallocated cases. Many front-line staff carried heavy workloads and were unable to action all the cases they were allocated, with a number of urgent tasks remaining incomplete or outstanding. The serious case review into Peter's death conducted by Haringey Local Safeguarding Children Board (2010, para 2.8.5) established that:

> the caseload of the social worker responsible for leading on the child protection plan for Peter had almost doubled from January 2007 to July 2007 and was 50% above the caseload recommended by Lord Laming in the Report of the Public Inquiry into the death of Victoria Climbié.

Ofsted, Healthcare Commission and HM Inspectorate of Constabulary (2008, para 50) inspected the operation of Haringey's Children's Services and found that:

> The high turnover of qualified social workers in some social care teams has resulted in heavy reliance on agency staff, who make up 51 of 121 established social worker posts. This results in lack of continuity for children and their families in care planning ... currently there are four unfilled social work posts. Some social workers have heavy caseloads,

exacerbated by the need for experienced staff to complete unfinished work for those staff who leave.

During the lead-up to Baby Peter's death, high staff turnover in Haringey absorbed additional social work time due to handovers and completing the work of departing staff. This occurred when social workers were already carrying heavy caseloads and were unable to accomplish work-related tasks. Doubtless, in Haringey, as in Brent, practitioners were frequently prevented from completing basic tasks due to the ceaseless volume of referrals that they were expected to deal with. The frustration–aggression hypothesis propounded by Dollard et al (1939) suggests that if social workers encountered repeated daily frustration of routine tasks, this would have caused them to feel angry. The report of the public inquiry indicates that practitioners were subject not merely to one frustration during an ordinary day at work, but to multiple numerous frustrations.

The situation that existed at Haringey London Borough Council can be generalised to practitioners working in other agencies in the present day. A social worker who planned to complete their file notes for an interaction with a child and a core assessment in connection with another family during that day might find this stymied by the unanticipated allocation of an urgent child protection case, which must be acted upon immediately. Additionally, they might be asked to perform a vital home visit in connection with a temporarily unallocated case, originally handled by an agency social worker whose contract finished the previous day. Within a short space of time, such a practitioner would have already experienced considerable frustration of their planned work goals for the day. The cumulative impact as the day proceeded, and as it was succeeded by a working week of similar disruptions, would have precipitated increasing levels of irritation. Aggressive behaviour sparked by countless frustrations is often expressed as tetchiness or argumentativeness and exhibited when front-line professionals easily find fault with one another.

High workloads and staff turnover occur in many other child protection agencies. Munro (2010, para 2.10), in her review of the child protection system in England commissioned by the government, observed that the negative publicity surrounding the trial of Peter Connelly's carers and the serious case review that followed had triggered an increased rate of referrals to children's services across the country, both from members of the public and from other professionals. In other words, the state of affairs at Haringey during 2006 and 2007, while exceptional in terms of their extreme nature, were not singular. Some social workers in child protection continue to practise in organisations where workloads are still above the recommended level and where they must cope with a revolving set of personnel.

Information and communication technology

Social workers reported to the Haringey Local Safeguarding Children Board (2010, para 2.8.5) inquiry that while the amount of administrative support to them had decreased over the years, the introduction of the new case-recording system, known as Framework 1, had generated a substantial number of additional administrative tasks. In this connection, Ofsted, Healthcare Commission and HM Inspectorate of Constabulary (2008, para 53) found that 'the existing social care electronic recording system operated by the council lacks sufficient flexibility and, although this impedes effective practice by social workers, there has been insufficient priority given to resolving this issue by managers'.

This is a widespread problem also identified by the *Munro review* (Munro, 2010). The online Integrated Children's System (ICS) has come in for particular criticism by social workers. It is a software system specified by central government, comprising a workflow that breaks down the social work task into a set of business processes with an associated set of timescales for the completion of each task. The ICS also incorporates a set of electronic pro forma for the recording of different types of information about families and children. Munro (2010, para 1.24) found that 'the micro-control of workflow and process in the ICS has had the unintended effect of increasing duplication and data entry at multiple stages, creating repetitive tasks that simply did not exist before its inception and now cannot be bypassed'. Contributions by front-line social workers to *Community Care* (2011c, pp 30–1) frequently express frustration about electronic case management systems. One practitioner employed by a London borough council captures the annoyance of many when she claims that:

> social workers here complain that the ICS is laborious. If the person [involved in the case] before you hasn't filled in all the relevant parts then you can't process it any further. Some of this work could be done by admin staff.

The nature of computerised records in combination with the vilification of child protection social workers after such child deaths as those of Victoria and Peter mean that practitioners feel compelled to spend considerable time inputting information. The same contributor to *Community Care*, speaking of her colleagues, explains:

> When they input information from a meeting or conversation many go into a huge amount of detail because there is a general culture of anxiety around whether they have done enough to cover their backs … that anxiety is a driver for much of the way we record things. (*Community Care*, 2011c, p 31)

Corroborating the perspective of this child protection social worker, a two-year study conducted by White et al (2010, p 410) found that social workers spent 60% to 80% of their available time (excluding periods travelling or at meetings) inputting data. For many social workers, the lengthy filling in of online forms is a work-related requirement that is often experienced as a burdensome distraction from vital face-to-face interaction with parents and children. Consequently, the restrictive, repetitive and time-consuming competition of electronic formats is a widespread source of stress and frustration in social work practice. They are a cause of daily irritation for many social workers and are sometimes the trigger for verbal aggression between overworked colleagues.

Performance management

The problems associated with computerised social work tasks, such as the ICS, are closely bound up with the adoption of New Public Management in children's services. This was core to New Labour's modernisation project, which was conceived to drive up standards in public services by introducing performance management through the use of indicators and targets collectively known as the Performance Assessment Framework (PAF). Alongside the introduction of 'value for money' and 'best value' requirements, the PAF obliges local authorities to make annual statistical returns regarding their revenue expenditures to inspecting bodies. Local government performance indicators of children's services in relation to child protection have included: the number of initial and core assessments completed within nationally prescribed timescales; the number of children on the child protection register; the number of children re-registered; and the duration on the register of children. Such performance indicators have been subject to a set of central government targets to, for example, reduce the number of re-registrations.

Ofsted, in turn, uses these performance indicators to measure the achievements of each local authority and whether it has met national targets. As Ofsted reports are made public, this places considerable pressure on senior management to ensure that front-line social workers are attaining the targets set for individual teams. This can add to the number of stressors with which practitioners are coping. The ICS incorporates the prescribed forms and timescales for completing initial and core assessments on children and their families. Since these forms are now computerised, the system records the performance of each social worker and team in completing assessments within the timescale. The central government has agreed to relax some of these timescales, but a number of local authorities have indicated that they will retain them. According to Broadhurst et al (2010), the use of performance management to this degree adds considerable pressure to workloads, distorts priorities and can result in poor data collection and input. White et al (2010, pp 406–7), investigating the impact of the ICS on front-line social work, opined that:

> the death of Peter Connelly brought to the fore a major concern that the post-Climbié reforms had resulted in too much organizational change, managerial scrutiny, data entry and e-enabled information sharing, all of which were causing social workers to spend excessive time at their desks.

An online system that records a social worker's every interaction with that system, tracking the completion of tasks, timescales and targets, can be incredibly intimidating. Such a situation exposes front-line practitioners to sustained, pervasive and heightened forms of stress. Simultaneously, they confront systemic frustrations, as interactions with children and families are curtailed in favour of data input at their desks. All of these factors contribute to workplace conflict and aggressive behaviour between colleagues. Taken together with the difficulties social workers faced at Brent and Haringey London Borough Councils already revealed in this chapter, they comprise a diverse range of stressors that can impinge on the disposition of a front-line practitioner, causing irritability, social withdrawal, passive-aggressive behaviour or unconcealed belligerence. These are listed as follows:

- Underfunding, resulting in constraints on office space, staffing levels and administrative support.
- Cramped, overcrowded and noisy office space.
- Understaffing due to funding cuts or sickness.
- High and complex workloads for front-line social workers.
- High staff turnover.
- High numbers of inexperienced or poorly inducted staff.
- Reorganisations that result in disruption to caseloads and teams.
- Organisational arrangements that contribute to disputes between social workers and teams.
- Poor administrative support, resulting in front-line workers undertaking administrative tasks.
- Timescales and performance management targets that interfere with professional judgement and priorities.
- Electronic filing and assessment systems that are time-consuming due to data input requirements, duplication of inputs or frequent software crashes.

Agency context and the fostering of conflict

The state of affairs within London boroughs is particularly acute in terms of recruitment and staff retention, with historically high vacancy rates for child protection social workers. But the circumstances revealed by the inquiries into the deaths of Victoria Climbié and Peter Connelly remain contributory factors to conflict in the workplace for practitioners across the country. Certainly, some local authorities will fund their social services for children better than others, have fewer vacancies, provide better office accommodation and engage in less detrimental reorganisations. Nevertheless, many of the factors just listed are likely to impinge upon the work of practitioners. Child protection activity is also mentally demanding and emotionally draining. Even the most well-adjusted professional will experience periods of heightened stress as he or she works with a child at risk of significant harm. All these aspects of the agency in conjunction with the nature of child protection work can fuel and perpetuate conflicts between colleagues. Disagreements can arise between administrative staff and social workers over who should be responsible for particular tasks, such as booking transport or inputting data into electronic files. One social worker may resent another's decision to transfer work with a family by means of what is perceived to be a self-serving re-categorisation of the young person from a *child in need* to a *child at risk*.

Front-line practitioners taking up the slack for a colleague who is off on frequent sick leave may feel that they are being taken advantage of to the detriment of their own work and health. This may be expressed as latent conflict or overt antipathy towards that colleague on his or her return to work. There can be tension between busy permanent staff and new or temporary workers when long-established practitioners find themselves answering multiple enquiries from poorly inducted or newly qualified social workers. Noisy and overcrowded open-plan offices may increase the potential for conflict between colleagues as they hot-desk and scramble for computer access. Team members can disagree over priorities as performance management requirements collide with child-centred social work practice. These sources of conflict, in turn, form the backdrop to professional differences of opinion over how to proceed with a particular family where children are at risk of significant harm. The causes of conflict have already been discussed in Chapter Two, where they were identified by Isenhart and Spangle (2000, pp 14–5) as revolving around disagreements over:

- data;
- interests;
- procedures;
- values;
- relationships;
- roles; and
- communication.

REFLECTIVE EXERCISE ON CONFLICT

Identify some recent conflicts involving you and a colleague that have occurred in your workplace. Having read the first section of this chapter, consider whether these conflicts were precipitated by purely interpersonal issues or whether aspects of your disagreement emanated from systemic problems in the agency.

Addressing conflicts stemming from the agency context

In the first instance, front-line workers need to distinguish between conflicts with colleagues, which can be experienced as exceptionally personal, but actually originate in the organisational architecture. Two social workers who find themselves squabbling over access to a computer are not essentially in conflict with one another so much as in conflict with management and the inadequate provision of computer terminals. Social workers who argue with each other as to who should accept a new referral at an allocations team meeting may well have issues with management regarding their bludgeoning caseloads rather than with each other. In any situation involving conflict, it is important to reflect on the deeper, often less apparent, causes rather than act precipitously to take issue with a colleague.

In this connection, the *conflict spiral*, identified by Carpenter and Kennedy (1988) and described in Chapter Two, is a salutary reminder of how rapidly a point of disagreement can conflate into a workplace battle. Once a problem emerges, the tendency is for the individuals involved to adopt positions that quickly become narrowed and rigid, and which are increasingly articulated through adversarial attitudes. The dispute then widens to pull in other members of staff who are co-opted onto different sides, culminating in the curtailment of viable options to achieve a resolution. It is crucial to forestall this *conflict spiral* by engaging in negation with the offending person from the outset. Box 3.2 outlines the principal strategies employed by individuals during negotiation.

Box 3.2: Principal strategies for negotiation

Lewicki et al (2010, p 23) identify five key strategies that people engage in when confronted with conflict, which are outlined as follows:

1. *Contending* (competing or dominating) – Protagonists tenaciously pursue their own outcomes with little regard for the outcomes of others. A person adopting this strategy attempts to impose their own aspirations upon others through such methods as 'threats, punishment, intimidation and unilateral action'.

2. *Yielding* (accommodating or obliging) – Protagonists using this strategy lower their own aspirations and are more interested in the other person achieving their goals than in achieving their own outcomes. Such protagonists in effect let the other person win.

3. *Inaction* (avoiding) – Protagonists appear to have little interest in whether either they or the person with whom they are in dispute achieves their desired outcomes. These protagonists engage in withdrawal, passivity, retreat, silence and inaction in the face of conflict.

4. *Problem-solving* (collaborating or integrating) – Protagonists evidence high concern both for achieving their own outcomes and those of the person they are in dispute with. The parties to the conflict 'actively pursue approaches to maximise their joint outcome from the conflict'.

5. *Compromising* – Protagonists engage in a moderate effort to achieve their own outcomes and those of the person they are in dispute with. This can constitute a lazy attempt to solve problems or easy yielding by the parties to the conflict.

Of course, individuals may use different strategies at different points in time in relation to the same issue or they may adopt a combination of strategies. As Lewicki et al (2010, p 24) emphasise, while the literature has historically advanced *problem-solving* as a normative approach to conflict resolution and therefore superior to other strategies, it is not necessarily apt in all situations. If your employer imposes cuts to staffing that fundamentally undermine the integrity of child protection services, *problem-solving* might be a counterproductive strategy and *contending* a responsible course of action. Likewise, where a child *is not* at immediate risk of significant harm, *yielding* to a father by a social worker might be an effective strategy to help buttress partnership-working with that parent and achieve longer-term goals that protect the child from significant harm. To take another instance, you could potentially vie with another team member for a desk in a particular bay of an open-plan office known to be quieter than others. The other team member has been supportive of you in the past and you value her friendship and guidance, so you minimise the importance of the outcome and decide on *inaction* as a strategy. In this way, you avoid damaging a supportive relationship with a colleague for the sake of a minor gain.

REFLECTIVE EXERCISE ON NEGOTIATION STRATEGIES

- Look again at the five negotiation strategies set out in Box 3.2. Which of these strategies do you typically engage in, and in what circumstances and with whom? Do you use some strategies more often than others and, if so, why?
- What are the different skills you would require to effectively implement each of the five negotiation strategies outlined in Box 3.2?
- Identify the attitudes or beliefs about yourself and others that underpin your use of different strategies. Do these explain why you tend to use some strategies more than others and, if so, are there any attitudes or beliefs you hold that undermine your ability to engage in a range of negotiation strategies? What are these unhelpful attitudes or beliefs?
- Identify your skills' strengths and weaknesses in relation to each of the five negotiation strategies. Does this explain why you tend to use some negotiation strategies more than others?

Integrative negotiation

A problem-solving approach is most likely to achieve an optimum resolution of conflict for the parities involved according to leading authority Lewicki et al (2010, p 72), who detail an integrative negotiation model based on problem-solving strategies, of which the key elements are:

- Focus on commonalties rather than differences.
- Attempt to address needs and interests, not positions.
- Commit to meeting the needs of all involved parties.
- Exchange information and ideas.
- Invent options for mutual gain.
- Use objective criteria for standards of performance.

These aspects of integrative negotiation are achieved through a number of processes, which includes the free flow of information. This means being upfront about your real goals and being prepared to listen intently to others to ascertain their desired outcomes. Understanding the possible alternatives that both parties to a dispute are willing to consider facilitates the identification of acceptable trade-offs during the ensuing negotiation. This initial process needs to involve inquiring into the values, preferences and priorities of the other party and sharing your own with them. It necessitates comprehending the other person's interests. Lewicki et al (2010, p 79) define interests as comprising 'underlying concerns, needs, desires or fears that motivate a negotiator to take a particular position'. The greater the understanding the parties to a negotiation have of each others' positions, the greater the likelihood of arriving at a win–win resolution. On sharing this sort of information, it may be possible to redefine what had appeared at the outset to be individual goals as joint or collective ones. This creates goals that all parties have a vested interest in achieving.

The advantages of this approach can be considered in the light of the circumstances uncovered by the investigations following the deaths of Victoria Climbié and Peter Connelly. In both instances, there were a set of systemic problems created by underfunding that manifested as understaffing and under-resourced existing staff. This was exacerbated in Peter's case by rigid timescales, prescriptive assessments and software not fit for purpose. For the social workers involved in events leading up to Victoria's death, their work was further impaired by a cramped and noisy working environment. In both investigations, high workloads and stress among front-line social workers were reported. In Brent Council, arguments between colleagues on the Duty Team, Child Protection Team and Long Term Teams as to who should carry a particular case were precipitated and sustained by the high caseloads carried by all social workers. This was intensified by an organisational structure that magnified rather than minimised the scope for dispute because of the often false distinction between a child in need and child protection referrals.

In this situation, colleagues ostensibly in conflict over the designation of a case, and thus its allocation, actually have a common goal in terms of reducing their high workloads and the potential for disputes between different teams that threaten to engulf many other social workers and the team leaders. Two colleagues able to exchange information about their real personal goals might be able to devise a common objective and thus become allies in searching for a common solution. This requires developing flexibility as to how your needs and interests as a worker are met. Such an approach avoids the detrimental impacts of interpersonal conflict identified by Lewicki et al (2010, p 19) and detailed in Chapter Two. These include competitive win–lose goals, misperceptions of one another's motives and goals, emotionally charged communications, and the exaggeration of differences. Moving from individually conceived to mutually agreed goals involves a number of processes, which are described by Lewicki et al (2010, pp 77–8) and set out in Box 3.3.

Box 3.3: The integrative negotiation process

1. *Define the problem* – This is a crucial stage as it sets the parameters for the ensuing negotiation. It must involve going beyond a simplistic view or gut reaction to the issue. A superficial examination of the facts will mean jumping to conclusions in ways that shut down negotiation. Problem definition has to include comprehension of the complexity of the circumstances in which disputes occur.

2. *Define the problem in a mutually acceptable way* – This requires maintaining an open mind and stating the problem in neutral terms. It means avoiding problem statements that appear to blame one side or only address the grievance, needs or priorities of one side. The parties to the conflict may need to revise the problem statement several times before they can agree a mutually acceptable definition.

3. *State the problem in terms of practicality and comprehensiveness* – This means stating the problem as clearly and distinctly as possible. It also necessitates stripping back the problem to its core elements, thus avoiding the distraction of more minor issues. However, this should not be done at the expense of acknowledging and articulating the complexity of the problem at the centre of the dispute.

4. *Restate the problem as a goal* – This necessitates concentrating on the goal that the parties want to achieve as opposed to the solutions to the problem. It is important to avoid vagueness and to be as specific as possible about the goal or sub-goals.

5. *Identify the obstacles to attaining the goal* – Parties to the dispute need to explore the impediments to obtaining the common goal they have identified. This step also involves determining which obstacles can be addressed and which cannot given the time and resources available to the parties. Obstacles that are immovable need to be openly acknowledged.

6. *Depersonalise the problem* – Strong negative emotions can easily feed into biases and perpetuate misconceptions. In such circumstances, each party views his or her own attitudes, actions and goals in a positive light while denigrating or dismissing those of the other person. Achieving a dispassionate standpoint is vital to successfully managing this aspect of integrative negotiation.

7. *Separate the problem definition from the search for solutions* – It is important to avoid pre-emptively arriving at preferred solutions before fully exploring and agreeing on the nature of the problem. Otherwise, parties can end up in prolonged dispute about solutions when the real issue is continued disagreement over the nature of the problem in the first instance.

8. *Develop standards against which alternative solutions can be measured* – These will be different depending on the nature of the problem. Parties need to agree

at the outset how they will know if the problem has been solved or the goals they have mutually defined are attained. These standards can then be used to assess alternative courses of action or solutions to resolving the problem.

9. *Generate alternative solutions* – This involves creating a list of viable options and evaluating each of these. Redefining the problem to produce win–win alternatives for both parties may be necessary.

REFLECTIVE EXERCISE ON THE PROCESSES OF NEGOTIATION

Read back over the stages involved in the integrative negotiation process set out in Box 3.3. Ask yourself the following questions:

- What challenges or difficulties might each stage of the negotiation process present for you?
- How would you go about addressing these challenges and what abilities or skills would you need to do so?
- Which of these abilities and skills do you already possess and which would you need to improve upon in order to effectively engage in an integrative negotiation process?

Conflict between individual social workers

Agency context can cause, heighten and sustain conflict between front-line workers, as the inquiries into the circumstances surrounding the deaths of Victoria and Peter testify. However, this is not to deny that even in the best of working environments, individual practitioners can disagree with each other or engage in prolonged disputes in the workplace. These conflicts may arise from: genuine differences of opinion in relation to practice; clashes of personal values; expressions of prejudice; power plays; or, indeed, for a myriad of idiosyncratic reasons. Whatever the cause, it is important to engage in discussion with the individual in question before widening the conflict to involve other people.

Before you enter into negotiations on any matter, you need to be clear about the issue at dispute and your own interests in relation to it. This means undertaking preparation before addressing the problem with a colleague. Not engaging in sufficient preparation leaves you in danger of being swept away by events, as claim and counterclaim, mutually exclusive goals, suggested trade-offs, and emotionality cram your opening discussions. You become vulnerable to precipitously agreeing to goals and solutions proposed by others that do not meet your needs or are not consonant with your values. Either that or you will become confrontational, adopting inflexible demands in the face of unexpected assertions or bargaining positions assumed by others. This fosters anxiety, which is often expressed as anger or impatience, resulting in the inadvertent sabotage of potential areas of agreement. Good preparation is, therefore, fundamental to effective negotiation. Lewicki et al (2010, pp 119–35) detail 10 components of good preparation, as summarised in Box 3.4.

Box 3.4: Preparing for integrative negotiation

1. *Defining the issues* – Dissect the problem to see if it consists of one issue or a number of issues, and, if the latter, consider how these interrelate. Which issues are interdependent and which can be dealt with separately during negotiations?

2. *Assembling the issues* – Create a comprehensive list of the issues and decide which are more or less important. This can suggest potential trade-offs, where some of the issues are less important to you than to the other party. Hence, you can give way on something of little consequence in exchange for an outcome that is significant to you. Determine your optimum and minimal outcomes for each issue.

3. *Defining interests* – Establish not just what you want, but why you want it. What are your motivations, needs and preferences? Ask yourself why you want a particular outcome.

4. *Knowing limits* – Establish your *resistance point*, which is the minimal position you would accept in the negotiation and beyond which it would be so disadvantageous to you that you would be better to abandon the negotiation. This restrains you from being talked into a poor offer during intense negotiations.

5. *Knowing alternatives* – Establish what alternative outcomes you could potentially achieve either with another party or with the same party to the negotiations. The more alternative agreements you identify, the less dependent you are on achieving a particular outcome with a particular party in negotiations.

6. *Setting targets* – This is a range of variations around your optimal outcome that would be acceptable to you. Targets need to be specific and realistic, even if challenging to attain. This will also involve packaging different targets together in a bargaining mix, which comprises the outcomes, priorities, optimal and minimum positions, and the range of acceptable outcomes.

7. *Assessing constituents and the social context* – Determine whether there are multiple parties to the negotiations and what sort of alliances they are likely to form. This requires giving consideration to others who may be constituents of the negotiation, meaning they have an interest in its outcome, such as a line manager.

8. *Analysing the other party* – Gathering information about the other party's interests is vital to understanding their overall perspective, together with their goals, targets, motivations, preferences, priorities, alternatives, *resistance points*, constraints and constituents. From this information, assess how the other party might negotiate, identifying the areas of likely agreement or disagreement or greatest dispute.

9. *Presenting issues to the other party* – Present as strong and substantiated a case for your outcomes as possible. Provide facts and assemble supporting arguments

> for your position. These can be gleaned from documentation or information from other people. Anticipate the facts and arguments of the other party in order to counter them with facts and arguments to justify your outcomes.
>
> 10. *What protocol should be followed* – Agree the agenda for the negotiation by deciding: what the issues are; the sequence in which they should be discussed; and whether they should be dealt with one at a time or grouped.

Preparing for an integrative negotiation with a colleague demands self-restraint to forestall pre-emptively engaging him or her in a discussion about the issue in dispute. It also means controlling stress-induced irritability, which often leads to spontaneous aggressive behaviour such as a sarcastic comment or the refusal to accede to an entirely reasonable request for assistance by another team member. Of course, this is not easy in a highly pressured workplace, especially if other colleagues are abrasive and unhelpful as they endeavour to cope with their own stress and anger. But, if social workers can manage to set aside time to examine the issues leading to conflict with another practitioner, this offers the possibility of initiating a constructive dialogue. Effective preparation, followed by engagement with integrative negotiating processes, has the potential to: support personal and professional development; improve problem-solving skills; and promote new approaches to perennial difficulties.

This deliberative approach to negotiations with colleagues is equally applicable to resolving a dispute with a manager, caregiver or young person. In all of these situations, desired outcomes may be circumscribed by agency policy, child protection procedures or the legal framework. At the same time, policy, procedure and statutory provisions can be successfully deployed to assist social workers to secure their entitlements in a workplace dispute or set limits on the outcomes sought by parents or their partners where a child is at risk of harm. Often, social workers find themselves pitched into conflicts with colleagues, managers and caregivers alike without sufficient preparation to deal in a measured way with the issues that suddenly confront them. Lack of preparation leaves social workers vulnerable to agreeing to outcomes that are unworkable or unsafe. Where workplace disputes arise unexpectedly, practitioners need to develop sufficient self-confidence to postpone discussion of them (when feasible) until they are adequately prepared to engage with them constructively. Entering an integrative negotiation process means neither seeking to impose a unilateral solution upon another nor acquiescing to outcomes that are unsatisfactory or highly risky.

Box 3.5: Research evidence: what makes a good negotiator?

Isenhart and Spangle (2000, pp 48–50), in their overview of research on negotiation, highlight a number of behaviours associated with successful negotiators, which are that they:

- build trust and are less likely to make positional statements;

- are more likely to share information;
- are courteous and personable;
- avoid making threats;
- ask many questions;
- do a considerable amount of listening;
- reflect back tentative understandings through paraphrasing and summarising;
- use *tagging*, which involves calling attention to procedures or behaviours that inhibit or promote negotiation;
- generate many options and come to a negotiation primed with a number of alternatives;
- demonstrate flexibility in relation to solutions to achieve goals; and
- generate trade-offs through acknowledging long-term versus short-term gains, differences in preferences between the parties, options over timing, and tolerance of risk.

REFLECTIVE EXERCISE ON INTEGRATIVE NEGOTIATION

Choose an unresolved recent workplace conflict in which you have been involved with another colleague. Using the guidance set out earlier to prepare for an integrative negotiation, take each element in turn and write out a bullet-pointed list for it. Ask yourself the following questions:

- What have been the most challenging aspects of this preparation for you and why do you think this is so?
- Would you normally engage in this degree of preparation before negotiating with someone and if not why?
- What are the obstacles to this kind of detailed preparation and how might you eliminate or reduce them at the outset of future negotiations?

When negotiation fails

Despite your best efforts, a disagreement with a colleague may not be resolvable. If you have engaged in a genuine negotiation process but have been unable to achieve a resolution acceptable to both parties, then it may be necessary to involve more senior staff. Doing so plainly runs the risk of escalating the conflict and widening it to encompass whole teams in addition to first or second line managers. This potentially damaging spread of the conflict needs to be weighed against the consequences of adopting a strategy of *yielding*, whereby you permit another colleague to do as they want without contention from you. In many situations, for example, in Brent Children's Social Services where the categorisation of a case as *child in need* or *child protection* was a cause of discord, an unresolved issue can lead to continual friction. In a child protection context, such friction can jeopardise the safety of children and sabotage best practice. Discussing your difficulty with a supervisor or first line manager may be vital to gaining greater insight into the basis of the dispute, and possibly your own contribution to sustaining it. A supervisor may support you to engage in a more considered and productive negotiation process with a colleague. Conversely, in circumstances where good practice in child protection is being compromised, it may be necessary for you to stand back and permit the disagreement to be resolved by team leaders at a higher level within the organisation. The conflicts created by an overcrowded open-plan office at Brent Children's Social Services during 1999 could not have been satisfactorily resolved through negotiation between colleagues. It plainly required action at management level. Negotiating with management requires front-line practitioners to develop and deploy an even greater repertoire of skills. These are considered in Chapter Four.

Points for practice

- Social workers tend to operate in challenging resource-constrained environments that increase the potential for conflict between colleagues, sometimes leading to stress and aggressive responses to other workers.
- Aspects of agency context such as high staff turnover, problematic computer software for recording assessments, filing and sharing information together with performance management requirements can be daily stressors for practitioners.
- Some practitioners may work in office conditions that act as additional stressors such as overcrowded or noisy open-plan offices.
- Practitioners need to reflect upon the interrelationship between workplace stressors and their own responses to stress, particularly if stress induces feelings of anger, resulting in aggressive behaviour towards colleagues, parents or children.
- Effective negotiation strategies can assist to prevent conflicts from escalating into divisive workplace arguments. Practitioners need to examine how their own habitual negotiation strategies may reduce their efficacy in resolving conflict.
- Integrative negotiation is a proven approach to conflict resolution that emphasises the importance of comprehending and working with the interests and priorities of the other party. Gaining familiarity with integrative negotiation can assist practitioners to de-escalate conflict and identify feasible solutions to mutual problems.

CHAPTER FOUR

Conflict with management

Conflict with managers

Team leaders are normally front-line managers and often provide supervision for social workers involved in child protection work. As such, they are a vital source of professional support for practitioners struggling with families who are hostile or aggressive. In highly pressured workplaces where resources are limited and caseloads high, front-line and middle management are crucial go-betweens in negotiating better working conditions. They may also be pivotal in resolving disputes between colleagues or teams as practitioners engage with a range of other professionals to intervene in families to safeguard children. Social workers may sometimes be in dispute with their managers when, for example, supervision is poor, workloads are excessive or resources are prohibitive of good practice with families. This chapter examines the circumstances revealed by the public inquiries into the death of Victoria Climbié and the sexual abuse of children in Welsh care homes in order to explore power relationships between front-line workers and their managers, alongside the skills of negotiation and assertiveness.

Case Study 4.1: Victoria Climbié

Laming (2003) *The Victoria Climbié inquiry*

This case study builds on the exploration of the public inquiry into the death of Victoria Climbié already considered in Case Study 3.1. It also moves away from events at Brent London Borough Council and disputes between colleagues to analyse conflicts between front-line staff and management at Haringey London Borough Council during the period when Victoria was allocated to a social worker there.

Excessive caseloads

The Laming (2003) inquiry investigated the supervisory arrangements in place during the period when Haringey London Borough Council was responsible for Victoria Climbié's welfare. When Victoria was admitted to hospital on the second occasion with a serious scald to her face, this time to North Middlesex Hospital on 24 July 1999, a referral was made by the hospital social worker to Haringey Children and Family Services, which was passed to the Investigation and Assessment Team. At the time the practitioner on this team was allocated to work with Victoria and her family she was already carrying 19 cases in contravention of the maximum 12 set out in the *Duty investigation and assessment team procedures*. She was also owed 52 days off for time in lieu. The high caseloads among social workers in the Investigation and Assessment Team were known to the commissioning manager, but apparently little was done to reduce them (para 6.15).

Excessive caseloads are not unique to Haringey London Borough Council. The Social Work Task Force (2009, paras 2.4, 2.6), in its own survey, found that 'concern about caseload size is widespread'. It concluded that:

> too many social workers are carrying caseloads which can be too high and make it hard for them to do their job well. There is very strong evidence that the absence of effective management of workload makes practitioners feel de-skilled, lowers their morale and can lead to poor health.

The Social Work Task Force (2009, para 2.5) opined that in situations of serious risk, excessive caseloads can impair the judgement and decision-making of practitioners. The survey they conducted (2009, para 2.8) indicated that almost half of all practitioners work more than their contracted hours as a result of high caseloads.

Kool (2008, p 137) contends that conflicts arise when two or more parties perceive themselves to have opposing interests, such that the achievement of one party's interest negates that of the other. If social workers are carrying disproportionately high caseloads, which persist despite being brought to the attention of management, they are confronted by a conflict between their interests and those of management. On the one hand, high caseloads undermine good practice. They leave children at greater risk, as overworked and stressed practitioners struggle to complete basic tasks such as finishing assessments on children or building rapport with caregivers for rehabilitative work. On the other hand, managers are subject to demands from local and central government to operate a cost-efficient child protection service within a limited budget. Performance indicators mean that the costs and outputs of individual teams can be measured, placing front-line managers under considerable scrutiny and pressure to deliver on targets. Greatly constrained local government budgets for children's social care, combined with increasing referral rates for suspected child neglect or abuse in many parts of the UK, compel social workers to carry high caseloads (*Community Care Online*, 2012e).

Within the context of Case Study 4.1 and the facts uncovered by the public inquiry, social workers and managers may have come to perceive their interests as win–lose outcomes, despite their common superordinate goal of protecting children. This would have led to disputes regarding the number of cases allocated to front-line practitioners. Lewicki et al (2010, p 19) suggest that there is a set of intertwined social dynamics that commonly play out in circumstances of conflict. Consequently, in similar situations of disagreement elsewhere, the perceptions that managers and practitioners have of each other may become progressively more critical and one-dimensional, as strong negative emotions such as anger and anxiety start to cloud judgements. As managers and front-line staff align themselves with those who agree with them and distance themselves from those who do not, workplaces become arenas of constant dispute. Demands by social workers and managers can become increasingly inflexible as meaningful communication in terms of negotiation over caseloads and staffing levels stalls. At this point, dissatisfaction can easily inflate to encompass an expanding variety of gripes unrelated to caseloads. As increasing numbers of issues and people are embroiled in the dispute, positions harden and flexibility becomes more difficult as people fear losing face. Ultimately, 'as the conflict progresses, each side becomes more entrenched in its own view, less tolerant and accepting of the other, more defensive and less communicative, and more emotional' (Lewicki et al, 2010, p 19).

Negotiating on workloads

Back and Back (2005, p 166) identify three key beliefs that inhibit employees from being self-assertive with managers over workloads. These are: first, the conviction that as a professional, one ought to be able to handle the pressure and the perception that everyone else is coping; second, the worry of many employees that if they complain about their workload, management will assume they cannot cope; and, third, the belief that a high workload is the norm and everyone else in the team or agency has a similar workload. These types of private internal dialogues undermine the capacity of social workers to challenge the size and complexity of their caseload with front-line managers. For those practitioners who conclude that their workload is intolerable and undermines good practice, they can raise this: on an ad hoc basis at the point when they are given additional cases; as a discrete issue during a supervision meeting; or by requesting a specific meeting with a team leader to address the issue. If dealt with ad hoc, objecting to the number of cases already allocated to the worker or to taking on additional ones can be less threatening to a front-line manager than requesting a specific meeting. People who feel less threatened are more amenable to compromise during a negotiation. However, such a strategy can make your workload concerns appear less pressing and, therefore, easier to brush aside. Nevertheless, voicing opposition to being given yet more cases can force a front-line manager to think twice before allocating you more cases in the future.

Alternatively, asking for a separate meeting to address problems of workload gives due weight to the issue. The timing of such a meeting needs to be right. Prematurely objecting to an increased caseload can make it appear that you are unwilling to work hard. It is also important to avoid requesting a reduction in caseload if this is short-term, perhaps when your increased caseload is due to another practitioner's temporary sick leave. In short, the timing of your request needs to communicate to a manager that it is reasonable. It is also crucial to ensure that you possess precise facts about your caseload, the quantity or the time each requires and so forth before entering into discussion with your manager. You must also be clear as to the number of cases or level of complexity you can deal with competently in terms of good practice with children and families in a safeguarding context. Except in the gravest of situations, such a position should constitute a basis for negotiation and not a rigid demand. Agreement is most likely in circumstances where both social workers and front-line managers feel that there has been some degree of compromise.

Knowing your legal rights, agency policies conferring entitlements, custom and practice within the workplace, and accepted norms of behaviour you should expect from others is vital to assertive negotiation with a manager. If you are not aware of your rights, it becomes far too easy for a stressed and irritable manager to simply tell you that these do not exist or do not apply in a given situation, or simply to ignore them. Not knowing your rights plays into passive and acquiescent responses when others make unreasonable demands on you. If a newly qualified social worker is unaware of their right to a lower caseload and more supervision than experienced practitioners during their first year of practice, then they will precipitately concede to a team leader's insistence that he or she is unable to reduce the caseload or provide regular supervision. Knowing your rights in this situation can buttress assertive statements and actions. It means that you already have a good foundation from which to argue your point of view. If you are unaware or unsure of your rights to have particular needs met or to have an opinion considered, you inevitably become hesitant or capitulate at the first challenge to your claim. Rights need not be legal; they can be based on good practice or social norms. One example of a non-legal right would be the right to a manageable workload. In terms of supervision, non-legal entitlements could include the right to make mistakes on occasion and to be supported through constructive criticism by a supervisor to correct or avoid them and not to be humiliated or made to feel foolish. Another would be the right to be consulted about decisions that affect you, or to have your opinion heard and given consideration at a team meeting.

REFLECTIVE EXERCISE ON WORKPLACE RIGHTS

List your workplace rights under the following headings: legal rights; rights based on local or national policies; rights based on custom and practice in your workplace; rights based on codes of practice; and rights based on accepted norms of behaviour. Drawing on knowledge of your rights, decide how you would respond to each of the following four attempts by a manager to dismiss your request not to be given an additional complex family situation to work with due to an already high caseload:

- 'Everyone else is taking on additional cases in the team.'
- 'Maybe you're not cut out for this job.'
- 'This is the work you're paid to do.'
- 'I'm disappointed that you're unable to handle additional work.'

Inadequate supervision

The team leader for the Investigation and Assessment Team was also the immediate superior and supervisor for the practitioner asked to work with Victoria. The team leader had recently returned from maternity leave and was only working two-and-a-half days a week. There was considerable disquiet within the team regarding her availability and competency as a manager. These concerns were relayed to the commissioning manager (who was the team leader's line manager) on a number of occasions. In particular, team members were worried by their team leader's poor knowledge of the cases for which she had supervisory responsibility, her chaotic approach to management and the unpredictability of when she would be in the office (paras 6.26, 6.30).

Victoria's allocated social worker criticised her team leader at the public inquiry and stated in evidence that: supervision was once every seven weeks instead of every two to three weeks; sessions were persistently cancelled or rescheduled without explanation; supervision was unsatisfactory, as the team leader discussed her personal life instead of the cases; and the team leader tended to simply agree to whatever course of action the social worker suggested (paras 6.39–40). The team leader's own line manager stated in evidence to the inquiry that he was unaware of any problems with her supervision of front-line social workers, although he admitted to being aware of her 'poor timekeeping, lack of availability for supervision, poor case management and case allocation' (para 6.42). It appeared that the team leader did not prioritise or rationalise the allocation of cases, neither was there any preliminary discussion with social workers as to how to proceed with a newly allocated referral at the outset (para 6.45). Given that the social worker assigned to Victoria had never actually conducted a child protection investigation, or been trained to do so, this of itself points to a misallocation of the case by the team leader.

The consequences of poor supervision were clearly demonstrated in relation to the strategy meeting held in the North Tottenham District Office on 28 July 1999. Professionals at that meeting agreed to 18 recommendations, which included: completing checks in relation to French social services; contacting the hospitals to which Victoria had been admitted; checks regarding her education and GP; arranging an interpreter; and completing an assessment. The case file was passed to the allocated social worker on 2 August 1999. The team leader, who had not read the file, was alleged to have simply told the social worker that the referral concerned a child with scabies. No date was set by the team leader as the supervisor to review progress on completion of the recommendations from the strategy meeting (para 6.212). Indeed, not until 20 September, almost two months after allocation of the case, did the social worker receive supervision relating to Victoria (para 6.357). Few of the recommended actions contained in the minutes of the 28 July strategy meeting were ever carried out. This was largely attributable to the fact that no supervisor read Victoria's file or checked the progress of the social worker assigned to work with her (para 6.451).

As Lewicki et al (2010, p 19) observe, interpersonal conflict results in: competitive win–lose goals; misperceptions; anger; decreased communication; defensive positioning; magnification of differences; and the proliferation of the dispute to other issues. All of these constitute additional sources of stress, which would have intensified the irritability of practitioners and managers alike, in turn contributing to an office environment in which arguments were easily sparked off. Many social workers on the Assessment and Investigation Team seem to have felt disgruntled, with malicious gossip about the team leader circulating among them and regular complaints about her being made to management. The team leader seems to have engaged in social withdrawal in the face of conflict marked by her frequent and unpredictable absence from the office. At the same time, the distance between front-line social workers, their team leader and more senior management appears to have widened over time, as practitioners wanted the team leader's removal and management failed to take remedial action.

Negotiating with front-line managers

For the vast majority of front-line social workers, their primary interaction with management is the supervisory experience usually provided by their team leader. The supervision given to Victoria's named worker was woefully inadequate because the team leader failed to: offer sufficient time for effective supervision to take place; monitor caseloads; inform herself of Victoria's situation; ensure the practitioner had adequate skills for the task; provide professional guidance; or oversee the social worker's performance. While the inadequacy of supervision by the team leader employed at Haringey was particularly egregious, the Social Work Task Force (2009, para 2.16) noted that time pressures on many front-line managers across the country mean that their time for supervision with each practitioner is often quite constrained. As a result, supervision can focus on 'tasks and processes, and on meeting indicators, at the expense of concentrating on outcomes for service users and quality of service'. The Social Work Task Force (2009, para 2.16) also discovered that most front-line managers are unable to avail themselves of training in supervision and many complain of being inadequately prepared for their role. This can lead to significant problems for front-line social workers, as supervision in child protection work is a composite of several different responsibilities, which are described in Box 4.1.

Box 4.1: The functions of supervision for front-line social workers
The Social Work Task Force (2009, para 2.13) formulated a comprehensive definition comprised of three key roles, which is reproduced as follows:

- *Line management* – This includes managing team resources, delegation and workload management, performance appraisal, duty of care, support, and other people-management processes.
- *Professional (or case) supervision* – Reflecting on and responding to the challenging questions thrown up by practice and cases, including: implications for the practitioner's welfare or safety; reviewing the roles the practitioner is taking on and their relations with the service-users and with other professionals; evaluating the impact of actions and decisions; and capturing what can be learnt for the future from day-to-day practice.
- *Continuing professional development* – Ensuring social workers are developing skills, knowledge and experience to do their job well and make progress in their careers. Observation of practice and constructive feedback should be part of the process.

It is the pivotal role of front-line managers in supporting good practice in child protection that makes it imperative for social workers to develop effective negotiation skills to successfully argue their points while remaining reasonable in their requests and open to engaging with the professional priorities and personal needs of managers. Back and Back (2005, pp 170–1) highlight a number of prerequisites for assertive negotiation with line managers, which are elaborated on as follows:

- *Own the issue* – This requires social workers to use 'I' statements to locate the problem with themselves and not their manager. This avoids sounding as if you are blaming the manager and creating a defensive reaction that will impede a successful negotiation over workload.
- *Show recognition of your manager's needs* – As already discussed, many managers are under considerable work pressures themselves and are often sympathetic to the plight of front-line staff. It is essential to recognise the responsibility of managers to ensure that work is completed, targets are met and good practice is observed. You also need to acknowledge the constraints that they may be labouring under in your negotiation.
- *State what you would like to happen* – Merely expressing dissatisfaction with the present situation can come across as an unconstructive complaint or purely grousing. You need to be specific about the changes in the workplace situation that would positively affect your working life and improve services for children and families.
- *Stress you want to explore alternatives* – It is crucial not to dwell on the past, which can deteriorate into blaming others. Instead, discussion should revolve

around possible alternatives to the present state of affairs. It is the feasibility of these alternatives that needs to be explored.

- *Focus on benefits* – The negotiation should focus on the potential benefits to you as a front-line worker, to the manager and agency, and to children and families. Describe the positive changes that would follow from a successful resolution of your concern.
- *Look for a win–win outcome* – This approach seeks to identify outcomes valuable to both the worker and management of a successfully negotiated resolution to the issue in dispute.

Legal action, or its threat, is one potential response when in dispute with a manager, but it ought not to be the first resort. Good negotiators do not threaten, intimidate or take up inflexible positions. As in negotiation with colleagues, it is important to bear in mind factors within the organisation that may impact on front-line managers just as detrimentally as social workers. Research by Broadhurst et al (2010) reveals the extent to which workload pressures, performance targets and software for assessment and file-recording combined to place team leaders under stresses comparable to those of front-line staff. While many front-line managers are deeply sympathetic to the workplace issues brought to their attention by social workers, they often find themselves caught between the demands of front-line staff for more resources and pressure from senior managers to cut costs or meet performance targets. It is salutary that a number of team leaders involved in the events surrounding the death of Victoria Climbié endeavoured to relay to middle and senior management the extent to which workloads were imperilling child protection in Brent and Haringey London Borough Councils. In tandem with giving consideration to the *interests* (motives, needs, preferences, sought outcomes) of front-line managers, practitioners experiencing unsatisfactory supervision should develop a reflective approach. Box 4.2 lists key questions for social workers to ask themselves before addressing any issues with their supervisor.

Box 4.2: Key questions to ask about unsatisfactory supervision
Hawkins and Shohet (2006, p 33) suggest a number of key questions to help social workers reflect on their supervisory experience before addressing the issues with their supervisor. These are reproduced in the following list:

- What are the strengths and weaknesses of your present resourcing system? What do you need to do about improving it?
- What are your specific needs from supervision and how far do your present supervisory arrangements meet them?
- Do you need to renegotiate the supervisory contract with your supervisor?
- Are there additional forms of supervision (peer supervision, etc) that you need to arrange for yourself?

- How open do you feel to supervision and feedback? If not, are there personal changes you could make to open up the communication?
- Are you frightened of being judged and assessed? Have you tried checking out whether your fears are justified or fantasy?
- Can you confront your supervisor and give him or her feedback? If not, are their constraints internal or external?
- What defensive routines do you fall into using? What do you need in order to move beyond these?
- Are you stuck in blaming others for what you yourself can change?
- Do you carry some of your supervisor's anxieties, so that you have to look after them?
- Is it feasible to have a more equal relationship? How far is it appropriate and is it what you want, given that more equality means more responsibility?

Assertive, non-assertive and aggressive behaviours

The previous questions should help practitioners to explore their own part in poor working relationships with supervisors or team leaders. If, having examined their contribution to unsatisfactory supervision and changing any attitudes or behaviours that perpetuate this, front-line workers are still experiencing problems, it is clearly time to address these with a manager. Resolving disagreements with supervisors or team leaders requires the same negotiation skills as those identified for dealing with colleagues. For practitioners who lack self-assertion, the best negotiation skills are likely to fail, particularly when their dispute is with a more senior member of staff. *Assertive behaviour* refers to forms of self-expression that lead to satisfying your own needs while not harming others, ignoring their rights or feeling guilty. *Non-assertive* behaviour means acting in ways that sacrifice your own needs and goals to meet someone else's. *Aggressive behaviour* is characterised by responses that seek to dominate others in order to impose your goals upon them and to do so regardless of their interests.

Assertiveness is based on a set of beliefs which are essentially that you have rights, needs and opinions that ought to be met and respected, while at the same time recognising that others also have rights, needs and opinions that they are entitled to have met and respected. This means that assertiveness demands both that you articulate your rights or desired outcomes in any given situation and that you are prepared to listen to how other individuals understand their rights and needs. It requires a willingness to both articulate one's own point of view and to be prepared to hear that of others. So, self-assertion is an important starting point for negotiation over entitlements, needs, preferences and opinions. However, it may also involve saying 'no'. Rejecting an unreasonable request, refusing to tolerate another person's unreasonable behaviour or censuring a prejudiced viewpoint are also forms of self-assertion. Assertiveness is therefore a way of thinking, verbalising and acting.

Non-assertiveness is either failing to voice your rights or desired outcomes or doing so in a way that they can easily be ignored by another person, who can then impose his or her demands upon you. If you express yourself in an apologetic, hesitant or self-effacing manner, this is likely to lead other people to disregard your point of view. Non-assertiveness also implies failing to challenge or contradict other people who you believe to be incorrect or behaving improperly. Non-assertive behaviour is generally underpinned by a number of core beliefs, such as other people's rights and needs being more important than your own or that you have less ability or less to contribute than other people. Actually attaining your needs in preference to someone else's can lead to feeling of guilt or relief that you have avoided imagined adverse consequences. Conversely, meeting someone else's desired outcomes at the expense of your own can lead to feelings of martyrdom and muted but persistent complaint. In essence, people who are non-assertive seek to evade conflict and please those they come into contact with. While avoiding conflict in the short term can reduce anxiety, if it means agreeing to something disadvantageous or ignoring objectionable behaviour, sooner or later it will generate resentment, stress and anger.

Non-assertiveness often produces secondary gains, such as reduced feelings of anxiety, a satisfaction in self-pity or pride in sacrificing one's own needs for those of someone else. These types of secondary gains act to reinforce non-assertive behaviour, leading to repetition of dysfunctional ways of dealing with conflict, which ultimately culminates in increased stress and anger. If anger is repressed, as is often the case for non-assertive people, this can manifest as depression, sometimes leading to physical illness. Non-assertiveness can be caused by low self-esteem, but it can also contribute to it. A person who fails to articulate or argue for their entitlements will most likely become increasingly irritated by their own habitual non-assertive behaviour and marginalised by others. People realise that they can take advantage of a non-assertive person, which, in turn, engenders disrespect for them. So, individuals who lack assertiveness are liable to have their self-esteem assailed from within and without, leading to a vicious circle.

Aggressiveness, on the other hand, is premised on the belief that you have either a greater number of or else more important rights and needs than those of others. This means asserting your own rights and needs in ways that violate those of other people. It means ignoring, belittling or minimising other people's entitlements and wants. Aggressive behaviour in this context emanates from a core belief that conflict is a zero-sum game in which there can only be a winner and a loser. Hence, people who act aggressively tend to be confrontational and seek to impose their demands on others through argument or behaviour that leaves little room for negotiation or contradiction. Those who deal with conflict through aggression are quick to stand up for their own rights and to voice their own needs, but often at the expense of others. They may develop a mistrust of others or view them as hostile. By contrast, some people can alternate between aggressive and passive behaviours, engaging in outbursts of anger or irritation to be followed by episodes of profuse apology and ingratiating behaviour.

REFLECTIVE EXERCISE ON NON-ASSERTIVE, ASSERTIVE AND AGGRESSIVE RESPONSES

Think of 10 different situations in a work context where you have been in conflict with a caregiver, child, manager or colleague. Ask yourself the following questions:

- What kind of verbal responses did you make in these situations; were they assertive, non-assertive or aggressive?
- Identify any patterns you notice in your verbal responses. Are you likely to be more assertive, non-assertive or aggressive with some people rather than others? If so, how do you account for this?
- Do your responses to work-related conflicts reflect those in your personal life as you react to disagreements with family and friends?
- If most of your responses were predominantly aggressive or non-assertive, what do you think accounts for this?

Socialisation and assertiveness

Comprehending what it means to be assertive is distinct from actually possessing the ability to be assertive. Many people want to act assertively but, often to their own frustration and incomprehension, find themselves held back by personal scruples or difficulty phrasing feelings or opinions in a manner that is assertive. Commonly, such paradoxical experiences are traceable to socialisation during childhood. Typically, children are encouraged by parents and teachers alike to be quiet, obedient and polite. Undemanding children are often rewarded for being compliant, while those who are uncooperative, obstinate or boisterous are more likely to be scolded for their behaviour or punished in other ways. Social learning through direct experience of reward and punishment, or observing the consequences for others of particular kinds of conduct, results in modelling behaviours. If, as a child or adolescent, the behaviours rewarded were those that put the needs of parents first or involved complying with parental instructions, then self-assertion is likely to be inhibited in adulthood.

This is in contrast with an individual who as a child had caregivers who encouraged him or her to express desires, but to also heed the needs of others. Such an adult is better able to be assertive, because their social learning involved rewards by parental figures for expressing their desired outcomes and negotiating with others to obtain them. Equally, a social worker who witnessed an overbearing parent usually getting their own way through emotional blackmail or explicit threats may tend towards aggressive interactions when confronted by opposition to their own interests and goals. They may find it difficult to distinguish between assertive behaviours with colleagues or managers and aggressive verbal responses to frustration of their plans or contradiction of their viewpoint. While much social learning within families, schools and peer groups is idiosyncratic and dependent on unique family and peer dynamics, it is also shaped by structural factors in society such as gender, class, religion and culture.

Role theory postulates that individuals learn to become masculine or feminine through learning a social role rather than expressing an essential nature. Masculinity and femininity are both socially constructed, with males and females subject to a set of social expectations from infancy that shape their gendered behaviour. The traits of competitiveness, rationality and physical strength associated with being masculine are internalised because boys and men are rewarded for exhibiting these kinds of behaviours. A boy who is called 'gay' by fellow pupils for helping a teacher in the classroom (essentially an accusation of effeminacy) will cease to offer this kind of assistance to others because he is punished for it. *Social learning theory* suggests that males learn sex-appropriate behaviour through observing other males and how social rewards and punishments are dispensed for different behaviours. Hence, a boy who witnesses his father voicing demands that his mother quickly caters to will be more likely to articulate his desires and preferences either assertively or aggressively as an adult. Similarly, if a girl observes that females are socially rewarded, for example, through receiving praise, for suppressing their own needs in order to meet those of others, such behaviours are reinforced and she will continue to perform them. If she also finds herself or witnesses other women who express their opinion being characterised as quarrelsome, then she will be inclined to mute her own point of view. A girl encountering these responses as she grows into womanhood will be predisposed to put others before herself and express her view timidly so as not to appear strident. Commonly, for adult men, the sex-role expectations that they have internalised can make it exacting for them to be assertive rather than aggressive, while for women, it can be a challenge to develop an assertive rather than a passive response to interpersonal conflict.

The class system is another form of social stratification that can shape upbringing and messages about approved and disapproved of behaviour. In surveys conducted in Britain, 95% of respondents stated that there was a class system, which they associated with differences in: earnings, education, lifestyle choices and self-presentation (Argyle, 1994, pp 3–4). People from upper-class or middle-class backgrounds are more likely to grow up with a sense of self-confidence derived from their experience of privilege, choice and control, which often flows from access to greater educational and financial resources. Conversely, people from lower-income groups may struggle with a sense of inferiority when interacting with apparently more powerful and affluent individuals from professional backgrounds.

Research evidence collated by Argyle (1994, pp 51–5) demonstrates that high-status individuals talk more in group contexts than low-status individuals. Concomitantly, individuals from low-status groups are more likely to behave deferentially and not interrupt those from high-status groups. They also tend to seek approval from higher-status individuals and inhibit their disagreements with them. As class is usually imputed to people based on their occupation, speech and often their clothes, this means that during interactions, class hierarchies tend to be asserted, with upper- and middle-class individuals assuming a high status and those from working-class backgrounds assuming a low status. Research also evidences some association between class and self-esteem, with upper- and middle-class individuals appearing to have higher self-esteem than those from working-class backgrounds (Argyle, 1994 pp 281–3). Case Study 6.1 reveals the relationship between self-esteem and self-assertion in a child protection context.

In the 2001 Census for the UK, three-quarters of households declared that they adhered to a religion. While over half the population identify as Christian, there exist sizable minorities practising Islam, Hinduism, Sikhism, Judaism and Buddhism. Since religious affiliation not only determines people's spiritual beliefs, but also generally their values and perspectives, it constitutes an important influence on behaviour (Furness and Gilligan, 2010). Religious faith can regulate an individual's level of comfort with self-assertion and his or her attitudes and responses to aggression. Some spiritual beliefs emphasise service to others and self-sacrifice, which may make it more difficult for individuals to articulate and advance their opinion or insist that their feelings are taken into consideration. Among some Christians, 'turning the other cheek' and not responding to aggression is an important spiritual obligation. Equally, for many practising Hindus, 'right behaviour' requires obedience to elders and neither causing harm nor offence to others. For followers of Taoism, the promotion of social harmony, often through the avoidance of conflict and confrontation, is a guiding principle. Religious beliefs may reinforce behavioural predispositions deriving from gendered norms of behaviour. Elements of both Christianity and Islam emphasise that women should show deference to men (King, 1993; Ahmadi, 2006). Therefore, individuals holding strong spiritual convictions can sometimes find it problematic to respond assertively to aggression or they may feel reluctant to act assertively for fear of causing hurt or discomfort to someone else.

Culture refers to common values, beliefs and norms of behaviour usually derived from the origin and history of a social group, its established conventions and shared assumptions. Cultural beliefs, values and behavioural norms that prioritise the welfare of the family as a whole over that of any one family member may hinder individuals of that cultural heritage from: articulating personal needs; using assertive behaviour to draw attention to them; and successfully negotiating how they will be met. For many families of South Asian heritage, their collective good remains more much important than that of any single family member (Stopes-Roe and Cochrane, 1990). Conversely, people influenced by a cultural milieu that promotes individualism, self-expression and competitiveness may struggle to avoid aggressive behaviour, as their tendency is to prioritise their own rights and needs above those of others. Such Anglo-centric values are strongly embedded in the white majority population of the UK (Laird, 2008, pp 44–5) and individuals influenced by an Anglo-centric culture may be more prone than those from some other heritage backgrounds to openly express anger and forcibly impose their choices upon other people during a conflict.

REFLECTIVE EXERCISE ON SOCIAL INFLUENCES ON PERSONAL ASSERTIVENESS

Consider your own background in terms of social learning within family and school, and in relation to your gender, class, religion and culture. Ask yourself the following questions:

• How have these influenced your ability to be assertive?
• What messages carried by rewards and punishments have shaped your use of assertive, non-assertive or aggressive responses to conflict in different situations and with different people?
• How do these family, school and structural influences affect your responses to interpersonal conflict in the office with colleagues and managers or in practice situations with parents, their partners or children?

Belief systems and assertiveness

Social learning, and the structural influences that they often channel, in turn shape beliefs about self and others. These can interfere with the ability of social workers to act assertively in child protection contexts. Back and Back (2005, pp 52–3) identify personal, but commonly held, beliefs associated with assertive, non-assertive and aggressive behaviours, which are reproduced in Table 4.1.

Table 4.1: Beliefs associated with non-assertion, assertion and aggression

Beliefs leading to assertion	Beliefs leading to non-assertion	Beliefs leading to aggression
I am responsible for what happens to me	I am not as important as others	Attack is the best form of defence
I am in control; I can choose how to behave	My opinions do not count	Aggression gets results
I can change	Other people will not like me if I say what I think	Other people cannot be trusted to do a good job
I can initiate actions to achieve results	It is safer to keep your head down in times of conflict	I am superior; I know best
I can learn from feedback	I should put others first	Other people should stand on their own two feet
I believe assertiveness does work	I must get this absolutely perfect	I must give as good as I get

The impact of beliefs that incline practitioners to non-assertive responses can be compounded if they confuse non-assertion with politeness or helpfulness. Such confusions often arise because of early parental messages that encouraged the social worker to comply with, rather than oppose, parental requests during childhood. Similarly, if social workers misperceive their assertive responses as aggressive (a particular tendency among women because of gender role socialisation), they will shy away from self-assertion. Social workers need to recognise factors deriving from their own background, socialisation and beliefs about interpersonal conflict that inhibit assertiveness. Only through introspection and challenging their own inhibitions surrounding assertion can practitioners then develop a range of assertive responses to conflict with others. Back and Back (2005, pp 84–91) identify six different types of assertion, which are outlined as follows:

- *Responsive assertion* – Used to elicit information through questions and probes about the needs, perspectives and feelings of others. It can be used to clarify your understanding or encourage a non-assertive individual to articulate their thoughts and emotions, and assists to ensure you are not violating other people's rights.
- *Basic assertion* – A simple short statement about a right, feeling, need or opinion.
- *Empathetic assertion* – Contains empathy as well as stating your own right, feeling, need or opinion and indicates an awareness of another person's situation or perspective.
- *Discrepancy assertion* – Identifies contradictions between what has been agreed with someone and his or her behaviour and includes a statement about your own entitlements or needs.
- *Negative feelings assertion* – Describes the negative effect of another person's behaviour upon you and ends with a request for a change in behaviour.
- *Consequence assertion* – States the adverse consequences for a person if he or she does not change his or her behaviour.

In essence, being assertive requires you to make other people aware of your feelings, needs and goals by using direct and honest communication. According to Bower and Bower (2004, p 90), assertive communication comprises four distinctive elements, which they draw together in the Describe, Express, Specify, Consequence (DESC) approach. This is designed to guide people in writing and then verbalising assertiveness scripts to articulate and negotiate their needs. The DESC approach is outlined as follows:

- *Describe*: Describe with as much objectivity and detail as possible what aspects of another person's behaviour or situation are problematic for you. This should be simple and pared down to minimise scope for the other person to dispute the facts; for example, describing the issue in terms of factual observed behaviour such as 'You start to type on the computer each time I approach your desk' as opposed to the vaguer more speculative claim 'You are avoiding me'. Similarly, generalising about a person's behaviour, such as 'You are always late', is much more open to his or her subsequent denial rather than a more exact statement of the concern, such as 'You arrived a half-hour late on Monday and Wednesday of this week to our scheduled meetings'. This very precise statement of the objectionable behaviour is much more difficult for the other person to refute, if true. The focus should be on the behaviour and not the character of the person who has given offence. So, for example, use a statement such as 'You

have disagreed with me over several minor issues this morning, which are ...',
rather than 'You are quarrelsome'.

- *Express*: Express your thoughts or feelings as to how the other person's
behaviour or the situation you have just described is impacting on you. Use
'I' statements to own your feelings and thoughts, for example, 'I feel ...' or 'I
think ...' as opposed to 'People feel ...' or 'Other team members think ...'.
This should be stated in neutral terms to minimise causing offence or injury
to the other person, otherwise your statement is likely to escalate conflict. It
should be framed in positive rather than negative terms. This means focusing on
shared values and common goals, avoid statements such as 'I feel upset by you'
as opposed to 'I think that your behaviour and my reaction to it are making
it difficult for us to work together'. There is less chance of the second phrase
being heard as an attack by the other person, who might counterattack in
response, thus intensifying the emotionality of the encounter and the likelihood
of magnifying the dispute.

- *Specify*: Be specific by identifying how you want the other person's behaviour
or the situation to change. Use 'I' statements and frame the desired change as a
request rather than a demand in order to encourage the other person to accede
to it. This means eschewing phrases such as 'You should ...' and 'I insist that you
...' and, instead, adopting more emollient language, such as 'I would prefer ...'
or 'I would like ...'. It is also important not to overwhelm the other person with
an assortment of changes you want. Instead, these should be restricted to just
a few and ought to be as detailed and specific as possible. Again, these requests
should refer to behaviour and not character traits. They must be reasonable
and ask for a change within the capability of the other person. Contrast 'I want
you to stop being lazy', which refers to a character trait and is vague in terms
of behaviour change, to the much more specific and, hence, grantable request
'I would like you to start coming to our meetings on time'. Taken altogether,
this guidance suggests that changes in another person's conduct may need
to be requested incrementally and not all at once, particularly if it involves a
number of problematic behaviours.

- *Consequence*: The consequence can be a reward of some kind for a positive
change in behaviour or of the situation. Depending on the nature of the
relationship, the reward for the other person could simply be that you will feel
better, or feel better disposed towards them. It could be the promise to return
a favour in the future or the gain of something tangible such as an item or
service. Alternatively, the consequence could be a punishment for refusing to
make any changes, for example, the refusal to cover for a colleague's sick leave
or the making of a complaint. This means spelling out to the other person
exactly what the consequence will be if there is change – 'If you do..., I will
...' – and what the consequences will be if little or nothing changes – 'If
you do not ..., I will ...'. Emphasising the reward for change rather than the
negative consequences for refusing to change is more likely to de-escalate
conflict and elicit a positive response to your request. Punishments can also

be clear, but implicit. If the reward for increased supervision by a team leader is a social worker agreeing to take on a particularly complex case, then the implicit negative consequence is a refusal to take on the case in the absence of additional supervisory support. The social worker does not need to foreground the potential punishment during his or her exchange with the team leader. Both positive and negative consequences must be realistic, plausible and within your capacity to execute. Exaggeration is likely to be counterproductive and your bluff will eventually be called, occasioning a loss of credibility. The use of punishments, rather than rewards, can inflame a dispute, particularly if these are perceived to be unreasonable, unjust or disproportionate by the other person.

The following is an example of a practitioner receiving minimal supervision using DESC scripting to formulate an assertive verbal response to a team leader who regularly cancels supervision sessions:

- *Describe* – 'When you schedule supervision sessions you frequently cancel them soon after, which means that often they are up to two months apart.'
- *Express* – 'I feel worried about the judgements I am being asked to make about children at risk without your guidance and professional opinion.'
- *Specify* – 'I would prefer it if we arranged supervision sessions once a month.'
- *Consequence* – 'If you provide more regular supervision, it will reduce my stress levels and enable me to make more accurate risk assessments for children. If you do not provide more regular supervision, it will undermine my ability to make accurate assessments of children who are at risk of significant harm.'

REFLECTIVE EXERCISE ON DEVISING A DESC SCRIPT

Devise a DESC script to respond to each of the following unsatisfactory situations with a colleague or manager (try to incorporate a range of different types of assertion):

- A colleague on the same team as you is regularly off work for extended periods due to stress-related illness. Your manager expects you to cover a third of the caseload of your absent colleague as well as your own.
- At team meetings, you think that your contributions are being consistently ignored by the team leader.
- Your team leader cancelled the last two consecutive supervisions and arrived an hour late for the most recent rescheduled session.
- A colleague persistently asks you to accompany her on joint home visits for which you can see no apparent necessity. You have previously accompanied her on several visits and this is now creating time pressures and interfering with your own work.
- You are accommodated in an open-plan office and the social worker at the desk next to yours often chats to friends and family on their mobile phone, which you find distracting.

Non-verbal communication and assertion

The most elaborately fashioned assertive statement will be undermined by a tentative verbal delivery (Greenberg, 2008, p 101). Research indicates that only 10% of a message is actually conveyed in the words used by a person, while 25% is carried by the tone, pitch and pace of their voice and 65% is expressed by body language (McBride, 1998, p 35). In practice, this means that if a social worker makes an assertive statement such as 'Please stop shouting at me or I will have to end this meeting', but delivers it in a hesitant quiet tone while adopting a cowering body posture, then the person shouting will pick up on the passive message implicit in the tone of voice and posture. They are likely to disregard or disbelieve the threatened negative consequences to end the meeting conveyed through words. That is why Back and Back (2005, pp 30–3) draw attention to the characteristics of assertive, non-assertive and aggressive speech, which are summarised in Table 4.2.

Table 4.2: Characteristics of assertive, non-assertive and aggressive speech

Verbal aspects of assertion	Verbal aspects of non-assertion	Verbal aspects of aggression
'I' statements	Rambling statements	Excessive use of 'I' statements
Statements that are brief and to the point	Fill-in words, such as 'you know' and hesitant phrases	Boastfulness
Distinction between fact and opinion	Frequent justification of self	Opinions expressed as facts
Suggestions rather than demands	Apologetic and seeking permission	Threatening questions
Constructive criticism	Self-regulatory statements, such as 'I should'	Requests in the form of demands or threats
Questions to discover the opinions and needs of others	Few 'I' statements	Advice given as a form of instruction
Oriented to practical problem-solving	Statements that dismiss own needs	Blaming others without constructive suggestions
	Self-deprecating phrases	Assumptions about people and events
	Saying nothing	Sarcasm and putdowns

As an illustration of the DESC approach set out earlier, take the case of a practitioner responding to unsatisfactory supervision. If their assertive statement is delivered in a hesitant apologetic tone, the supervisor may think that the practitioner lacks confidence and is not prepared to persist in their request for improved supervision, and the supervisor will suppose that the practitioner can be ignored without penalty. Likewise, posture, facial expression and gesture all have the potential to strengthen an assertive verbal statement or to completely negate it. Back and Back (2005, p 41) identify a number of behaviours that can undermine the most carefully crafted of assertive statements. These are replicated in Table 4.3.

Table 4.3, listing the facial expressions, gestures and body postures associated with assertive, non-assertive and aggressive behaviour, is helpful in drawing the attention of practitioners to their physical presentation. However, it needs to be used with caution. Back and Back (2005, p 41) identify the predominant features of assertive, non-assertive and aggressive behaviour among the white majority populations of the US and the UK. These are culture-bound and it would be a mistake to assume that everyone, regardless of their heritage background, adopts similar non-verbal forms. Some people from a South Asian background may avoid eye contact with a superior or with a member of the opposite sex as a gesture of respect, not of non-assertive evasion. Social workers practising in cross-cultural contexts must take the time to research the influences on behaviour for families of different heritage backgrounds. This, of course, does not imply that everyone from a particular minority ethnic group uses the same postures or gestures to convey their feelings. It simply means that some members of that ethnic community may be greatly influenced by culturally determined norms around the expression of aggression and passivity.

Table 4.3: Common assertive, non-assertive and aggressive non-verbal expressions

Physical feature	Assertive non-verbal expression	Non-assertive non-verbal expression	Aggressive non-verbal expression
Facial expression	Smiles when pleased Frowns when angry Otherwise open expression Features steady, not wobbling Jaw relaxed	Ghost smiles when expressing anger or being criticised Eyebrows raised in anticipation (eg of rebuke) Quick-changing	Smile may become wry Scowls when angry Eyebrows raised in amazement/disbelief Jaw set firm Chin set firm
Eye contact	Firm but not a staredown	Evasive Looking down	Tries to stare down and dominate
Body movement	Open hand movements (inviting to speak) Measured pace hand movements Sits upright or relaxed (not slouching or cowering) Stands with head held up	Hand-wringing Hunching shoulders Stepping back Covering mouth with hand Nervous movements that detract (shrugs and shuffles) Arms crossed low for protection	Finger-pointing Fist-thumping Sits upright or leans forward Stands upright with head 'in air' Strides around (impatiently) Arms crossed high (unapproachable)

Source: Adapted from Back and Back (2005, p 41).

REFLECTIVE EXERCISE ON SELF-AWARENESS

The next time you are in conflict with someone, try to be aware of your facial expressions, how you are standing, gesticulating and speaking. Ask yourself the following questions:

- What messages are these other forms of communication sending?
- Are they consistent with what you are saying or do they contradict it?
- Does your non-verbal communication convey assertiveness, non-assertiveness, aggressiveness or a mixture of these?

- How might you change your non-verbal communication to convey assertiveness?

Case Study 4.2: Lost in care

Waterhouse (2000) *Lost in care*

An inquiry was commissioned by the House of Commons in 1996 following a series of convictions of white British residential care staff during a 20-year period running from 1976 to 1995 for sexual offences against children in their care across a number of local authority children's homes in North Wales. During the 1980s, a series of complaints made by an Officer-in-Charge of one of the residential homes involved in the scandal had culminated in a police investigation in 1986/87. Social services were not involved in this and no criminal convictions arose from it. The Officer-in-Charge continued to make complaints regarding the activities of other members of staff in relation to children and to bring this to public attention. In 1987, she was suspended from her duties. There followed a further police inquiry during 1991–93, which resulted in a number of criminal proceedings and convictions. In 1994, Clwyd County Council set up a private investigation, which became known as the Jillings Inquiry, but the report of this inquiry was not published by the local authority. There was media speculation of a cover-up and public disquiet continued to grow, resulting in the inception of a public inquiry in 1996. It reported in 2000 to reveal the widespread sexual abuse of children in a number of public and private children's homes in North Wales. Physical abuse of children was found to be equally prevalent.

Mr Howarth, a Deputy Principal Officer, was convicted of buggery and seven offences of indecent assault against seven boys resident at Bryn Estyn committed during the period 1974–84. He was sentenced to 10 years' imprisonment. A number of other residential social care workers were also convicted of indecent and common assault.

Conflict with front-line management

Case Study 4.2 details just one example of the many documented in the voluminous report of the Waterhouse (2000) *Lost in care* inquiry into sexual abuse by some residential care workers and their managers. Peter Howarth, of white British heritage, was Assistant Principal and subsequently Deputy Principal during 1973–84 at Bryn Estyn. This was a special home owned by the local authority with places for 49 boys who had behavioural problems, some of whom had a history of offending. Mr Howarth obtained his Certificate in the Residential Care of Children in 1965. He lived in a flat attached to the home to which he invited some of the children for refreshments, including alcohol, and to watch television or play board games in the evening from around 8.30pm to 11.30pm. He created a 'flat list' of those boys welcome to attend these activities, which was regularly posted on his flat door. Boys attending were required to wear pyjamas without underwear and their attendance was entered in the residential home's logbook. In a statement to the public inquiry, Mr Howarth argued that these evenings were conceived to give the boys a sense of domestic normality and as an opportunity to provide counselling (para 8.05). The Deputy Principal also had a number of favourites, who were known within the home as 'bum boys'. Within the home, the 'flat list' practice was common knowledge.

As the inquiry found, among staff:

> a majority viewed the practice with disfavour. They objected, for example, to the principle of selecting boys for special favours and the impact of such favouritism on discipline generally. Some of them spoke themselves of these boys in derogatory terms and many were aware that the boys were called 'bum boys' or the like by their fellows. Many thought it highly unwise of Howarth to place himself in such a vulnerable position, open to allegations by the boys of sexual misconduct. (para 8.11)

At the inquiry, two members of staff admitted that they suspected sexual impropriety by the Deputy Principal. However, the inquiry concluded that many more members of staff must have shared these suspicions at the time and had done little to intervene to stop Howarth's activities at the flat (para 8.21).

At the very least, and permitting the most innocent interpretation of Mr Howarth's behaviour, it violated basic social norms at the home concerning the equal treatment of the boys. This contravention of accepted norms led a number of residential social care staff to feel uneasy, regardless of whether they suspected more sinister motives for Mr Howarth's conduct. Many other staff may have felt angry with Mr Howarth as they witnessed the flagrant breach of established norms of behaviour in the home. As already discussed in Chapter Two, more powerful members of an organisation are often able to break its informal rules with impunity, creating a situation of *latent conflict*. No action was taken against the Deputy Principal by lower-status residential workers, most probably for fear of creating disharmony within the home or disadvantage to themselves. A number of staff undoubtedly wanted to avoid conflict alongside the additional stresses and divisive discussions it would have generated, as some individuals remained fiercely loyal to Mr Howarth. For others, the knowledge that a residential care worker who fell into disfavour with Mr Howarth was plainly vulnerable to retaliatory action by him would have greatly inhibited any overt criticism. As the Deputy Principal of Bryn Estyn, Mr Howarth held considerable power and could certainly have abused his position to block career progression or assign onerous duties to a residential care worker. Consequently, *latent conflict* prevailed at Bryn Estyn, with neither Mr Howarth nor residential staff openly alluding to the 'flat list', but with social aggression in the form of gossip continuing to circulate among residential care workers.

While the situation that transpired at Bryn Estyn is rare, the social dynamics that inhibited workers from challenging their seniors are certainly not. Employees commonly hold beliefs about management that restrain them from being assertive with managers. For example, believing that management knows best, are uninterested in the views of front-line staff or will penalise an employee who appears to be complaining are all likely to inhibit assertive interactions with line managers. Some of these sorts of beliefs may have underpinned the muted responses of individual social care workers as events surrounding the abuse of children unfolded at Bryn Estyn. Such commonly held beliefs in relation to management also have implications for social workers outside of residential settings when confronted by behaviours, decisions and guidance by supervisors, team leaders or more senior managers with which they disagree or that cause them disquiet.

In contrast to these inhibiting beliefs, which stymie open disagreement with managers, ones that could facilitate self-assertion by front-line social workers include recognising that while managers have more expertise, they do not always know best, as they may not be as familiar with the family as the practitioner. Just like anyone else, a manager can, of course, simply make a mistake. Possessing the capacity to be assertive with more senior personnel requires a social worker to believe that it is possible to respect a manager without being deferential and that questioning their decision or advice, if done tactfully, need not be either impertinent or aggressive. The difficulties created by deferential attitudes to more senior colleagues are explored further in Case Study 5.1, which concerns interactions between medical and social work professionals during events surrounding the death of Victoria Climbié. Conversely, social workers who believe that they have superior knowledge because of their front-line interactions with families are liable to behave aggressively with managers and possibly further imperil a child already at risk.

REFLECTIVE EXERCISE ON BELIEFS ABOUT MANAGEMENT

Re-examine the common beliefs about managers mentioned in the previous two paragraphs. Ask yourself the following questions:

- Which of these do you hold?
- Are there any other beliefs you have about managers or consequences that could inhibit your ability to be assertive with a more senior professional and, if so, list these?
- How might these beliefs have affected your behaviour with managers in the past?
- What alternative beliefs could you develop and adopt to support assertive behaviour at work with supervisors, team leaders and other managers?

Conflict with senior management

It is accepted that the Principal of Bryn Estyn, who held a teaching qualification and a Senior Certificate in Residential Child Care, was well aware of Mr Howarth's evening activities but did not intervene. Indeed, to the very contrary, at one staff meeting, he stated that there were a number of rumours circulating at Bryn Estyn concerning the Deputy Principal and some of the boys at the home. Residential care staff were warned by the Principal that these rumours were to cease immediately and that any staff member discovered to be repeating them would be summarily dismissed. The Principal insisted that his Deputy was merely 'taking a special interest in some of the boys but that there was nothing in the rumours' (para 8.14). As the *Lost in care* inquiry was to observe:

> members of staff generally were obviously in some difficulty in these circumstances if they wished to voice complaints or suspicions about Howarth. He had been placed in a dominant position by [the Principal] and the latter was manifestly unsympathetic to any criticism of him. (para 8.17)

Residential care staff rarely met as a staff team and this hampered their ability to share concerns and take coordinated action (para 8.21). In any event, many of them were either overawed by Mr Howarth or actively disliked him, albeit that a number remained loyal to him, testifying as witnesses for the defence at his trial (paras 8.17, 8.19). Some members of staff tried other avenues of complaint about Mr Howarth. One sought to inform the Principal Officer Residential Services based at social services headquarters and responsible for community homes such as Bryn Estyn to be told that making a formal complaint against Mr Howarth could result in 'serious repercussions' (para 8.18). The inquiry concluded that there was a 'reluctance of headquarters staff to respond to complaints with thorough investigation' (para 29.89).

Many staff members felt cowed both by Mr Howarth and the Principal who, as his line manager, protected him and threatened to dismiss anyone casting aspersions. For a minority of residential workers, their loyalty to the Deputy Principal meant a refusal to acknowledge or act on what they witnessed. Their position persisted as a source of division within the staff team, which doubtless undermined concerted action by residential workers to confront management with Mr Howarth's malpractice. Workers were confronted by aggressive tactics by management, which constituted a coercive deployment of power designed to impose a one-sided outcome in a situation of dispute. The Principal explicitly threatened residential care workers with dismissal from their employment if they articulated any criticism of Mr Howarth concerning his behaviour towards *looked-after* children. The Principal Officer Residential Services issued a more subtle threat against a staff member by insinuating that making a complaint about Mr Howarth could lead to detrimental consequences for the complainant. Faced with this aggressive response to their concerns by much more powerful opponents, it is hardly surprising that residential care workers eventually took 'flight' and thereafter avoided confrontation with aggressive managers.

Power relationships in the workplace

A number of issues bearing upon power dynamics can be drawn from the *Lost in care* inquiry. In the first instance, there were gross power differentials, which enabled both the Principal and Deputy Principal to either intimidate or explicitly threaten care staff with dire consequences if they challenged the conduct of management. Care workers who attempted to go above the heads of the Officer-in-Charge and his Deputy found themselves discouraged by senior management from pursuing their concerns. The absence of a forum in which residential care workers could voice their shared disquiet was a further obstacle to addressing concerns with line management. Front-line workers can make the mistake of assuming that faced with an apparently obdurate manager, they are powerless to effect change. While negotiation with a senior colleague can seem more intimidating than that with a colleague, power is fluid and not fixed. A manager may, of course, draw some initial advantage from their position of authority, but front-line workers also have sources of power. They can, for instance, manage the negotiation process by gaining some control over the venue, agenda and timing of discussions on the issue in dispute. Lewicki et al (2010, pp 217–18) give further advice to negotiators dealing with someone more powerful than themselves, as summarised in Box 4.3.

Box 4.3: Negotiating with a more powerful individual

- Avoid doing an all-or-nothing deal with a more powerful single party, as this can leave low-power negotiators very vulnerable if the more powerful party changes their mind or reneges on the agreement.
- Endeavour to build multiple relationships and enter multiple negotiations with a number of more powerful parties, thus making each one of them less powerful in relation to a low-power negotiator.
- Build coalitions and alliances with other parties, as these can increase the leverage of a low-power negotiator relative to a high-power party during negotiations.
- Attempt to complete a number of less significant agreements in sequence in order to build a relationship with a high-power party and to then use this as a foundation for more important negotiations.
- Seek out information likely to strengthen the low-power negotiating position. Ensure the facts are organised and presented in the most persuasive way.
- Ask as many questions as possible to identify the underlying interests of the high-power party. This approach also conveys a willingness to cooperate.

When negotiation fails

A front-line worker, despite good self-assertion skills and proficiency at negotiation, may still be confronted by a lack of remedial action on the part of a team leader or senior manager. In this instance, to return to the DESC approach to self-assertion, the *consequences* for a manager of not taking any action could be the social worker warning that they will: raise the matter at a team meeting; take the matter to their union representative; involve their professional body; or put a complaint in writing to a more senior manager. While all of these options are perfectly legitimate courses of action, they plainly contain an element of threat. Before resorting to this sort of unilateral response, a practitioner must ensure that they have:

1. Reflected on their own contribution to problems with a supervisor or manager and made what improvements they can to resolve the difficulty.
2. Endeavoured to forestall the *conflict spiral* by genuinely entering into negotiations with a manager.
3. Used effective self-assertion in articulating and addressing the problem with their manager.

HM Government's (2010, para 2.11) *Working together to safeguard children* requires 'a clear line of accountability and governance within and across organisations for the commissioning and provision of services designed to safeguard and promote the welfare of children and young people'. It also compels agencies delivering services to children to put in place 'procedures for dealing with allegations of abuse against members of staff' and to adopt 'appropriate whistle blowing procedures and a culture that enables issues about safeguarding and promoting the welfare of children to be addressed' (HM Government, 2010, para 2.11). In effect, this creates an entitlement for front-line staff to pursue concerns or complaints up through the line-management structure. Similar provisions exist in Scotland and Northern Ireland. Ultimately, if practitioners believe that concerns about aspects of the agency or colleagues are not being taken seriously by their line manager, they can take their complaint outside of line management through the whistle-blowing procedure.

  Some child protection social workers voice caution about pursuing complaints and whistle-blowing due to fears of dismissal in a climate of cutbacks or budgetary constraint (*Community Care Online*, 2010). It is salutary that the *Lost in care* inquiry revealed that one Officer-in-Charge of a children's home found that her attempts to raise concerns about the sexual abuse of residents by staff during the 1980s were either followed by inadequate investigation or blocked by senior managers. She eventually resorted to involving her local councillor, the Welsh Office and the media in voicing her concerns. This resulted in her suspension from her duties and, thereafter, she pursued a claim for unfair dismissal through the Employment Tribunal and later accepted financial compensation in settlement of this claim.

She was, of course, vindicated by the findings of the *Lost in care* inquiry, which revealed the widespread physical and sexual abuse of children in residential homes across North Wales. The conclusion to be drawn from Case Study 4.2 is that social workers who find their concerns or grievances ignored by line managers, despite attempts at constructive negotiation, should seek guidance and support from their union or professional body before pursuing matters any further with more senior management or through a whistle-blowing procedure.

Points for practice

- Developing self-awareness in relation to their own characteristic assertive, non-assertive and aggressive responses to disagreement and conflict with others is essential if practitioners are to develop effective negotiating styles.
- Social workers are dependent on front-line managers for the allocation of their workloads and supervision. They also rely on them to mediate with senior management and colleagues when there are workplace problems.
- The power differential between team leaders and front-line social workers can inhibit practitioners from articulating their concerns, dissatisfactions and disagreements regarding workplace issues.
- Social workers need to develop assertiveness skills and examine how their suppositions about management may inhibit assertive behaviour and undermine integrative negotiation.
- Before tackling concerns with a team leader through the use of assertive communication skills, practitioners need to explore their own contribution to the problems that they are encountering with their team leader.

CHAPTER FIVE

Conflict between teams and agencies

Conflict between multidisciplinary colleagues

Inquiries and serious case reviews reveal the extent to which conflict between multidisciplinary colleagues can create impasses and antagonisms that undermine the effectiveness of child protection interventions. In this chapter, events leading up to the death of Victoria Climbié and events concerned with the sexual abuse of looked-after children by their foster carers are used to explore the nature of these disagreements. How power relationships between professionals from different professional backgrounds can influence their interactions is also examined. The interplay of personal beliefs with the expression of professional opinion is investigated, particularly in relation to the pivotal role of self-confidence. Differences of opinion inevitably arise among multidisciplinary colleagues in the course of pursuing a child protection investigation or implementing a child protection plan; therefore, the use of assertiveness and skilful negotiation to resolve conflict is discussed throughout the chapter.

Case Study 5.1: Victoria Climbié

Laming (2003) *The Victoria Climbié inquiry*

Drawing once more on events leading up to the death of Victoria Climbié, as summarised in Case Study 3.1, this case study centres on the interactions between multidisciplinary colleagues. The encounters between social workers at Brent and Haringey London Borough Councils, medical professionals and police officers are examined in some detail.

Conflict between social workers at Brent and medical colleagues

When Victoria was admitted for the first time to the Central Middlesex Hospital on 14 July 1999, she was referred to Brent's children's social work department by a locum paediatric registrar who examined Victoria on admission and concluded that her injuries, which included bruising to her arms, legs, buttocks, feet and hands, were non-accidental. The following day, the senior social worker on the Child Protection Team to whom the referral was allocated telephoned the hospital to be told by a different doctor that a consultant paediatrician considered that Victoria was suffering from scabies and was therefore a *child in need* rather than a child requiring protection. The senior social worker accepted this medical diagnosis at second hand and did not speak personally to the consultant paediatrician. Children's Services, however, is the agency charged to investigate and decide on child protection matters. Therefore, it was not the consultant paediatrician's decision as to whether Victoria should be treated as a *child in need* or not. This decision should ultimately have been the decision of Brent Social Services based on a multidisciplinary assessment.

Moreover, given the other information that Brent Children's Social Services held regarding the extent of Victoria's injuries, there was scope for questioning the paediatrician and requiring her to explain the inconsistencies between her diagnosis and that of her more junior colleague (paras 5.1.37–8). The consequence of not probing further into the contradictory diagnosis from two hospital doctors was that the Police Protection Power, which could confine Victoria to hospital for up to 72 hours, and had been invoked after receipt of the first doctor's referral alleging non-accidental injury, was lifted. Victoria was thereafter removed from the hospital by Ms Kouao without any social worker or police officer having seen or spoken to either of them. The use of a Police Protection Power should automatically trigger a child protection enquiry under the Children Act 1989. Brent children's social work department never commenced such an investigation, as Victoria's case file was re-designated 'child in need' rather than 'child protection'. The failure 'to respectfully challenge' multidisciplinary colleagues is not restricted to events surrounding the abuse and death of Victoria Climbié. Is it a familiar problem in circumstances where professionals from different agencies and disciplinary backgrounds are collaborating to protect a child, as the analysis of serious case reviews by Ofsted (2010, paras 101–2) attests:

> Some of the reviews identified a second form of challenge which had been inadequate. This was the absence of rigorous questioning by professionals of accepted views about the family, of the decisions being taken and of the action being planned. These shortcomings related to a lack of challenge both within and between agencies, insufficient persistence if the initial questioning did not receive the necessary response, and a failure to hold others to account for doing or not doing what they said they would do ... all too often practitioners failed to challenge their colleagues.

Brandon et al (2009), in their examination of serious case reviews, come to much the same conclusion, noting that social workers and police officers were often reluctant to question the decisions of medical practitioners in the mistaken belief that they possessed more expertise in the arena of child protection, as opposed to greater diagnostic expertise. Brandon et al (2009, p 45) averred that 'professionals with low levels of confidence will struggle to challenge the decisions and behaviour of their multi-agency colleagues when they feel the child is at risk of harm'. The widespread reluctance to challenge other professionals, and especially senior colleagues, had ramifications for multidisciplinary intervention with the family. For, as Brandon et al (2009, p 45) concluded, 'in this context of uncertainty and diffidence, clear decision making and action does not take place, and children remain unprotected'.

Power in negotiations with multidisciplinary colleagues

Disagreement between professionals is not unusual and social workers may from time to time be confronted with differences of opinion among those providing information or assessments in relation to a child protection inquiry. In Victoria's case, a paediatric consultant disagreed over medical evidence with a more junior, though well-qualified, doctor. There are two issues raised by this incident. First, social workers may sometimes need to enter into a dispute between other colleagues from the same organisation or disciplinary background. Second, they may themselves be in direct dispute with another multidisciplinary professional. At Brent Social Services, the situation that confronted the senior social worker, and ultimately Victoria's allocated worker, was of a paediatric consultant who was both an expert in her field and held a high status within a multidisciplinary context. This made it problematic for a front-line practitioner to question her diagnosis or, indeed, to explicitly challenge her usurpation of the social work role when she declared that Victoria was a *child in need*. Indeed, in her evidence to the public inquiry, the senior social worker concerned stated that:

> I was told this child was seen by Dr. Ruby Schwartz, who is a consultant paediatrician who is highly respected in Brent ... I felt that if Dr. Schwartz had seen the child, her diagnosis would have been correct, and I did not feel I could have disputed that. (para 5.137)

Social workers appeared to be overawed by the consultant's power and status, as a result of which, they baulked at the prospect of challenging her opinion. It is widely accepted in the literature that there are five different sources of power, which are summarised as follows:

- *Informational power* – This could be based on expertise, knowledge or experience in a particular area of practice and is commonly associated with formal training and qualifications. Professionals, including hospital consultants and social workers, possess this kind of power.
- *Position-based power* – Known also as legitimate power, it is derived from the position an individual occupies within an organisation. It includes 'resource power', meaning the ability to reward or penalise other people depending on their degree of compliance. Child protection social workers often hold this kind of power in relation to families. Line managers also exercise it over front-line professionals.
- *Relationship-based power* – A shared past, common goals or the mutual dependence of people upon each other in relation to desired outcomes shapes the deployment of this power. It will also be influenced by the relative statuses

of the people involved, whether they belong to the same group or not, and what access they have to information or resources via social or professional networks.

- *Personal power* – This refers to the diversity of beliefs people hold about the exercise of power, the skills they possess to deploy power effectively and their motivation to control others. A social worker who feels anxious or guilty about making demands upon others is much less likely to exercise power in relation to service-users or multidisciplinary professionals.
- *Contextual power* – This stems from several sources. Partly, it derives from having alternatives to a negotiated agreement with a particular person, which, in turn, reduces dependence on that person regarding decision-making and attaining desired outcomes. If a social worker can make the same request of several different professionals to complete a task, they are less reliant on any one of them. Contextual power is also framed by the norms of organisations and groups that determine if the exercise of power is deemed acceptable.

At the time of Victoria's discharge from the Central Middlesex Hospital, social workers possessed power based on their own specialist training, that is to say, *informational power*. In addition, they should have been in possession of a body map detailing the bruising to Victoria's body and the medical opinion of the locum paediatric registrar. They were also vested with a statutory duty under the Children Act 1989 to investigate the circumstances of any child suspected of being at risk of significant harm. Social workers held this legal power in addition to their *position-based power*, deriving from employment in the local government organisation charged to undertake this investigative duty. However, the relatively poor liaison between Brent Children's Social Services and medical staff meant that they exercised much less *relationship-based power*. It is also significant that the senior social worker in Brent's Child Protection Team felt that she could not contradict the consultant paediatrician in direct contrast to the team manager of the Investigation and Assessment Team at Haringey, who dismissed concerns about Victoria expressed by a consultant paediatrician from North Middlesex Hospital, as discussed later. This illustrates the importance of *personal power* in the exercise of power, which witnessed the senior social worker at Brent not deploying personal power. It also hints at the fluid nature of power and the degree to which it has to be owned by a social worker and proactively exercised by them. Lewicki et al (2010, p 202) allude to this when they observe that:

> Power is in the eye of the beholder. For power to be effective, it does not necessarily have to be fully and completely possessed; rather, the actor must convey the appearance that he or she has power and can use it at will. Power is therefore somewhat self-fulfilling. If you – and others – think you have it, you have it. If you – and others – don't think you have it, you don't have it. Perceived power is what creates leverage, and many power holders go out of their way to create the image of power as the critical element of effective influence.

Making requests to others

It is worth re-examining the senior social worker's explanation for not questioning the diagnoses of Dr Schwartz; she told the inquiry: 'I did not feel I could have disputed that'. Certainly, the social worker and consultant were liable to be in conflict with each other if the practitioner asked the doctor to reconsider her decision. But there were other ways of framing this; perceiving it not as a disputation of the consultant's diagnosis, but as a request to appraise or explain other evidence. Making a request to a multidisciplinary colleague, rather than directly challenging him or her, has the potential to lower defences and opens up the possibility of productive exchanges about a child at risk. Of course, sometimes, a more direct challenge may be indicated, but reformulating disagreements as pertinent requests can assist deliberations within multidisciplinary contexts. The beliefs of social workers can also greatly hinder assertive responses. For example, individuals who feel uncomfortable exercising their authority because of a belief that it puts others in a difficult position to refuse, that they should not make demands on others or that requesting help is a sign of weakness will be unassertive with colleagues. Similarly, social workers who perceive the refusal of their requests by other professionals as a personal rejection are unlikely to bring to bear different sources of power in pursuance of a legitimate request. Conversely, practitioners who think that others have no right to refuse their request are likely to be verbally aggressive towards colleagues or professionals from other disciplinary backgrounds.

The key to making requests assertively is the belief that you have the right to ask, but that the other person has the right to either point out that there is some problem with your request, in which case you may need to modify it, or they have the right to refuse. Being doubtful as to whether you have the right to ask a health visitor or consultant paediatrician to produce evidence to substantiate their opinion or position is likely to lead to a non-assertive hesitant verbal request, one easily brushed aside by another busy professional. Conversely, believing that other colleagues or multidisciplinary professionals should respond to any request you make assumes that they have no right to refuse or to query your request. Such a viewpoint is likely to lead to you making an aggressive verbal statement such as insisting on a police officer's attendance at a prearranged core group meeting. Adopting a trenchant position in this case ignores the time pressures on other professionals and the importance of negotiating mutually agreed aspects of a meeting to discuss a child protection issue. Back and Back (2005, pp 58–9) set out a helpful list of dos and don'ts for making a request in a work situation. These are, in brief, *do not*: apologise; justify yourself; take advantage of a friendship or a person's good nature; flatter or offer benefits to induce compliance; and take it personally if the other person refuses. While avoiding these common pitfalls, *do*: be direct rather than hint; keep it short and to the point; give a reason to justify the request; and respect the other person's right to say 'no'.

REFLECTIVE EXERCISE ON MAKING REQUESTS ASSERTIVELY

Formulate and write down a short written request for the following situations:

- Ask a general practitioner to medically examine a child when he is reluctant to do so.
- Ask a health visitor to accompany you on a joint home visit to see a child when she states she is extremely busy and the family is not a priority.
- Ask the manager of a Youth Offending Team to explain why her opinion about a child at risk of further offending contradicts that of several other professionals on her team.
- Ask sceptical colleagues to attend a core group meeting about a child at risk.

Conflict between social workers at Haringey and medical colleagues

There were also difficulties between medical staff at North Middlesex Hospital, to which Victoria was admitted on 24 July 1999, and Haringey Children and Family Services. At the inquiry, a consultant paediatrician at that hospital complained that on a number of previous occasions, members of the Haringey social work team had failed to recognise the child protection concerns raised by medical staff (para 6.22). Neither the manager responsible for ensuring good liaison between Haringey Social Services and the hospital, nor the consultant paediatrician herself who sat on what is now the Local Safeguarding Children Board, effectively addressed the poor working relationship between the two organisations. As a result, there were negative feelings within the medical staff team towards social workers in the Investigation and Assessment Teams for Children and Family Services at the North Tottenham District Office (para 6.22).

The consultant paediatrician based at the North Middlesex Hospital sent several letters to Haringey Children and Family Services after Victoria's discharge from that hospital expressing concerns about the child. These were not properly acted upon either by Haringey's Child Protection Advisor and link-worker to the North Middlesex Hospital or by Victoria's allocated social worker at the time. In evidence to the inquiry, the social worker claimed that she had informed her team leader of the consultant paediatrician's concerns during supervision, to which the team leader is alleged to have responded 'she always gets it wrong, she got it wrong in a child death that I was working on'. The team leader denied this allegation (para 6.343). Nevertheless, these incidents appear indicative of the poor working relationships that existed between the hospital's medical staff and social services at the time.

level, the interactions between doctors and social workers could be d as a form of *distributive bargaining* (Lewicki et al, 2010, p 33). This conflict is characterised by a win–lose contest in which the goals and one individual or group are believed to be mutually exclusive to those of the other. Resources are perceived as fixed and limited, forcing the individuals or groups in dispute into a competition with each other to maximise their share. Such an approach is generally confrontational, with individuals developing hard bargaining skills such as withholding information, using threats or emphasising the costs to the other person or group of not making concessions. Patterns of *distributive bargaining* are not confined to tangible goods or services, but can relate to intangible matters such as who has authority to make decisions in a given situation or who should be responsible for a safeguarding task in relation to a particular family. Integrative negotiation offers the individuals or groups involved in a dispute the opportunity to examine the commonality of their interests and goals, and to expand the number of possible alternatives to realise mutual interests and goals. Ultimately, both the hospital and social services had a primary and mutual interest in safeguarding children such as Victoria. The individual motivations and character traits of some professionals subverted multidisciplinary cooperation, transforming it from an *integrative negotiation* into a personal struggle to dominate decision-making.

Victoria was referred to Haringey Social Services from the North Middlesex Hospital on 24 July 1999, the day she had been admitted for suspected non-accidental injuries. According to Haringey's local child protection guidelines, if the child concerned is in hospital, then the strategy meeting should take place at that location. This procedure was designed to ensure that those directly involved in the child's medical care would be present and that professionals would have better access to the child concerned. However, the strategy meeting was held at Haringey's North Tottenham District Office. As a consequence, only four people attended the meeting, namely: the hospital social worker who had made the initial referral; a police constable from Haringey Child Protection Team; the duty social worker at Haringey; and a senior practitioner from the Investigation and Assessment Team at the North Tottenham District Office. No medical staff were present and none of the attendees had seen or spoken to Victoria or anyone connected with her care. At the inquiry, there was some confusion as to whether medical staff had even been invited to attend the strategy meeting (paras 6.194–6.196).

Mutual antagonism arose between medical professionals and the Investigation and Assessment Teams at the North Tottenham District Office. Arguably, this was acted out by the professionals responsible for safeguarding Victoria in relation to a strategy meeting, which was characterised by a failure to issue clear invitations, poor attendance and a venue that was less suitable for some individuals than others and contravened procedure. Events at Haringey during 1999 are certainly not unique in child protection work. *Flight* as a response to conflict can be acted out in any strategy meetings, case conference or core professionals' meeting through the exclusion or absenteeism of multidisciplinary professionals. *Passive-aggressive* behaviour on the part of social workers can be manifested as an omission to issue invitations to a meeting, failure to provide sufficient notice or arranging it in an inconvenient location for other attendees. In these circumstances, social withdrawal from colleagues and the avoidance of interaction becomes the predominant and dysfunctional means of dealing with interdisciplinary disputes. This, of course, is not to deny that professionals can have other reasons for neglecting to attend multidisciplinary forums, such as pressure of work or assigning safeguarding a low priority.

Self-assertion in integrative negotiation

It appears from evidence presented to the public inquiry into the death of Victoria Climbié that personal scruples and power struggles between individuals overtook the imperative to engage in productive deliberation and genuine negotiation to safeguard children. If parties hold negative stereotypical views of each other, the likelihood is that distributive bargaining will ensue. For social workers who maintain respectful, but not deferential, perceptions of multidisciplinary colleagues, integrative negotiation offers an effective route for resolving disputes. However, the best preparation for a negotiation will be entirely undermined if, as a social worker, you lack self-assertion during the subsequent one-on-one or multidisciplinary meeting and are therefore unable to articulate your point of view during discussion. Back and Back (2005, pp 59–61) identify a number of beliefs determining people's ability to articulate their opinion in work contexts when confronted by disagreement with a colleague or manager. Some of these are reproduced in Table 5.1. Patently, social workers who believe that a difference of opinion can lead to fruitful exploration of an issue are much more likely to articulate their view compared to those who worry that any disagreement with another professional's opinion will cause irritation and lead to unproductive conflict.

Table 5.1: Beliefs underpinning assertion, non-assertion and aggression when stating an opinion

Beliefs underpinning assertion in stating opinion	Beliefs underpinning non-assertion in stating opinion	Beliefs underpinning aggression in stating opinion
Disagreements do not necessarily lead to conflict Opinions are not necessarily right and wrong, merely different	People will think I am just being awkward if I raise doubts Other people will always be upset or annoyed if I disagree If I state my point of view, I stand the risk of being wrong/ridiculed	Other people can only be right if I am wrong: both parties cannot be right I am more vulnerable if I am seen to be wrong Other people have no right to disagree with me

As previously explored in Case Study 4.1, it is not only personal beliefs that influence whether social workers assertively articulate their opinions during a meeting, but also their views on the rights they hold. Back and Back (2005, pp 174–5) identify rights workers are entitled to at any work-related meeting, many of which are equally applicable to social workers. For example, the right to: state opinions; be listened to; attend productive meetings; understand the points under discussion; and know in advance the agenda and purpose of the meeting.

Only if social workers claim these rights can they actually exercise them in a team meeting, multidisciplinary forum or during exchanges between agencies. If a social worker takes seriously their right to understand what is being said at a meeting, they will feel confident to interject and ask for further clarification of a point being made by another professional. Likewise, if they are convinced about their entitlement to be furnished in advance with the agenda for the meeting and this does not happen, they will assert this right by objecting and insisting on being given sufficient notice. Conversely, a social worker who thinks that they are too unimportant to really hold these kinds of rights will be non-assertive when they do not understand a point during a meeting or are not given time to prepare for it because of inadequate notice. Beliefs about expressing an opinion and determining what rights are held in relation to a meeting are crucial to the acts of self-assertion in team meetings and inter-agency and multidisciplinary contexts. There are a number of ways to improve your own assertiveness at strategy meetings, core professionals' meetings and case conferences that build on basic beliefs and rights supporting self-assertion:

1. It is essential to use 'I' statements to make your views clear and distinguish fact from opinion. For example, 'Based on my experience of this family, I think we should place the child on the register' is a statement of opinion that unequivocally associates it with your own personal view, which is also a professional judgement in this context. This type of contribution to the meeting indicates self-confidence and certainty about a position, in this case, a particular course of action. Beliefs such as 'I do not have an important contribution to make' or 'Others have more expertise than I do' will inevitably produce deferential, hesitant and vague non-assertive responses. Such interjections can effortlessly be ignored by others at the meeting. If you fail to articulate your viewpoint with ownership and conviction, other professionals are unlikely to listen to you.

2. Explicitly agree or disagree with other people's views at the meeting and do not just use non-verbal behaviour to indicate your perspective. Offer clarification as to why you agree or disagree with another colleague's opinion at the meeting. However, if you disagree with a position, it is important to offer a constructive alternative and not come across as impeding general agreement. It is also helpful to highlight any points or aspects you agree with in the proposition being considered: 'I agree that we need to put a family support worker in place for this child. But I think it would be better if instead of doing this immediately as proposed, we were clearer on the tasks of the support worker and what outcomes we are seeking to achieve'.

3. People at a case conference or other meeting will be more amenable to your proposals if you articulate them as suggestions rather than demands. An example of this would be: 'How about if we postpone this decision until we have the report of the medical assessment on the child'. Contrast this to the same proposal framed as an imperative statement, such as: 'Postpone this decision'.

The latter can come across to other attendees as abrasive in tone and, therefore, aggressive, which could, in turn, elicit hostility towards you and possibly derail agreement with your position.

4. Requesting clarification of someone's contribution during a child protection discussion is an essential skill. In a public setting, such as a case conference, social workers can sometimes retreat from asking for an explanation of a point made by another professional that they have not fully understood. Often, such reticence is due to a fear of being perceived as foolish by other attendees at the meeting, which may also include their own line manager, if present. Understanding what is being said is a basic right in any forum and it is crucial to enforce this right, most particularly when a child is at risk. Beliefs such as 'Others are cleverer than me' will inhibit you from asking for more explanation of an essential point that another professional has made during the meeting. Invariably, not comprehending all the issues raised during a discussion undermines your own ability to make a pertinent contribution to child protection decisions.

5. Avoid interrupting others, as this is aggressive behaviour that indicates a belief along the lines of 'What I have to say is more important than that of others'. Exceptionally, there are two occasions in which interrupting other attendees is justified. First, if someone at the meeting has misunderstood your point and is, in turn, misleading the meeting as to what you actually meant; in which case you might begin your interruption with 'Before you continue, I need to say that you have misunderstood my last point'. Second, you should be prepared to interrupt someone who attempts to speak over you at a child protection forum; for example, 'Let me just make this one point, before you respond'. Permitting someone to interrupt or talk over you indicates a belief that other people's needs are more important than your own and leads to reluctance to insist on your rights at a meeting.

6. Assertiveness at a meeting can also involve soliciting the views of others or asking them to expand on something they have said. If you value and respect other people's opinions, then actively asking for these at a meeting is another demonstration of assertiveness. Asking a police officer to relate his impressions of the home he visited on a call-out to a domestic violence incident where it is known a child may be at risk also demands assertiveness skills. If you believe that, as a social worker, 'you know best', then you are unlikely to seek out or respect the contributions of others. You will devalue or dismiss them or simply not bother to ask for the contributions of others at all. Such behaviour at a meeting is aggressive rather than assertive. On the other hand, if you lack conviction in your right to information in order to make an effective contribution to the discussion, then silence is likely to be your non-assertive choice.

7. Assertive contributions at child protection forums do not just depend on what you say, but also on when you say it. If you disagree with another professional's viewpoint or proposition, you need to voice this early rather than later in the meeting. Certainly, you need to do it before that particular topic is

closed or agreed upon. Otherwise, you run the risk of a hostile reaction from other professionals who perceive you as holding up the meeting or possibly sabotaging a tentative agreement on a course of action to safeguard a child. Intervening late in this discussion can come across as aggressive behaviour by your colleagues. Ironically, a late contribution may actually be attributable to a belief that what you have to say is not very important, resulting in hesitation to make a contribution in the first instance. This ambivalence leads to delay in articulating a view, as the social worker attempts to work up the courage to say something in front of a full meeting of multidisciplinary colleagues.

REFLECTIVE EXERCISE ON BELIEFS ABOUT EXPRESSING OWN OPINION

Reflect on what beliefs you hold about articulating your opinion and disagreeing with others in your personal and professional life. Ask yourself the following questions:

- Do these beliefs tend to support assertive, non-assertive or aggressive interactions with others?
- What rights do you think you possess in relation to work with professionals from other agencies or teams?

Assertive non-verbal communication in meetings

Being heard, in the sense of having other colleagues take on board and respond to your point of view in their deliberations, necessitates realising that at a team or multidisciplinary meeting, you are competing with possibly eight or 10 different sources of information, viewpoints and professional opinions on further action. Therefore, it is vital to use non-verbal communication in a manner that supports and draws attention to your assertive contributions. Back and Back (2005, p 180) suggest a number of ways in which non-verbal behaviour at meetings can buttress assertive verbal interventions. These build on the discussion around assertive non-verbal communication in Case Study 4.1. Speak a bit more loudly than you would at a one-to-one interaction to ensure you are heard by everyone at the meeting. This does not mean shouting at people, which would be perceived as aggressive. The volume you settle on should take into consideration the size of the meeting and the acoustics of the venue.

Use more eye contact. If you are responding to one particular person at the meeting, you should look directly at them, without appearing to stare them down, which would, of course, be experienced by the other professional as aggressive. It is important to be seen to give that professional your full attention. By contrast, if your contribution is one that you are addressing to the whole meeting, for instance, to object to a course of action that is gaining a consensus, then sweeping round everyone with your eyes is more likely to gain the attention of all those at the meeting. As previously discussed, a social worker from the white majority community who is non-assertive will tend to look down or avoid eye contact. This will undermine the most assertive of statements at the meeting. Social workers from heritage backgrounds influenced by social norms that regard members of the opposite sex looking at each other as immodest, or a younger person looking an older person in the eyes as disrespectful, need to be mindful of how avoidance of eye contact in a cross-cultural context may convey passivity rather than respect. Use gestures to draw attention to yourself and what you are saying. Open gestures can reinforce verbally assertive messages. Equally, producing too many hand movements or using such gestures as pointing can be a distraction for other professionals at the meeting or appear aggressive. Like the use of volume, gestures need to be carefully calibrated during a discussion. Altering body posture can also be used to considerable effect in conveying assertiveness. Leaning forward when you wish to make a point can emphasise a verbally assertive statement while also catching the attention of other professionals at the meeting.

REFLECTIVE EXERCISE ON NON-VERBAL COMMUNICATION

Recall the last time you were at a multidisciplinary forum or, indeed, a team meeting. Ask yourself the following questions:

- To what extent did you employ non-verbal communication to support and reinforce your spoken contributions?
- During the next multidisciplinary or team meeting you attend, endeavour to be aware of your own non-verbal communication. Do you think this is assertive, non-assertive or aggressive?
- To what extent does it reinforce or undermine your verbal assertiveness at the meeting?
- How might you improve your non-verbal communication to support assertive statements during future meetings?

Conflict between social workers and police colleagues

Medical staff at the North Middlesex Hospital were not the only professionals to report difficulties in their working relationships with social workers. There were also tensions between some of Haringey's Child Protection Teams and the police. In evidence to the inquiry, Victoria's social worker at Haringey described hostility towards the police and other agencies because there was a widely held belief that 'social services knew best'. The Detective Sergeant attached to the Haringey Child Protection Team of the Metropolitan Police Service conceded that working relationships were not always productive between the two organisations. Despite the existence of protocols for joint investigations, there were disagreements between social services and the police as to how to conduct these. The police contended that, at times, social services thwarted them. A Metropolitan Police Service internal letter referring to the North Tottenham District Office of

Haringey Children and Family Services described the 'difficulty of working with what seems to be an "aggressive" social work unit' (para 6.24).

Disputes between the Child Protection Team of the Metropolitan Police and the social work Investigation and Assessment Team had undoubtedly entered the *conflict spiral*. This probably started out as an initial difference of opinion over a particular safeguarding issue between individual social workers and police officers. Left unresolved, this would have developed into coalitions of colleagues aligning themselves behind oppositional positions. At this point, social workers and police officers were predisposed to side with their own fellow professionals, followed by a hardening of their respective positions and an insistence that it was the only correct one. As communication faltered between the two professional groupings, their view of one another certainly narrowed, possibly to the point of stereotype. While police officers began characterising social workers at the North Tottenham District Office as 'aggressive', many social workers seemed convinced that police officers generally had limited contributions to make to safeguarding. Communication between front-line police officers and social workers deteriorated, as indicated by their inability to even agree on how to follow laid-down procedures. The individuals involved sought out more powerful figures to support their viewpoint, with managers becoming embroiled in the dispute, as evidenced by the internal letter sent by a police officer regarding the matter. As the conflict escalated to encompass ever more people, those involved would have increasingly lost their objectivity.

At the bottom of the *conflict spiral* was an apparently shared perception within the police child protection unit and the Investigation and Assessment Team of social workers that differences were irreconcilable. By this point, the fixed positions and constrictive views of these adversarial coalitions of multidisciplinary colleagues made it impossible for either side to formulate mutually agreeable goals. As Lewicki et al (2010, p 19) observe, during sustained conflict, 'the parties become anxious, irritated, annoyed, angry, or frustrated. Emotions overwhelm clear thinking, and the parties may become increasingly irrational as the conflict escalates'. It appears that as both police officers and social workers became angered by one another, their discussions deteriorated into abrasive exchanges and, at times, verbally aggressive interactions, while wrangles over the minutia of joint investigations evidenced irrational self-defeating choices.

The interactions between the police and social workers in Haringey London Borough Council can also be understood within a web of common multidisciplinary dynamics that can interfere with productive working relationships between these professional groups. Brandon et al (2009, p 45), in their overview of serious case reviews, found that police officers regularly reported hesitation in questioning the decisions or actions of medical doctors or social workers in child protection situations due to the conviction that these professionals were more experienced in this area. Indeed, Brandon et al (2009, p 45) noted that 'in spite of a raft of procedural guidance, practitioners and managers were often unclear about what they could or could not do, or should or should not do in these cases'. The result was that 'everyone seemed to be frozen into inactivity'. Certainly, the mutual antagonism that developed between some practitioners at Haringey Children and Family Services and some officers in the Metropolitan Police Service may have been fuelled by assumptions on the part of social workers that they 'knew best' and diffidence on the part of police officers. In such circumstances, an ostensible expression of professional judgement by a social worker can be experienced by multidisciplinary colleagues as an aggressive imposition of opinion, which ignores the perspectives, insights and expertise of others. The events at Haringey illustrate how social workers can sometimes abuse their *information power* and *position-based power*, engendering aggressive responses to challenges by multidisciplinary professionals.

Box 5.1: Using power in negotiations

Research by Lytle et al (1999) reveals a number of important considerations in the use of power during negotiations. The lessons from this study are drawn out by Lewicki et al (2010, p 199) and are reproduced as follows:

1. Starting a negotiation by conveying your own power to coerce the other party could bring a quick settlement if your threat is credible. If the other party calls your bluff, however, you are left to either carry out your threat or lose face.

2. To avert a conflict spiral and move towards an interests-based exchange, avoid reciprocating messages involving rights or power. Shift the conversation by asking an interests-related question. It may take several attempts to redirect the interaction successfully.

3. If you can't avoid reciprocating negative behaviours (which may be a natural response, but not necessarily effective), try a 'combined statement' that mixes a threat with an interests-oriented refocusing question or statement.

4. Power tactics (and rights tactics) may be most useful when the other party refuses to negotiate or when negotiations have broken down and need to be restarted. In these situations, not much is risked by making threats based on rights or power, but the threat itself may help the other party appreciate the severity of the situation.

5. The success of power tactics (and rights tactics) depends to a great extent on how they are implemented. To be effective, threats must be specific and credible, targeting the other party's high-priority interests. Otherwise, the other party has little incentive to comply. Make sure that you leave an avenue for the other party to 'turn off' the threat, save face and reopen the negotiations around interests.

REFLECTIVE EXERCISE ON THE USE OF POWER IN MULTI-AGENCY SETTINGS

During the next multidisciplinary meeting you attend, observe how different professionals deploy *informational, position-based, relationship-based* and *contextual power* to assert their positions and question or challenge other professionals in attendance. Also consider how people at the meeting are using these different sources of power in conjunction with aspects of their own personalities. Ask yourself the following questions:

- How skilfully and appropriately do they employ these different kinds of power?
- How do they tactfully assert their own professional opinion and challenge others in ways that facilitate the discussion?
- Does their manner of articulating their power during deliberations appear to antagonise other professionals and, if so, why?
- How does it affect the dynamics of the multidisciplinary meeting?
- What might you do differently at a future multidisciplinary meeting to draw more effectively on your power?

Case Study 5.2: Child sexual abuse by foster carers

Wakefield City Council (2007) *Independent inquiry report into the circumstances of child sexual abuse by two foster carers in Wakefield*

Craig Faunch was 29 years old and Ian Wathy was 38 years old at the time of these events. They were both of white British descent and had purchased a house together early in their relationship. They had been living together for seven years. In August 2002, both men made an application to become foster carers. An assessment was undertaken and they were registered as short-term foster carers from July 2003. In all, 18 children aged 11–15 were placed with the couple between August 2003 and January 2005. In June 2004, a family support worker was told by two foster children, Child F and Child G, that Mr Faunch had taken a number of photographs of both of them urinating, defecating and washing in the bath and shower. The support worker informed both the children's mother and their social worker. The mother demanded that her children be immediately removed from the foster carers, which was duly done. The incident was also reported by the children's social worker to management and although the foster carers were challenged over their behaviour, no further action was taken against the couple. Children continued to be placed with Mr Faunch and Mr Wathy.

The relationship between social workers and the couple became increasingly strained, resulting in a deterioration of collaborative working. In October 2004, the mother of Child F and Child G reported that she had seen Mr Faunch and Mr Wathy near her home and her children's school on a number of occasions. No action was taken regarding the couple's presence near the children's home. On 31 January 2005, Child T ran away from his foster care placement with the two men and informed his brother's girlfriend that he had been sexually abused by them. The police and children's services were alerted. A strategy meeting was convened the next day at which it was agreed to suspend all foster placements with the couple. Subsequently, other children placed with them also made allegations of sexual abuse. The couple were deregistered as foster carers in June 2005.

A Crown Court hearing in June 2006 convicted both men of multiple sexual offences against children in their care. Craig Faunch was given a six-year custodial sentence while Ian Wathy was jailed for five years.

Conflict between social work colleagues in different teams

Child F and Child G, during a car journey with a family support worker, showed her a photograph taken by their foster carer of Child G urinating. Both children claimed that Mr Faunch had taken many photographs of them urinating, defecating or in the bath, and that these were kept in a drawer. The family support worker informed the children's social worker, who showed the photograph to a front-line manager within Wakefield Children's Services. This Children's Team manager in turn spoke to the Fostering Team manager about the incident. According to the Children's Team manager in evidence to the independent inquiry, the Fostering Team manager was 'defensive and not open to a full debate about the potential implications of the photograph' (para 9.183). She recalled that the Fostering Team manager 'did not seem able to understand the view of the Children's Team, and was not supportive of their view that a Strategy Meeting in the context of Working Together children protection procedures needed to be convened' (para 9.183). The Children's Team leader stated that she felt angry and frustrated that she could not prevail upon the Fostering Team leader to collaborate with her on an agreed way forward. The Fostering Team manager did, however, discuss the matter with her own line manager, who advised that the children be asked to clarify what had occurred, as there was insufficient information to proceed directly to a strategy meeting. The Foster Team manager believed that the matter was being treated as a 'standard of care issue' and not a child protection matter.

This disagreement fundamentally affected the action that was then taken. The children's social worker and the family support worker made a joint visit to see the children, who were now back living with their mother. As the matter was being treated as a 'standard of care issue', routine child protection procedures for investigating potential abuse were not observed. The children's social worker had no specialist training in evidential interviews. Child F and Child G confirmed their story. The children's social worker then made a joint visit with a family support worker to explain to the two foster carers why Child F and Child G would not be returning to their care and also to outline the allegations they had made. This meant that the foster carers were alerted to the incriminating evidence and had the opportunity to dispose of it or hide it. The photographs referred to by Child F and Child G were never found.

Subsequent to this, there continued to be disagreement between the Fostering and Children's Team managers regarding the necessity of a strategy meeting. In the end, no strategy meeting took place and, instead, a carers' annual review was to be arranged. Moreover, at no stage was the disclosure by the children treated as a child protection matter and child protection procedures were not invoked. There was considerable confusion at management level as to which team should take the lead on dealing with the foster carers. This was because there was dispute as to whether the incident brought to the attention of children's services by the two children was a complaint, 'a standard of care' issue or a child protection matter. The independent inquiry established that Wakefield Children's Services had, in fact, clear policies in place for dealing with exactly the sort of allegation that the children had made. But the disagreement between the Fostering and Children's Team managers meant that this was not acted upon.

In the midst of the continuing conflict between the teams, the children were taken on a farewell visit to the foster carers' home, during which they were left unsupervised with Mr Faunch and Mr Wathy. This presented the foster carers with a final opportunity to intimidate the two children into silence about their sexual abuse. The visit took place against the better judgement of the children's social worker and her manager, who both came under pressure from the Fostering Team to accede to it. It is significant that the Fostering Team social workers had themselves come under considerable pressure from the foster carers for the farewell visit to take place (para 9.210). The social worker responsible for supervising Mr Faunch and Mr Wathy later approached the Children's Team to ask that the foster carers be allowed to speak to the parent of Child G and Child F, as the foster carers wished to have some contact with the two children. The children's social worker and her team leader refused this contact (para 9.348). As the inquiry noted, this episode meant that the Children's Team:

> continued to worry about what the actions of the foster carers might mean. However, they felt defeated in their attempts to get this across to the fostering service which they saw as unquestioningly supportive of [Mr Faunch's and Mr Wathy's] wish for continued contact with the children. (para 9.350)

The events at Wakefield took place against a backdrop of poor working relationships between the Fostering and Children's Teams. According to the inquiry, this was evident in: the lack of knowledge about one another's practice and responsibility; 'superficial and distant' professional relationships at managerial level; and a 'silo' approach to practice within the teams (para 9.229). Colleagues in disagreement with each other were apparently reluctant to meet face to face and, instead, over-relied on email and telephone conversations. These embedded dynamics within the wider organisation actively hindered the resolution of disputes. Endorsing the finding of the independent inquiry into the abuse of foster children in Wakefield, Brandon et al (2009, p 96), on examination of almost 200 serious case reviews, concluded that: 'Professional challenge is also said to be easier in the context of good trusting professional relationships where a disagreement is not seen as a threat, or a slight, or a comment on professional competence'. Reliance on communication via the telephone and email rather than face to face by social workers and their managers in both the Children's Team and the Fostering Team almost certainly contributed to the lack of rapport among practitioners. This would have made it difficult for a social worker to challenge the opinion of his or her colleagues without appearing to fault their professional competence. In such circumstances, it would have been easy for offence to be taken and aggressive exchanges to ensue.

As explained in Chapter Two, conflicts involve opposing interests between individuals, groups or organisations such that positive outcomes for one are perceived to have negative outcomes for the other. At an institutional level, social workers and front-line managers in both the Fostering Team and the Children's Team at Wakefield had the common goal of protecting children from abuse, they certainly both had the legal obligation to safeguard them. But at a team level, they had opposing perspectives on the same incident, with the Fostering Team believing the inappropriate photograph of *looked-after* children was a standard of care issue, while the Children's Team believed it to be a child protection issue. Both teams had a degree of vested interest in their interpretation of events. Social workers on the Fostering Team were resistant to the notion that the two foster carers their agency had assessed and contracted were in fact paedophiles, as this would have grave repercussions for Wakefield's fostering service. At the same time, social workers on the Children's Team perceived their primary duty as protecting children, even if this meant uncovering abusive foster carers employed by their own local authority. Failing to identify child abuse would have negative consequences for the foster children in the social workers' care and for the practitioners themselves if either management or the media found them wanting in their safeguarding responsibilities. It was this perception of divergent adverse consequences that each team sought to protect itself from while simultaneously carrying out their primary functions of, respectively, placing *looked-after* children and safeguarding children.

As epitomised by this case study, most conflicts are not in fact over material resources, but revolve around intangible issues identified in Chapter Two as disputes over: data; values; interests; procedures; relationships; roles; and communication (Isenhart and Spangle, 2000, pp 14–15). In particular, colleagues located in the Fostering and Children's Teams disagreed over: the reliability and interpretation of information provided by the children; the procedures that should be invoked to address the inappropriate behaviour of the foster carers; and the respective roles of social workers from the two teams in tackling the issue with the foster carers. There was also disagreement between the front-line managers in respect of their working relationship, with the Children's Team leader claiming that her judgement was not being given the consideration it ought to have commanded from the Fostering Team leader. Finally, there were plainly differences of opinion over the necessity of sharing more information about Mr Faunch and Mr Wathy and how such communication should occur, with the Children's Team urging the convening of a strategy meeting and the Fostering Team arguing that there remained insufficient grounds for organising one. As in Case Study 5.1, the dispute quickly entered into a *conflict spiral*, with more senior managers being pulled into the conflict and social workers on both teams becoming angry with one another amid a growing perception of practitioners on the other team as obdurate and obstructive. As a result, the perception of the Fostering Team that Mr Faunch and Mr Wathy had merely acted inappropriately and that the matter was therefore a 'standard of care issue', and the contrasting view of the Children's Team that Mr Faunch and Mr Wathy might be acting abusively, making it a child protection matter, remained the entrenched positions of the two teams up until the point of formal police involvement.

Addressing conflict between teams and agencies

The independent inquiry concluded that differences of opinion within the same organisation were not unusual or unexpected and could, indeed, be viewed 'as information rather than taken personally, where points of view are respected and openly debated and another professional's experience is valued and given credence' (para 9.229). The failure to convene a strategy meeting meant that professionals did not meet in a face-to-face forum with representatives from outside agencies, such as the police. Had such a strategy meeting or child protection strategy discussion occurred, children's and fostering social workers and their team leaders would have had the opportunity to air their points of view and bring the conflict into the open. Under an experienced independent chair for the meeting, and with the presence of representatives from outside agencies to act as a buffer, this could have offered a forum for resolution and an agreed way forward (paras 9.223–9.224, 9.230). At such a meeting:

> everyone could have seen the photograph and been aware that there were alleged to have been many more photographs. It might have provided a forum to make sense of different people's viewpoints, to identify whether there was a need for any further investigations and to plan a coherent way ahead under a clear procedural framework. (para 9.224)

Discussions between social workers on the teams responsible for foster placements and child protection at Wakefield had deteriorated into repetitive arguments in which maintaining established positions overtook procedural requirements and professional judgement. Coming face to face in a multidisciplinary setting would have provided some scope for movement from entrenched perspectives. Yet, without some commitment to negotiate differences rather than simply impose one particular view upon everyone else, it is conceivable that social workers would have replayed their dispute even in the presence of other professionals. In these circumstances, other professionals might have been swayed to take sides, resulting in the escalation of the conflict and the formation of alliances. Child protection forums attended by colleagues from different social work teams or disciplinary backgrounds are, in one sense, negotiations between professionals about how to protect a child. As discussed in Case Study 5.1, these interactions involve the deployment of power, which Lewicki et al (2010, p 197) define as 'the capabilities negotiators can assemble to give themselves an advantage or increase the probability of achieving their objectives'. Skilled negotiators also utilise influence, which comprises 'the actual messages and tactics an individual undertakes in order to change the attitudes and/or behaviours of others'. Sole reliance on *informational power* or *position-based power* in the midst of a long-standing conflict is likely to intensify defensive reactions rather than reduce them. Lewicki et al (2010, pp 223–9) propose ways of influencing the motivation of the other party to enter into integrative negotiations, which are summarised in Box 5.2.

Box 5.2: Making integrative negotiation attractive

- *Make the offer attractive* – Emphasise the advantages for the other party of agreeing to your proposal. This means that it is particularly important to understand the other party's interests.
- *Frame the message so that the other party will agree* – Individuals who agree to one proposal, regardless of how minor, are more likely to agree to a further proposal. So, starting with smaller requests can help build a relationship that predisposes the other party to agree to more exacting proposals.
- *Make the message normative* – Individuals prefer to act in ways consistent with their own values and self-image. Knowing the other party's interests can assist you to frame messages that persuade the other party that your proposal is consistent with his or her beliefs and values.
- *Agreement in principle* – When there appears to be intractable conflict over details, getting a broad agreement in principle early on can help to build a basis for more thorough negotiation.
- *Two-sided messages* – Outline the other party's position as well as your own, explicitly acknowledging their arguments and interests. This assists to refute the other person's arguments.
- *Message components* – Break your argument down into smaller, more easily comprehended components instead of articulating a single complex proposition. This approach can also be used to identify the elements of a proposition that both parties can agree to and what remains in dispute.
- *Repetition* – Repeating your point or several key points assists to reinforce your core argument. However, overdoing repetition can annoy the other party to the negotiation.
- *Conclusion* – Make the conclusion of your arguments and propositions explicit.
- *Pitching the message* – This includes engaging the other party in meaningful conversation prior to negotiations in order to build rapport, as this reduces the sense of confrontation. Deciding on the intensity of the message and whether

to use threats or not depending on the nature of the negotiation are further considerations.

According to Isenhart and Spangle (2000, p 49) effective negotiators also deploy a tactic known as *tagging*. This is the act of drawing the attention of another negotiator to aspects of his or her behaviour that are inhibiting or facilitating the process of reaching an agreement. If another negotiator is threatening to renege on an already-settled matter that forms part of the dispute, a tag would highlight the way in which this behaviour was undermining the negotiation process and jeopardising a successful conclusion. Conversely, if a negotiation is becoming stuck, one negotiator might point out to the other which of their behaviours had been an aid to reaching accommodation in the past, and how a small concession by him or her previously had helped the negotiation to move forward. *Tagging* is a means of signalling to other negotiators what aspects of their behaviour are helping or hindering the negotiation. The idea of the tag is to either stop destructive negotiating tactics by the other negotiator or to encourage him or her to engage in more facilitative behaviours.

REFLECTIVE EXERCISE ON INTEGRATIVE NEGOTIATION

Recall a recent conflict with a colleague from a different team or agency concerning a child protection matter that remained unresolved or was unsatisfactorily resolved in your opinion. Using the methods of influencing negotiations suggested by Lewicki et al (2010, pp 223–9) set out earlier, rework the conflict, noting down how you could have presented your interests, goals, outcomes, needs and opinions in a way that might have been more acceptable or attractive to your colleague.

Latent conflict within and between agencies

During the independent inquiry, the children's social worker stated in evidence:

> I think that one of the problems was that the family placement team were very clear that we've got these carers and they are unique ... the fact that they were a gay foster couple ... we need to do everything to support them, to help them remain foster carers really and that was very clearly coming across even though we were sort of saying, although not stating specifically that we felt the boys were being abused but were saying that we've got numerous concerns about these carers that need dealing with. (para 9.228)

According to the independent inquiry, beyond the disagreement between the Fostering and Children's Teams regarding the nature of the foster carers' behaviour, there was also a widespread fear of articulating views that might be interpreted as homophobic. This pervasive fear affected both teams.

There appeared to be a general reluctance to link evidence of paedophilia to the activities of a homosexual couple. As a result, anxiety that the couple were, in fact, abusing the children in their care was restricted to conversations between the children's social worker, a number of family support workers and the Children's Team manager. In other words, it was not articulated in any procedural way. As the inquiry was to note: 'beyond this front-line social work level within a specific team context, it was not possible to think, articulate or debate this possibility – to think the unthinkable. Why?' (para 9.323). The inquiry sought to answer its own question by suggesting that:

> the fear of being seen as prejudiced, the risk of talking about the words gay and paedophile together was too great. There was a pervasive anxiety that if this view was put forward whether in writing or verbally that the person putting it forward would be accused of being prejudiced and homophobic. (para 9.232)

The independent inquiry described the impact this had on the organisation as a whole at length:

> Not allowing the hypothesis to surface (that the boys might have been exposed to sexual abuse, or to 'grooming' with sexual abuse in mind), or if it did surface, allowing it to be immediately discarded due to the internal anxiety it aroused, resulted in the usual rules of professional social work practice not being followed. Gathering information through mobilising the network, analysing the information and then planning an informed multi-agency way forward within a clear procedural framework did not happen.... This had two aspects: first, that these concerns might really be generated from a personal prejudicial response to their being gay; second, that real suspicions, if voiced, might be reacted to by others as if they were prejudices – including by the carers themselves, were they to be made aware of these suspicions. Our major criticism is of the organisation's failure to create a 'culture of inquiry', in which such feelings, suspicions, concerns and unconscious prejudices could be explored – without fear of being seen as deficient or homophobic. (paras 9.233, 10.12)

Social workers, together with their frontline managers, whether on the Fostering Team or the Children's Team, were hesitant to articulate a suspicion that Craig Faunch and Ian Wathy, who happened to be gay, might also be paedophiles. This hesitancy emanated from a fear that they might actually be, or they might be accused of being, homophobic, either by other colleagues or by the foster carers. Understandably, social workers committed to anti-oppressive practice baulked at the prospect of colluding with prevalent negative stereotypes of gay men that characterise them as paedophiles. The processes of self-censorship that quelled private misgivings and silenced public expression led to the repression of conflict. Consequently, apart from scattered private conversations between a few close colleagues, the possibility that Craig Faunch and Ian Wathy were sexually abusing *looked-after* children was not mooted. It was never opened up to debate and remained a source of *latent conflict*; an unacknowledged disagreement, which nevertheless affected the dynamics within the organisation and impeded the ability of social workers to safeguard children in their charge.

Anti-oppressive practice and professional self-assertion

The preoccupation of the social work profession with social justice has made anti-oppressive practice a key focus of training and intervention with families. Seminal social work texts on combating discrimination and oppression emphasise the capacity of practitioners to hold negative stereotypes, be prejudiced, perpetuate inequality and be intolerant of difference (Dominelli, 1997, 2002a, 2002b; Thompson, 2006). There is very much less consideration given to how the sexism, racism, homophobia, disablism and ageism of service-users can be directed against social workers in ways that are hurtful and offensive. Such instances can detrimentally impact on both the well-being and practice of front-line professionals. There is little in the social work literature on how to tackle the problem evidenced by some inquiries and serious case reviews, which show anti-oppressive approaches being actively subverted by caregivers to prevent social workers from intervening to protect children. In Case Study 5.2, Craig Faunch and Ian Wathy, as gay men, probably played upon their oppressed minority status as homosexuals to discourage social workers from following through on suspicions that they were, in fact, paedophiles. Social workers are predisposed by their training in anti-oppressive practice, in conjunction with their professional codes of practice and standards of proficiency (which emphasise respect for diversity), to shy away from any supposition that inclines towards a negative stereotype. The linkage of male homosexuality with paedophilia is an enduring prejudicial and predatory archetype of gay men. Professional assertiveness and the personal self-confidence necessary to give expression to it make substantial demands upon practitioners. One-sided anti-oppressive perspectives, which minimise the capacity of unscrupulous caregivers to turn this approach to their own advantage by alleging they are being discriminated against in order to conceal their abuse of children can lead to professional self-doubt. Ultimately, as in this case study, it can undermine good child protection practice.

REFLECTIVE EXERCISE ON PRACTITIONER POSITIONALITY

Consider your positionality, meaning your ethnicity, gender, sexuality, age and so on, in relation to the parents, children and other family members you have worked with or currently work with. Ask yourself the following questions:

- Have any of them accused you of prejudice or discrimination and, if so, how did the accusation make you feel, what were your thoughts and how did you react?
- Did you discuss the interaction with anyone else and, if not, why?
- Did you think there was some justification for the caregiver's or child's accusation or not?
- How did the accusation affect your practice with that family or with other families from a similar background?
- Having read the events that occurred in Wakefield regarding two gay foster carers, how might you approach a similar occurrence in the future?

Points for practice

- Practitioners carrying out child protection-related roles operate in a multi-agency context and conflicts can arise between multidisciplinary colleagues or social work colleagues from other teams.
- Power dynamics between higher- and lower-status professionals can undermine the assertiveness of practitioners when a conflict or disagreement arises with a higher-status colleague.
- Understanding the different types of power exercised by professionals in interdisciplinary contexts is crucial to improving assertive communication skills.
- Social workers should be cognisant of how colleagues can express their disagreement or anger about issues through *passive-aggressive* behaviours, which undermine effective inter-agency working.
- The use of assertive communication skills, in conjunction with integrative negotiation strategies, can diminish tensions with colleagues from other agencies or teams and reduce the potential for *conflict spirals*.
- Differences of opinion and perspective can arise between social workers from different teams or agencies when they have diverse roles and responsibilities in relation to children. Lack of face-to-face interaction between practitioners can play into *conflict spirals*.
- Latent conflict can arise when practitioners fail to articulate concerns about a caregiver or child because of fears that they will be perceived as prejudiced.

CHAPTER SIX

Conflict and substitute carers

Conflict with substitute carers

Social workers are often required to work with substitute carers, who may be guardians, local government-contracted foster carers or those involved in private foster care arrangements. Like interventions with parents or their partners, engagement with substitute carers can be challenging if they perceive social workers to be interfering or if they are attempting to hide the abuse of children in their care. This chapter centres on two case studies, the first deriving from an independent inquiry into the sexual abuse of children in foster care. The second is sourced from a serious case review into the death of a child at the hands of a young care-leaver and her male partner while in a private fostering arrangement. These case studies together explore the challenges confronting practitioners when substitute carers behave in evasive or aggressive ways. The detrimental impact that prolonged exposure to hostile behaviour by caregivers can have on the well-being of social workers and their practice is also examined. Advanced negotiating and assertiveness skills are described and how they can be deployed to work effectively with defensive or hostile caregivers is explained.

Case Study 5.2: Child sexual abuse by foster carers

Wakefield City Council (2007) *Independent inquiry report into the circumstances of child sexual abuse by two foster carers in Wakefield*
This study revisits events set out and discussed at the beginning of Case Study 5.2 based on the investigation and findings of Wakefield City Council's (2007) *Independent inquiry report into the circumstances of child sexual abuse by two foster carers in Wakefield.* However, Case Study 6.1 moves away from a focus on exchanges between professionals to examine the interactions of social workers with the two foster carers, Craig Faunch and Ian Wathy.

Non-compliance with a programme of activity

Mr Faunch and Mr Wathy contacted Wakefield Council in July 2002, asking to be considered as foster carers of a young boy with a view to adopting. They were duly invited to be assessed for fostering by the local authority. As part of this assessment, Mr Faunch and Mr Wathy, who had never parented before, were provided with work experience at a local Family Centre where they were asked to help weekly with a group of 20 children aged 9–13 years old. This was to be undertaken from January through to March 2003. On 11 March, the assessing social worker telephoned the Family Centre to discover that Mr Faunch and Mr Wathy had ceased attending two weeks previously without either informing the Family Centre or the assessing social worker of their decision. During the inquiry, the assessing social worker admitted that she had felt angry with the couple and that 'she had spoken to them about the unacceptable nature of their actions and asked them to ring Family Centre Y to make contact to explain their absence' (para 9.27). She told the inquiry that she did not know if Mr Faunch and Mr Wathy actually returned to the Family Centre to complete the agreed period of work experience. According to the assessing social worker, she 'moved on with it' and took no further action regarding the matter. She later summarised the couple's time at the Family Centre as positive, which comprised part of their formal assessment as foster carers. As neither a note of their actual attendance at the Family Centre nor their failure to explain their absence was recorded, the couple were never subsequently challenged by the assessing social worker or the fostering panel.

From the earliest stages of contact between the couple and the fostering service, they were both given the impression that they could contravene requirements and procedures with impunity. The failure to challenge Mr Faunch and Mr Wathy when they withdrew from the work experience arranged by the assessing social worker during their application process as foster carers was only the first in a series of behaviours that were neither challenged nor led to any adverse consequences. The lack of challenge or penalties encouraged rather than discouraged the couple to push the boundaries at each stage. It would also have reinforced behaviours that contravened the stipulations of social workers. Deliberating on the responses of practitioners and agencies to the non-compliance of Mr Faunch and Mr Wathy, the independent inquiry opined that:

> An approach which was informed more strongly by the safeguarding of children would have given [Mr Faunch and Mr Wathy] a message about the 'tightness' of the fostering services' systems and the layers of oversight and scrutiny to which they would be subject. They would have had an experience whereby any irregularity or non-compliance was quickly picked up and challenged. This was particularly pertinent in relation to the carers' failure to comply with the agreed voluntary programme at Family Centre Y. We believe the way non-compliance with expectations is dealt with at an early stage in an intervention communicates a critical message. To the person who has failed to comply, the response or lack of it gives information about the robustness of the system in which he/she is operating; to the system that expects compliance, it gives information about the capacity of the non-complier to work within set boundaries and expectations and lines of authority. (paras 9.33–9.34)

Challenging substitute caregivers, parents and partners

Challenging is one component in a range of communication skills widely employed by social care professionals. It has received considerable attention in the psychotherapeutic literature, from which it informs social work practice. Egan (1990, p 184) offers a helpful definition of challenge as 'an invitation to examine internal or external behaviour that seems to be self-defeating, harmful to others, or both and to change the behaviour if it is found to be so'. According to Nelson-Jones (2008, pp 81–2), there are seven major types of discrepancies that a worker may challenge, which are outlined in Box 6.1.

Box 6.1: Types of discrepancy

- Inconsistency between verbal, vocal and/or body messages.
- Inconsistency between words and actions.
- Inconsistency between values and actions.
- Inconsistency between giving and keeping one's word.
- Inconsistency between earlier and present statements.
- Inconsistency between statements and evidence.
- Inconsistency between own and others' evaluations.

To take Case Study 6.1, there was a blatant contradiction between the avowed desire of Mr Faunch and Mr Wathy to foster children and yet their unwillingness to attend a Family Centre to gain experience of working with children in order to increase their prospect of being accepted as foster carers. This revealed an inconsistency between words and actions. Given that the assessing social worker contacted Mr Faunch and Mr Wathy to insist that they telephone the Family Centre and explain their absence – a demand they almost certainly acceded to, but likely never undertook – this demonstrated inconsistency between giving and keeping one's word. As the social worker admitted to the independent inquiry, neither of these inconsistencies was concertedly challenged. It needs to be appreciated that challenge, because it is a form of confrontation that often provokes a dispute, demands emotional and mental energy together with sufficient time to deal with a caregiver's response, which may well be defensive. As the assessing social worker acknowledged, she decided to move on and let the matter drop. In a stressful, time-pressured environment, this is an ever-present and understandable temptation.

Challenges, however, are not merely exercises in drawing attention to discrepancies in the thinking and behaviour of caregivers, they must constitute a constructive endeavour to *make a demand for work*. Shulman (1992, p 138) describes the nature of this work for service-users as an endeavour that 'often requires lowering long-established defences, discussing painful subjects, experiencing difficult feelings, recognizing one's own contribution to the problem, taking responsibility for one's actions, and confronting people and systems that are important to the client'. *Making a demand for work* in child protection means persuading caregivers to make changes in their values, attitudes or behaviours in ways that reduce risks to, or improve, the welfare of a child. It involves the skilful deployment of challenge to maintain a caregiver's focus on the work he or she must do to accomplish that change. The ability to successfully confront caregivers with their own discrepant and, sometimes, self-serving perspectives or actions rests on assertive verbal communication and the avoidance of aggressive interjections.

Ideally, challenges should be offered after rapport has been established with a caregiver. Realistically, in child protection situations, where urgent action is required to safeguard a minor, this may not always be possible. The crucial ingredient of offering an effective challenge is that there exists a degree of trust within the context of partnership-working between the caregiver and the social worker. The caregiver's trust in the social worker reduces the likelihood of either a blunt refusal to hear the challenge or defensiveness characterised by aggressive argumentation or multiple excuses. Patently, none of these hostile responses to challenge progresses the work needed from the caregiver for productive change to occur. Reducing defensive reactions to challenge involves a number of micro-skills in communication, which are outlined as follows:

- *Timing of challenge* – Should be used after rapport has been established and the social worker judges that the caregiver has some trust in him or her. Any challenge needs to be integrated into wider processes that assist a service-user to make a particular change. A challenge should be offered at a point when there is a clear goal determining its use. They should also be spaced to prevent placing too many simultaneous demands on a service-user.
- *Degree of challenge* – Build from mild challenges to stronger ones as the working relationship develops through the caregiver coping successfully with more minor challenges. The minimum amount of pressure should be used, only that necessary to achieve the goal of a given challenge. At the same time, challenges should be as forceful as the working relationship can tolerate without being weakened at a given point in time.
- *Form of challenge* – Must be explicit, specific and unambiguous. Where possible, challenge service-users' strengths, such as drawing attention to the resources, abilities and social support they have to assist them to achieve change. Challenges concerning cognitions, emotions, attitudes and behaviour must ultimately relate to challenges about taking action to change.
- *Delivery of challenge* – Body posture and gestures should be relaxed while the tone of voice should convey friendliness. Verbal communication should be assertive and avoid any aggressive elements, such as 'putdowns' or blaming. A challenge ought to be offered as an invitation for the caregiver to explore an aspect of his or her life, rather than as a demand to account for an inconsistency. Tentative, but unapologetic, challenging can lower service-user defences, while a categorical challenge can come across as an accusation, provoking a retaliatory response from a service-user or caregiver. By using probes, immediacy and

advanced empathy, social workers can encourage service-users to self-challenge, as these communication skills assist them to identify and question their own inconsistencies.

• *Frequency of challenge* – Persistent challenging can leave a caregiver feeling emotionally unsafe, leading to reluctance to engage with the social worker. There is a balance to be achieved between appropriate challenges that *make a demand for work* and overusing this communication skill to the extent that it alienates the caregiver and actually creates an impediment to the work.

• *Reactions to challenge* – Acknowledge a service-user's defensive reactions to challenge and use empathy and probes to help him or her work through these in order to reduce resistance. However, do not be diverted from the subject matter of the challenge by prolonged discussion of service-user reactions, as this may lead to avoidance of the challenge.

Even the most considered, best-timed and well-formulated challenges can meet with opposition from caregivers. Egan (1990, pp 206–7) identifies five common reactions of clients to challenge during counselling, which are adapted to social work practice as follows:

1. *Discredit challengers* – Essentially this is a form of counterattack in which the service-user endeavours to question the legitimacy, expertise or entitlement of the social worker to make the challenge.
2. *Persuade challengers to change their views* – The service-user argues with the social worker in an attempt to demonstrate that the challenge is misconceived and is based on mistaken assumptions or interpretation of events on the part of the social worker.
3. *Devalue the issue* – The service-user or caregiver minimises the issue that is the subject of the social worker's challenge.
4. *Seek support elsewhere for the views being challenged* – The service-user or caregiver discusses the challenge with others in his or her social network to elicit support and then confronts the social worker with the opinions and perspectives of others that contradict the basis of the challenge. In an extreme form, the service-user or caregiver can express this by demanding a different social worker, one that they hope will agree more with them and challenge less.
5. *Agree with the challenger but do not act on the challenge* – The service-user or caregiver agrees with the social worker as a means of disregarding and quickly moving on from the challenge to a different topic or issue. This can be a tactic for avoiding constructive change.

Egan (1990, p 208) warns that counsellors, like social workers, can be 'beguiled' and lulled into a false sense of achievement by the apparent insights of service-users or their agreement with challenges. The test is always whether such insight or agreement has resulted in action and constructive change in the life of the service-user or caregiver. He also highlights the 'Mum effect', which is the reluctance of counsellors, but equally of trained social workers, to cause anxiety or discomfort to service-users through challenge. Many social workers may also want to avoid the stress and discomfort that comes with conflict. As high numbers of people are attracted into the social care professions to assist others, they may feel deeply uneasy when engaging in a dispute with service-users that plainly unsettles or distresses them. Social workers are often very comfortable with helping activities, such as providing practical support, but uncomfortable with boundary-setting, challenging and pursuing legal action or its threat against a caregiver. This makes social workers particularly susceptible to the 'Mum effect' and, therefore, they need to be particularly vigilant in identifying any failures to challenge caregivers when this was plainly required.

As in other arenas related to child protection, such as supervision or multidisciplinary meetings, social workers can hold beliefs that impair their ability to act assertively. The beliefs practitioners have about challenging caregivers are crucial to how they actually go about setting boundaries and making demands on parents or their partners in order to safeguard children. Social workers who think that it is wrong to ask personal questions, that they must never hurt others, that they will be rejected by people they disagree with or that they are unable to cope with the anger and distress of others will retreat from challenging. Practitioners holding these types of beliefs will be: apprehensive about intruding upon caregivers' privacy; anxious about hurting them; afraid to prompt the caregivers' dislike; or worried that the caregiver's problems will overwhelm the practitioner. Social workers of this frame of mind are unlikely to behave assertively. Of course, it is imperative to balance the rights of caregivers to privacy against the necessity of pursuing intrusive questions, or to be cognisant of the potential for causing a caregiver pain so as to endeavour to minimise it. But such proper concerns should not be at the expense of beliefs that undermine vital challenges to caregivers. Egan (1990, pp 185–6) suggests a range of situations in which challenge can be positively employed to push service-users to engage with issues (see Box 6.2).

Box 6.2: When to use challenge with service-users

- Talk about their problems when they are reluctant to do so.
- Clarify problem situations in terms of specific experiences, behaviours and feelings when they are being evasive.
- Develop new perspectives on themselves, others and the world when they prefer to cling to distortions.
- Review new scenarios, critique them, develop goals and commit themselves to reasonable agendas instead of wallowing in the past.
- Search for ways of achieving goals in the face of obstacles.
- Spell out specific plans instead of taking a scattered, hit-or-miss approach to action.
- Persevere in the implementation of these plans when they are tempted to give up.

REFLECTIVE EXERCISE ON CHALLENGING A CAREGIVER

Recall three instances in which it was appropriate to challenge a caregiver. Ask yourself the following questions:

- Were you able to challenge him or her or did you retreat from this and, if so, why?
- If you did challenge, what were your thoughts about this?
- How did you feel before, during and after you challenged the caregiver?
- Do these thoughts and feelings facilitate or inhibit your capacity to challenge caregivers?
- Based on previous discussion about verbal and non-verbal assertiveness in this book, do you think your challenges were assertive, non-assertive or aggressive?
- If some of your challenges were non-assertive or aggressive how do you account for this?
- How might you improve your capability to offer effective challenges to caregivers in the future?

Building hostile alliances

Mr Faunch and Mr Wathy came into contact with a number of parents by virtue of providing short-term foster care to their children. At times, the couple used these contacts to form alliances with parents, many of whom had grievances themselves with children's services. Parent B acknowledged that she was initially well disposed towards the couple, as they had provided respite care to her 14-year-old son who had Asperger's syndrome and attention deficit hyperactivity disorder (ADHD) at a point where she was exhausted by his challenging behaviour. The foster carers made Parent B feel as if she was their confidant and all three of them frequently shared their dissatisfactions with children's services. Parent B was to actively align herself with Mr Faunch and Mr Wathy when, unknown to social workers, they invited both her and her father to attend a planning meeting with members of the Fostering Team. During the ensuing discussion, the foster carers argued that Parent B's son should be placed with them through a shared care arrangement and not via respite, as the former paid more. The inappropriate invitation extended to Parent B to attend the planning meeting was to the consternation of social workers, who were faced with both the foster carers and the parent arguing for a particular type of fostering placement. The planning meeting acceded to the foster carers' demands (para 9.314). Neither Mr Faunch nor Mr Wathy was challenged over their conduct in this instance.

The invitation extended to parent B and her father appeared to be a deliberate attempt by the foster carers to create a coalition of people to exert greater influence over the outcome of the deliberations of the planning meeting. Coalitions are defined as situations in which more than two negotiators are involved and where each still negotiates for their own interests, but with mutual goals that they pursue together. In this case, Parent B had a different interest from that of the foster carers, as she wanted respite from the care of her child, but she had a mutual goal in having the child placed with them. Coalitions also form to attain outcomes that meet the shared objectives of negotiators or to avoid a less optimum outcome if the negotiator were to act in a purely self-interested manner and just negotiate individually. By virtue of adding more parties arguing for similar outcomes to the negotiation, coalitions commonly increase the power and leverage of any one negotiator through this collective approach. At the same time, by adding certain parties, but not others, such coalitions may act to exclude potentially important negotiators. A mother may bring along her male partner to a negotiation with social workers in an effort to increase leverage in a situation in which social workers are insisting upon changes to parental care to safeguard a child. At the same time, the mother excludes a grandmother who commands influence within the wider family, because she is aware that the grandmother is sympathetic to the concerns of children's services about the care of her grandchild. Effective Family Group Conferencing is one way to avoid this sort of exclusion.

The forging of alliances in order to place pressure upon the Fostering Team and sometimes to intimidate was not confined to parents. As the supervising social worker for Mr Faunch and Mr Wathy during the second half of 2004 was to discover, they were capable of identifying others who had grievances with social services and co-opting them to support their demands. The social worker recalled that towards the end of her time supervising the foster carers, they insisted on having a neighbour present at meetings, who also had a number of issues with social services that she gave vent to during these meetings. The social worker described how she was subjected to 'a barrage of complaints and issues' and confessed to 'feeling bullied and intimidated by [Mr Faunch and Mr Wathy]', believing that they were 'out of control' (para 9.501). Mr Faunch and Mr Wathy actively sought out others who either felt dissatisfied with children's services or whose occasional gripes could be encouraged and magnified. This enabled them to confront social workers with the diverse issues, grievances and complaints of a number of people and successfully fog the concerns about them as foster carers. As a result, Mr Faunch and Mr Wathy continually diverted the attention and energy of social workers away from their problematic behaviour as foster carers. These hostile alliances also assisted the couple to bring additional pressure to bear upon the Fostering Team to get their own way on fostering placements and financial arrangements.

Bystanders and audiences

Within the context of a negotiation, *bystanders* are people who have some stake in its deliberations due to an interest in how it is conducted or the result. They do not formally participate in the negotiation, nor are they officially represented at it. Instead, *bystanders* follow the negotiation and express public and private views about its progress, process or outcomes to the negotiators. An *audience* is any person or group of people who are not directly involved in the negotiation, but who are nevertheless present at it and who may offer input or critical commentary to the negotiators. These observations can encompass any aspect of the negotiation. *Bystanders* may be present or absent during actual negotiations. If they are present, then they become an *audience* to that negotiation and their presence may start to affect how the negotiators behave. This social phenomenon is referred to as the *audience effect*. Essentially, any occurrence that results in a negotiator directing his or her attention away from the other negotiator and the negotiation in hand towards the *audience* is an *audience effect*.

Research on negotiation has established a set of common *audience effects* that alter the behaviour of negotiators when an audience is present (Lewicki et al, 2010, pp 331–5). These indicate that when negotiators are being observed, they 'try harder' and 'act tougher'. Practically, this means that they are more liable to use threats and putdowns and less likely to pursue integrative bargaining approaches. They have also been shown to achieve poorer joint outcomes when compared to unobserved negotiators. When confronted with a choice between maintaining a favourable self-image or an acceptable trade-off to achieve an agreement, negotiators with an audience tend to choose their image over reaching an agreement. This occurs because negotiators generally seek a positive appraisal from the audience. Research evidence suggests that so strong is this social dynamic that negotiators can engage in self-defeating behaviours during negotiations if the audience indicates that they appear foolish for pursuing a particular course of action. As a result, negotiators may abandon effective strategies for achieving their optimal outcome to the negotiation. A negotiator can sometimes also act as an audience in situations where one negotiator comes to believe that the other negotiator perceives him or her to be feeble or stupid. Fear of losing face in front of an audience composed of *bystanders* or other negotiators often makes a negotiator 'act tough'.

Lewicki et al (2010, p 334) note that face-saving can be an important consideration for negotiators when there is an audience. Some negotiators have a higher 'face threat sensitivity' than others, meaning that they are more susceptible to criticism or being hurt and sensitive to criticism. Hence, a negotiator with a high 'face threat sensitivity' may be easily taunted by bystanders or other negotiators when they are acting as an *audience*. This will invariably increase the likelihood of that negotiator adopting a tough stance towards the negotiation or retaliating by perhaps withdrawing a previously agreed trade-off. In a child protection context, this might mean the caregiver reneging on an agreement to attend a parenting programme or the allocated social worker revising their offer to argue at the next case conference for more contact between a father and his son in foster care. Research evidence indicates that negotiators who believe that their reputations are at stake during a negotiation are more likely to take higher risks and encounter a greater number of impasses than those who do not (Wheeler, 1999). Caregivers or social workers who have low self-esteem are likely to experience a higher 'face threat sensitivity'.

In Case Study 6.1, Mr Faunch and Mr Wathy refused to be interviewed by the social worker on their own and, therefore, acted as an audience for each other. Mr Faunch tended to dominate discussions with social workers in the presence of his partner. It could be speculated that this was likely to increase Mr Faunch's espousal of more inflexible and excessive negotiating positions with practitioners, particularly in relation to placements and payments. The couple also co-opted *bystanders*, who were predominantly parents with an indirect interest in the outcome of their negotiation with Wakefield Children's Services. The foster carers would have endeavoured to mobilise support from *bystanders* by persuading them of how reasonable, fair and justified their position was and how unreasonable, inflexible and unfair the other negotiator in the guise of the supervising social worker was being. In effect, Mr Faunch and Mr Wathy were building alliances to pressure the social worker into concessions that she would not otherwise have made. For the social worker, preserving her professional self-image would have involved appearing helpful and supportive. If the foster carers and members of the audience they had assembled indicated that the social worker was not behaving in a helpful manner, this would have pressured her to negotiate a suboptimal outcome for the fostering service and, ultimately, for fostered children.

The actions of Mr Faunch and Mr Wathy are far from unique. Many social workers find themselves interviewing, assessing and negotiating with caregivers in the presence of other family members. Sometimes, this is entirely appropriate, while, on other occasions, as in Case Study 6.1, it distorts the negotiating process and places undue pressures on practitioners. Parents negotiating in the presence of their spouse or partner may also feel pressured to adopt inflexible positions or refuse to make concessions that they would compromise on if negotiating alone. Conversely, some caregivers, like Mr Faunch and Mr Wathy, may deliberately use the presence of a partner or family friend to manipulate the negotiation in their favour through the use of *audiences* or threats to involve *bystanders*. A number of caregivers are known to have written to the newspapers or contacted their local councillor or Member of Parliament when they were not successful in obtaining the concessions they wanted during negotiations with social workers. These are attempts to widen the *audience* to a negotiation by involving *bystanders* and through developing alliances with those not directly involved in the negotiation to bring to bear greater pressure upon social workers to accede to the caregivers' demands.

REFLECTIVE EXERCISE ON THE PRESENCE OF AUDIENCES

Recall three instances in which you have been involved in negotiating with a caregiver where another family member or friend of the family was present. Ask yourself the following questions:

- How do you think this affected the positions adopted or the concessions made by the caregiver?
- How did it affect the positions you adopted or the concessions you offered?
- How do you think the presence of others affected the negotiation process?
- Do any patterns emerge in your approach to negotiation in these circumstances and, if so, what are they?
- Do these facilitate or hinder a successful negotiation process in terms of reducing risk to a child?
- How might you improve your negotiation strategies with caregivers in the future?

Personal and professional self-confidence

The foster team social worker allocated to supervise Mr Faunch and Mr Wathy during the period May 2004 to January 2005 was an agency worker. She admitted to the inquiry that she was not sufficiently conversant with 'the procedures, expectations or the framework for the remuneration of carers'. Furthermore, she 'had a difficult experience in her previous employment, which had left her with low self-confidence' and 'had a tendency to blame herself' (paras 9.499, 9.503). By August 2004, the supervising social worker was noting on the foster carers' file that 'she was struggling to carry out her role in relation to [Mr Faunch and Mr Wathy]' (para 9.500). She described them as preoccupied with financial matters and insistent on discussing these to the point where it interfered with addressing other aspects of their fostering role. When the fostering social worker attempted to discuss issues with Mr Faunch and Mr Wathy that were of concern to the agency, she found them 'aggressive and dismissive'. By November 2004, the social worker was noting on file that 'our working relationship is very difficult and does not seem to be getting any better'. Regarding the ending of a placement for a foster child, the social worker wrote 'I did not speak to [Ian Wathy or Craig Faunch] as I felt that any discussion would be hated and pointless'. In December 2004, around six months after she had taken on responsibility for the foster carers, she stated: 'they feel punished at times and perceive my involvement sometimes as negative, rather than constructive – this is not helpful to working together' (para 500).

Giving evidence at the inquiry, the social worker described the foster carers as 'arrogant, refusing to compromise, always insisting on being seen together'. She admitted to the inquiry that 'she had felt overwhelmed and out of her depth working with [Mr Faunch and Mr Wathy] and at one point had asked to be removed from the case' (para 9.501). The social worker recalled that her line manager's response to her request to be removed from the case was that 'we all get difficult carers you know you cut your teeth on them' (para 9.501). Indeed, the social worker recalled that her supervision had been 'irregular and ineffective'; a contention endorsed by the inquiry (paras 9.502–9.503). However, the social worker also recognised that 'she found it difficult to make demands of people' and had perhaps not been sufficiently clear or firm with her team leader as to her professional needs (para 9.502). Given the surrounding circumstances, the inquiry concluded that the social worker's team leader should have accompanied her to meet with Mr Faunch and Mr Wathy in order to directly challenge them about their behaviour in a face-to-face encounter. Instead, the couple were left with the impression that as long as they pushed hard enough, they could get exactly what they wanted (para 9.503). Summing up, the inquiry concluded:

> Key staff lost their professional confidence and competence when dealing with these men. Their experience was of being bullied by them, of being bombarded and psychologically pressurised, of dreading encounters with them and of consequently sometimes avoiding these encounters. This was not treated at the time as evidence that there was a problem, or that the carers might be intimidating in order to get the professionals to back off. Instead it was interpreted personally by staff, as a failure on their own part to be robust enough to manage 'challenging' but valuable carers. (para 10.12)

Self-esteem and social work

Self-esteem is a form of self-appraisal about one's merits and abilities. High self-esteem involves possessing confidence and satisfaction in one's self together with feelings and attitudes of self-respect. It also includes feelings of personal efficacy and having the resources to overcome challenges and the competence to accomplish tasks. Personal efficacy is related to motivation, as being willing to act rests on the belief that an action can bring about a desired outcome. People low in self-esteem lack confidence in their abilities to successfully complete tasks or realise personal or professional goals. As a consequence, they are often inhibited from taking action. Shelton and Burton (1995, p 14) identify low self-esteem as a major impediment to being assertive. People generally have low self-esteem who: feel insecure; view themselves as having limited knowledge or abilities; retreat from disagreement; or easily lose their temper during a dispute. This commonly results in passive or aggressive responses to situations.

In Case Study 6.1, the supervising social worker felt inadequately informed about the requirements for foster carers. In addition, she had suffered adverse experiences in her previous employment that undermined her self-confidence. This was reinforced by a team leader whose tendency was to focus on the social worker's personal failings in the management of Mr Faunch's and Mr Wathy's behaviour. In the absence of good supervision, the opportunity for the social worker to reflect on the couple's behaviour and to consider whether it was intended to frustrate legitimate social work activity was lost. The combined effect of this was to leave the social worker feeling out of her depth and overwhelmed by the aggressive behaviour of the foster carers. Her admission to the independent inquiry that she found it difficult to make demands on people such as caregivers, colleagues and managers is suggestive of her inability to assertively articulate her rights, needs or opinions. Unable to successfully manage the hostile behaviour of the foster carers, the social worker seems to have resorted to avoiding it, as evidenced by her decision not to discuss the ending of a child's placement with them. It is pertinent that her reasoning in this instance was that any such discussion would be 'pointless'. A belief that action cannot change circumstances or progress a goal is one that undermines motivation and endeavour. Practitioners confronted by hostile or aggressive caregivers may feel that their knowledge or skills are inadequate to the task of partnership-working while protecting a child at risk of significant harm. If this plays into feelings of low self-esteem, then the likelihood is that assertiveness will be impaired. Social workers need to be aware of the linkages between their levels of self-esteem and their ability to behave assertively. Problems with self-esteem that interfere with professional practice should be openly discussed in supervision.

A person's self-esteem is a function both of other people's appraisal of them and of their own self-observation. Throughout a person's life, they are subject to the evaluations of parents, teachers, partners, employers and other authority figures. If these evaluations tend to be negative, then they will be internalised as feelings of inadequacy, which produce low self-esteem. While if many or most of these authority figures offer positive appraisals of a person's abilities and behaviour, then this will be internalised as a belief in one's efficacy, thus promoting high self-esteem. Related to, but distinct from, these external evaluations are those that an individual makes about him or herself based on personal experience. If a person experiences a number of successful social or professional encounters, he or she will draw increased confidence from this, contributing to feelings of self-liking, potency and a belief in his or her ability to deal with similar situations or accomplish similar tasks in the future. It follows that someone who encounters a succession of failures in relation to interpersonal relationships or professional activities will be susceptible to self-defeating thoughts, which provoke anxiety. The combination of self-defeating beliefs and anxiety will, in turn, undermine assertiveness and, hence, satisfactory or positive interactions in the future. Shelton and Burton (1995, p 17) suggest that, ultimately, low self-esteem results in a self-fulfilling prophecy, as individuals who feel inadequate either avoid the situations that cause them to experience failure or become so anxious that they undermine their own ability to successfully manage the situation. Self-defeating beliefs in the form of negative self-talk can both exacerbate and perpetuate low self-esteem alongside the inaction and lack of assertive behaviour that follows from it. Shelton and Burton (1995, p 17) set out the processes that lead to negative self-talk, which are reproduced in Box 6.3.

Box 6.3: Processes of negative self-talk

1. As a situation occurs, you compare the circumstances to past experiences.

2. Because your past experiences have been negative in some way, you choose not to assert yourself in the present situation.

3. After the situation is over, you feel that you should have responded assertively rather than non-assertively or aggressively.

4. As a non-assertive person, you realise that you did not act assertively because you did not want to experience the feeling of anxiety or failure again. If you are aggressive, you may feel the same way.

5. Because you are anxious, worried and nervous in this situation, you begin to feel bad about not asserting yourself. You start telling yourself, 'I am incapable', 'I won't be able to do it' and so forth. You get on the low-esteem treadmill.

Shelton and Burton (1995, p 26) aver that raising self-esteem requires, first, increasing the frequency of positive self-statements together with providing rewards for doing so. In this context, self-statements comprise the beliefs people hold about themselves and the internal messages they vocalise when confronted by challenges. Second, it necessitates reducing how often individuals recount their perceived weakness to themselves or dwell upon negative thoughts about themselves. Devising means of punishing negative self-talk will help to extinguish it. Bower and Bower (2004, p 38) insist that individuals should never attempt to 'cheer themselves up' with food or television when they are experiencing self-defeating thoughts, as this simply rewards the habit and thus reinforces it. They also propose close scrutiny of self-statements in conjunction with efforts to manage a negative-to-positive shift in these self-statements, for example, moving from a self-statement such as 'I'm afraid' to 'I can manage my fear', or 'I'm inarticulate' to 'I can say what I mean'. These revised positive self-statements are, in effect, 'propaganda messages' that an individual repeats to themselves for sustained periods and usually when faced with the challenges that provoke negative self-statements. Over time, such positive self-enhancing statements become integrated into a person's self-image, promoting more confident engagement with the challenges presented by interpersonal relationships.

REFLECTIVE EXERCISE ON AWARENESS OF NEGATIVE SELF-STATEMENTS

- When you are working with a caregiver you find difficult or challenging, what self-statements do you make?
- Are these positive or negative?
- Write down any negative self-statements; rewrite these as positive self-statements.
- Devise a set of penalties for saying the negative self-statement and rewards for repeating the positive self-statement as you continue to work with

caregivers, who may be substitute carers, parents, step-parents or their partners.

The impact of aggression on social workers

The supervising social worker's lack of confidence and ability to challenge the two foster carers is also demonstrable in her documentation for the Foster Carers' Annual Review in September 2004. According to the inquiry, the social worker's report played down all the incidents of concern regarding the couple's conduct and some were not mentioned at all. When weaknesses were cursorily mentioned, these were counterbalanced by emphasis on their strengths. Adverse comment about the foster carers, for example, by Parent A, who withdrew her children from their care, was discounted by the social worker and, instead, she empathised with the foster carers, describing them as having 'experienced betrayal' by the mother (para 9.332). Indeed, the inquiry criticised the social worker's contribution to the Annual Review for being 'passive' and that 'rather than confidently presenting the full set of data and exploring the meaning, she continually found excuses for why the foster carers had made errors of judgement' (para 9.332). This meant that the supervising social worker's report reflected the perspective of the foster carers and not an objective evidentially based assessment of their performance (para 9.332). In accounting for her incompetent report for the Annual Review, the social worker described feeling a 'sense of helplessness and inability to focus on the tasks of a fostering social worker as the carers were so resistant, and distracted her by insisting that she focus primarily on financial issues' (para 9.335).

Other fostering social workers also admitted to difficulties working with Mr Faunch and Mr Wathy, but failed to take any action. The tendency to placate rather than challenge Mr Faunch and Mr Wathy was, in part, driven by the shortage of foster carers in the Wakefield Council area, resulting in fears that if pushed too hard, Mr Faunch and Mr Wathy would resign from the local authority as foster carers (para 9.503). The inquiry speculated that the fostering team 'knew but did not know', because knowing, admitting that there was a grave problem with Mr Faunch and Mr Wathy, would have meant re-examining their own decisions and the implications for the team and fostering service of discovering that they had employed two paedophiles as foster carers (para 9.504). As the inquiry was to conclude: 'if staff had allowed themselves to "know" they would then have been faced with the turmoil that came from the "knowing"' (para 9.504). In short, because of these factors, Mr Faunch and Mr Wathy were able to 'split, manipulate, intimidate and confuse the system in which they operated' (para 9.505).

The fixation of Mr Faunch and Mr Wathy with payments for fostering placements was an effective issue with which to deflect any criticism of their conduct. When this occurred in conjunction with a supervising social worker who already lacked professional self-confidence due to a previous employment experience and was unable to avail of effective supervision, the result was a passive and captive professional who capitulated to the foster carers' demands. This was also evident in her contribution to the Annual Review of the foster carers, which reflected their perspective rather than presenting an objective factual account of their behaviour and social work interactions with them. The supervising social worker eventually sought to cope with the stressful and frightening situation created by the foster carers, which was intensified by the agency's priority to retain their services, by acceding to the demands of Mr Faunch and Mr Wathy.

Hostage theory

Stanley and Goddard (2002), in their investigation into the impact on social workers in Australia of prolonged exposure to hostility and aggression from caregivers, conclude that they sometimes react in a manner similar to those taken hostage. During the 1970s, there was a spate of hostage-taking by extremist groups in Europe. Psychologists were astonished by the paradoxical behaviour of some hostages, who identified with their captors and, on being rescued, endeavoured to justify their captors' conduct. Particularly notorious was the kidnapping of adults in Stockholm, who negotiated on behalf of their captors and, on release, refused to testify against them (Wardlaw, 1982). This effect of captivity became widely known as Stockholm Syndrome. It has since also been related to the behaviour of some women and children who, when subjected to violence by a man within the family, appear to adopt the perpetrator's view of his aggression while displaying partiality and liking towards him (Barnett and LaViolette, 1993; Stanley and Goddard, 1995). Such victims typically blame themselves for having committed some wrong to incur the abuse, rather than blaming the perpetrator for an unjustified attack. They often describe the perpetrator in positive terms. Hostage theory, as applied to social work by Stanley and Goddard (2002), explores the psychological impact of intervening with aggressive caregivers and how this, in turn, affects their practice.

People taken hostage are denied institutional and social support during a period when they are subject to sustained threats to their life, bodily integrity and identity, sometimes accompanied by unpredictable violence. The combined effect of this is to overwhelm normal physical and psychological defence mechanisms, resulting in feelings of helplessness and the destruction of self-confidence and a positive self-image. As Wardlaw (1982, p 155) points out, hostages in such extreme situations have 'to understand, co-operate or even love their captors in order to save themselves'. They may suppress negative feelings towards their captors, as acting on these could threaten their survival or well-being; positive feelings may predominate, such as sympathy for the captors or perceiving them to be in some sense also victims (Soskis and Ochberg, 1982).

In hostage situations, the hostage-takers deliberately use violence or its threat to instil fear in the kidnap victim. They aim to dominate their captives by making them feel isolated and powerless. This renders victims totally dependent on their captor, making them compliant and open to easy manipulation. A victim's level of anxiety can be further increased by making vague and unpredictable threats, which are difficult to interpret or anticipate, but leave the victim feeling frightened of committing any infraction likely to attract the wrath of the captor (Wardlaw, 1982). At the same time, where captors appeared in other respects fairly ordinary, came from a disadvantaged background or indulged in small acts of kindness or affability, it was more likely that their victims would positively appraise them (Stanley and Goddard, 2002, p 14). Drawing on research in this area, Stanley and Goddard (2002, p 119) list the psychological defences used by hostages to alleviate severe stress, which are reproduced as follows:

- Denial of the threat.
- Rationalisation.
- Intellectualisation of the situation.
- Identification with the aggressor or adopting the aggressor's viewpoint.
- Reaction formation, or adopting a viewpoint opposite to what the person truly believes.
- Creative elaboration.
- Black humour.

Stanley and Goddard (2002, p 123) contend that these mental defences are deployed by a victim in circumstances of 'overwhelming fear and anxiety where he or she is unable to use other coping behaviour'. Generally, coping mechanisms involve some variant of a 'fight' or 'flight' response, but in a hostage situation, neither of these courses of action is available to successfully manage an aggressive captor. It is for this reason that hostages rely on maladaptive, often subconscious psychological defences. Stanley and Goddard (2002) postulate that when social workers are engaged in medium- to long-term interventions with aggressive caregivers, they too can become traumatised in a manner similar to that of hostages. As a result, they may employ some of the psychological defence mechanisms and defensive behaviours exhibited by kidnap victims. While this will be most pronounced among social workers subjected to acts or threats of violence, those experiencing other forms of intimidation over a sustained period may also exhibit some reactions akin to those of Stockholm Syndrome.

Learned helplessness

Those subjected to situations in which 'fight' or 'flight' responses are unavailable must, nevertheless, make some response. The maladaptive behaviours of both animals and human subjects in uncontrollable, and harmful situations were extensively researched by Seligman and his colleagues. Based on numerous observations and psychology experiments, Seligman (1975) concluded that when any organism is subjected to repeated unpleasant stimuli that it cannot avoid, regardless of which course of action it adopts, the organism ceases to make any response at all and enters a state of helplessness. In these situations, a person experiences a harmful event occurring no matter what he or she does to try and prevent it. A young child is physically assaulted by his mother, regardless of what responses he makes to try and placate her; a social worker faced with a hostile caregiver finds that whether she resists their demands or gives in to them, she faces persistent threats of violence or complaints against her. Both the child and the social worker are locked into these situations, the child because of dependence on the caregiver and the practitioner because of her child protection responsibilities. Discovering that whatever response they make in the face of actual or threatened harm makes no difference to the outcome ultimately produces a state of apathy in which the child or social worker ceases to make responses to avoid the harm. Seligman (1975, p 17) encapsulates this when stating that: 'a person or animal is helpless with respect to some outcome when the outcome occurs independently of all his voluntary responses'.

Experiencing oneself as helpless retards 'fight' or 'flight' courses of action, because the motivation to take some action is completely undermined by the belief that no action can change the situation and remove the harm. Not only do detrimental motivational and behavioural consequences arise from experiences of helplessness, but cognitive deficits are also produced. In states of learned helplessness, individuals subjected to uncontrollable harm in one situation transfer their learning from this to other situations in which they are confronted by the harmful behaviour of others. The boy who is physically abused by his mother becomes apathetic when bullied at school by another pupil, even though were he to complain to a teacher, the situation would be immediately resolved. Likewise, a social worker who behaves helplessly in the face of one intimidating caregiver may transfer their learning from this to a parent who is aggressive towards them. In this instance, the social worker has developed not only a motivational deficit, but also a cognitive deficit, which leads her to believe that it is pointless to attempt to challenge the threatening behaviour of a caregiver.

Learned helplessness and hostage theory in practice

As Seligman (1975, p 38) succinctly describes it: 'learned helplessness produces a cognitive set in which people believe that success and failure is independent of their own skilled actions, and they have difficulty learning that responses work'. He continues: 'a past history of uncontrollability will make it difficult to believe that an outcome is controllable, even when it actually is' (Seligman, 1975, p 60). The fear that individuals experience when confronted with the possibility of harm is reduced if they believe that they can exercise some control over it through alternative responses, but fear and anxiety will be heightened when people are faced with harmful behaviour by others in situations where they believe they cannot alter this adverse outcome. Returning to Case Study 6.1, the priority of the agency to retain Mr Faunch and Mr Wathy as foster carers pressured the social worker to placate them in order to avoid confrontations that might lead to their decision to resign. The agency's imperative generated two effects: it made 'flight' impermissible while discouraging 'fight' responses in a situation where the social worker could not escape from the stressor constituted by the foster carers' aggressive behaviour.

It was against this background that the supervising social worker, already low in self-confidence due to a previous professional experience, was particularly vulnerable to responses associated with Stockholm Syndrome. She was confronted by a team leader who failed to offer adequate support and reinforced feelings of self-blame. Hence, the supervising social worker experienced herself as having little institutional backing or assistance. She was also poor at making demands on others and asking for help when she needed it, which reduced the social support from colleagues, family and friends otherwise available to her. By inhabiting a relatively isolated position, she was much more susceptible to the detrimental psychological effects of the aggressive behaviour of Mr Faunch and Mr Wathy.

The supervising social worker's report to the Foster Carers' Annual Review presented a positive portrayal of Mr Faunch and Mr Wathy, despite their lack of compliance and already concerning behaviours. In doing so, she appeared to identify with their emotional reactions to events, such as feelings of betrayal surrounding Parent A's withdrawal of her child from their care. She also incorporated their perspective into her reports, making it, in turn, her professional judgement, by portraying them as good foster carers through either muting their failings or presenting excuses for them. In short, the supervising social worker appeared to exhibit one of the coping mechanisms used by hostages, which is to identify with the aggressor and adopt his or her viewpoint. She also described to the independent inquiry 'a sense of helplessness and inability to focus on the tasks of a fostering social worker'. It is these very feelings of powerlessness which led to the belief that events cannot be controlled and produced inaction. The supervising social worker's testimony to the independent inquiry illustrates the detrimental impact of prolonged exposure to aggressive behaviour by caregivers.

REFLECTIVE EXERCISE ON IMPACT OF AGGRESSIVE CAREGIVER RESPONSES

Recall a past or current working relationship with a caregiver who has behaved aggressively towards you, who may be a substitute carer, parent, guardian or a partner. Ask yourself the following questions:

- How have you reacted to his or her aggressive behaviours?
- Re-examine the effects of prolonged exposure to aggression predicted by hostage theory and learned helplessness. Might some of your perspectives of the caregiver and some of your decisions been subject to these influences and, if so, how?
- In future interactions with caregivers who are aggressive towards you, how might you mitigate these cognitive and emotional effects on you?

Case Study 6.2: Ryan Lovell-Hancox

Wolverhampton Safeguarding Children Board (2011) *Executive summary Child J*

All those involved in this case were of white British heritage. Ms Hancox was a 20-year-old single mother with no formal qualifications who was experiencing mental health problems and some difficulty caring for her two young children. She also wanted the opportunity to decorate her flat. In November 2008, Ms Hancox arranged for her three-year-old son, Ryan, to be looked after by her cousin, Ms Boleyn, aged 18 years old, and her partner, Mr Taylor, aged 23, in their flat for a weekly payment. Technically, this was a private fostering arrangement. Earlier in 2008, a duty social worker and police officer became involved when Ms Hancox was discovered to have left Ryan's younger sibling in the care of unsuitable people. The initial assessment conducted by the social worker at the time concluded that no further action was necessary. As for Ms Boleyn, she had been the subject of care proceedings and at the time of being asked to care for Ryan was in receipt of Leaving Care Support and the Intensive Specialised Supported Living Service. This service provided a flat together with intensive visiting and practical support to enable a young person to work towards independence. The service was actually provided by a charity under contract with Wolverhampton City Council.

The police had previously been involved with Ms Boleyn during 2005 when they investigated a family member's report that Ms Boleyn had hit her six-year-old sibling causing minor injury, but this was not recorded. The Youth Offending Team was also involved in 2005 when a Referral Order was made against Ms Boleyn. After Ms Boleyn moved into her flat in 2008, she was shortly joined by her partner, Mr Taylor. He was on probation and had recently been convicted for assaulting someone with a golf club and was deemed to be of 'medium level risk of serious harm to children'. Although the probation officer was aware that Mr Taylor was in the company of a young child, no action was taken. Mr Taylor also had a history of drug and alcohol addiction and of abusing his partners. On 22 December 2008, a telephone call was received by the emergency services stating that Ryan had slipped in the bath and had a seizure. The toddler was rushed to hospital by ambulance but died there two days later. At the time of his death, Ryan was discovered to have over 70 injuries.

Mr Taylor and Ms Boleyn were sentenced in 2010 to life imprisonment for the murder of Ryan Lovell-Hancox, with minimum terms of 15 and 13 years, respectively.

Diversion by caregiver

Shaftesbury Young People, a charity in Wolverhampton, tendered for and was awarded a contract by the local authority to work with care-leavers. As the serious case review acknowledged, these were some of the 'most needy young people in Wolverhampton' who could on occasion be difficult to work with or uncooperative (para 5.13). This should have alerted both Wolverhampton City Council and the charity to the importance of employing qualified and experienced staff who could meet the needs of such vulnerable young people. Yet, the contracting charity employed staff with 'limited experience and qualifications' and provided them with 'minimal training' (para 5.13). Despite statutory and contractual duties to make frequent visits to Ms Boleyn as a vulnerable care-leaver, shortly after she moved into her flat, visiting tailed off. Partly, this was due to Ms Boleyn's initial intensive engagement with a number of agencies declining as she came under the increasing influence of Mr Taylor, who was living with her in the flat. Evidence put before Wolverhampton Crown Court indicated that both Ms Boleyn and Mr Taylor were heavy users of cannabis and alcohol. The serious case review noted that Ms Boleyn's 'cooperation with the contractor and other agencies was patchy, and visiting by the contractor was sporadic' (para 4.4.4). Nevertheless, support staff did observe Ms Boleyn, Mr Taylor and Ryan together on several occasions, although they do not seem to have been aware that either Mr Taylor or Ryan was actually resident at the flat.

On 20 December, Ms Hancox attempted to gain access to Ms Boleyn's flat in an attempt to see her son, but this was denied. At the time, Ryan's face would have been severely bruised and maltreatment clearly in evidence. On 22 December 2008, Ms Boleyn's case worker from the charity visited the flat and noticed one of Ryan's legs sticking out from under a pile of bed clothes, but assumed he was asleep. She was in any case quickly distracted by Ms Boleyn, who drew the worker's attention away from the child and towards a puppy that Mr Taylor had given to her as a birthday present. The support worker then took Ms Boleyn to a job centre appointment in her car and dropped her back at the flat, but the support worker did not enter it. It was later that same evening that the emergency call was made and Ryan was discovered to be unconscious in the flat by the ambulance crew. Giving an interview to the press, the chairman of Wolverhampton Safeguarding Children's Board said of Ms Boleyn's case worker that:

> her focus had been in engaging with Boleyn and forming an affirming, supportive relationship with her, which she felt she had done successfully ... it was possible that she did not ask challenging questions of Boleyn when she saw a child in the flat, because she did not want to jeopardise that relationship which she considered to be her job. (*BBC News Birmingham and Black Country*, 2011)

Ms Boleyn's case worker was not a qualified social worker; however, the tactics used against her by Ryan's substitute carers are instructive. She was required to befriend and support a vulnerable yet uncooperative care-leaver who abused alcohol and was in the process of disengaging from services as she fell increasingly under the adverse influence of a male partner. At the same time, the case worker was required to exercise vigilance around child protection concerns and to intervene if necessary. In this particular instance, intervention would have meant contacting children's services and requesting them to assess the situation. As Ms Boleyn became less cooperative, it is likely that engagement with any service became more tenuous. This creates a dilemma for workers, who are afraid that challenging a user will result in damaging a good working relationship or result in the user declining a needed service.

Alcohol misuse, with the erratic aggressive behaviour it induces, often makes it difficult for workers to achieve consistency in their interactions with caregivers. Ms Boleyn's ability to accurately interpret the verbal and non-verbal responses of the case worker during conversations between them would have been impaired. Consequently, entirely reasonable enquiries into Ms Boleyn's circumstances were probably construed by her as hostile intrusions, provoking verbally aggressive reactions. The insidiousness of this social dynamic would have made the worker reluctant to confront Ms Boleyn about the presence of a toddler in the flat. Indeed, the case worker appears to have avoided conflict with Ms Boleyn by reducing her visits to the flat and adopting a non-assertive response to Ms Boleyn's lifestyle choices and conduct. Managing Ms Boleyn in this way would have resulted in mentioning her substance misuse tentatively, or even apologetically, so as not to offend or anger her. Invariably, this would have enabled Ms Boleyn to easily sidestep the topic or dismiss the case worker's concerns. It almost certainly meant that she permitted herself to be easily distracted away from the child lying still in the bed by the antics of Ms Boleyn in relation to the puppy. In the context of a supportive professional relationship, drawing attention to a puppy that Ms Boleyn may well have been genuinely excited at receiving would have appeared as an entirely innocent diversion, although, in this instance, it was plainly not. This incident is illustrative of the potential for apparently innocuous, even pleasurable, diversions of attention to hide sinister motives. Such tactics do not have to be overtly aggressive; indeed, their very artlessness and innocence may be more effective in catching a social worker off guard and dulling his or her vigilance.

Resistant and reluctant caregivers

Adopting the definitions used by Egan (1990) and widely applied in the social work literature, resistance refers to the reaction of an individual against feelings of being coerced into a particular course of action. Commonly, this occurs when a person is subject to uninvited social work interventions, such as during child protection enquiries, the assessment or examination of a child, the production of a Child Protection Plan, or, as in Case Study 6.2, when a care-leaver remains under the supervision of a case worker. Such reactions may not be directly related to social work interventions, but reflect wider issues, for example: opposition to being helped by anyone; a perception that nothing is wrong; or antipathy towards all third-party interference. Resistance is the caregiver's (or, in this case, care-leaver's) means of reasserting control in the context of unequal power statuses and in opposition to the coercive authority possessed by the practitioner. Often, this resistance is not overtly expressed in order to avoid retaliatory action from the social worker. It is usually not articulated as an outright refusal to work with the practitioner or the agency; instead, it expresses itself as: belligerence; an unwillingness to build a working relationship; successive missed appointments; failure to institute changes through action; or aggressive behaviour towards the practitioner. Any situation in which a substitute carer, parent, partner or child feels compelled to interact with a social worker may engender feelings of resistance alongside obstructive conduct. Resistant behaviour that thwarts social work activity can sometimes be subconscious and not within the caregiver's or child's awareness.

Reluctance refers to the ambiguity many individuals experience when they are aware that they need to make changes in order to improve their lives, but are hesitant to actually make the required changes because of the effort involved or costs imposed of doing so. Such individuals confronted with social work activity act out their ambiguity through: appearing unsure of what they want; confining conversations to unimportant or minor issues; setting unrealistic goals that they cannot possibly achieve; being slow to own responsibility for the circumstances of their lives; and concealing inactivity behind an enthusiastically cooperative façade. Egan (1990, pp 171–2) avers that this reluctance is engendered by fear of intensity, change or disorganisation. It may also be attributable to lack of trust or feelings of shame. While resistance and reluctance are distinctive responses to child protection interventions, they frequently occur in conjunction with each other during different stages of partnership-working. Social workers can be disconcerted by behaviours associated with resistance and reluctance, resulting in confusion, panic or anger. All of these emotions clearly have the potential to impede good practice. Egan (1990, p 174) describes the adverse reactions of counsellors to resistance and reluctance, which are equally pertinent to child protection social workers and are reproduced as follows:

- They accept their guilt and try to placate the client.
- They become impatient and hostile and manifest these feelings either verbally or non-verbally.
- They do nothing in the hope that the reluctance or resistance will disappear.
- They lower their expectations of themselves and proceed with the helping process, but in a half-hearted way.
- They try to become warmer and more accepting, hoping to win the client over by love.
- They blame the client and end up in a power struggle with him or her.
- They allow themselves to be abused by clients, playing the role of a scapegoat.
- They lower their expectations of what can be achieved by counselling.
- They hand the direction of the helping process over to the client.
- They give up and terminate the counselling.

These responses can be divided up into 'flight' or 'fight' responses to difficult service-users as the source of stress. Many seek to avoid confrontation with the service-user through conciliation, appeasement or simply ignoring the problem. Strategies incorporating 'fight' include becoming accusatory with caregivers or engaging in a power struggle with them. These are clearly responses that are detrimental to partnership-working and to challenging evasive or aggressive caregivers. In their place, Egan (1990, pp 174–6) suggests alternative approaches, which neither ignore feelings and behaviours generated by resistance or reluctance, nor reinforce them. These are considered in relation to social work in Box 6.4.

Box 6.4: Responding to reluctant and resistant caregivers

- *Resistance is normative* – Assist caregivers to recognise that resistance is a common experience when encountering social work interventions.
- *Reluctance as avoidance* – Reduce the caregiver's tendency towards avoidance by demonstrating the advantages of the helping process and the benefits of positive change.
- *Self-exploration of resistance and reluctance* – An examination of the social worker's own experience of these processes can assist them to better understand caregivers.
- *The quality of practice* – Social workers need to consider whether aspects of their own practice precipitate resistance in caregivers by reflecting on interactions that appear to trigger more numerous or intense resistant behaviours.
- *Accept the reluctance and resistance* – Do not ignore these processes but acknowledge them as part of a caregiver's reactions to intervention. Then use the communication skill of *immediacy* to bring these out into the open for discussion.
- *Be realistic and flexible* – Social workers need to be realistic about the capacity of individual caregivers to make changes and the limits on their own ability to assist in this process.
- *Establish mutuality* – Social workers should discuss and address the caregiver's experience of being coerced.
- *Invite participation* – Through partnership-working, encourage caregivers to engage with all aspects of social work activity, except where this creates unacceptable risk to a child.
- *Identify resistance-supporting incentives* – Assist caregivers to identify the sources of their resistance and the pay-offs that sustain it.
- *Incentivise overcoming resistance* – Assist caregivers to identify incentives to engage in partnership-working, including their self-interests, and thus reduce their resistance to social work activity.
- *Engage significant others* – Encourage the caregiver to use family members, friends or other organisations as resources to help them work through their resistance to social work interventions.
- *Employ caregivers as helpers* – Use role-play or other tools to enable the caregiver to recognise the resistant or reluctant behaviours they are employing.

REFLECTIVE EXERCISE ON RELUCTANT OR RESISTANT CAREGIVERS

Consider the behaviours of reluctant and resistant caregivers described earlier. Recall three different instances of work with caregivers who were either unwilling or ambivalent about engaging with social work intervention. Ask yourself the following questions:

- What behaviours did they exhibit?
- How did you react to these behaviours?
- Try to recall what you thought, felt and did when confronted by the caregiver's reluctant or resistant behaviour. To what extent did these reactions lead you to engage in 'flight' or 'fight' responses?
- Utilising a number of the strategies suggested earlier for working successfully with reluctant or resistant caregivers, what alternative approaches could have been employed in partnership-working with these caregivers?

Employing personal and professional rights

Social workers have a number of statutory rights and powers under various laws, for example, the legal duty and, thus, entitlement to pursue a child protection inquiry if they have cause to suspect that a child is at risk of significant harm. Outside of this narrow and specific right, identifying your personal and professional rights in a given situation is also essential in order to assess whether caregivers are behaving reasonably or unreasonably towards you. What are your rights when faced with reluctance or blatant opposition to your request to see or interact with a child? Are your rights different depending on whether a formal child protection inquiry has been initiated? To what extent can you insist on access to a child by a caregiver? What are your rights if a caregiver starts screaming at you or makes a derogatory comment about your appearance? Assertiveness is predicated on the ability to articulate and claim rights. These may sometimes be legal entitlements, but they often concern social norms regarding conduct and issues of mutual respect and fairness, or else relate to the right to express and have acknowledged personal feelings, opinions and wants.

Professional practice is commonly more difficult when social workers are called upon to use self-assertion in the absence of a specific statutory right or power. In Case Study 6.2, there was no child protection inquiry in process; nevertheless, Ms Boleyn was a vulnerable care-leaver still in receipt of services and known to be in a relationship with Mr Taylor, who had a violent history. Moreover, Ms Boleyn was herself known to be uncooperative and aggressive on occasion. It was in this context that it was necessary to ascertain whether Mr Taylor was cohabiting with Ms Boleyn and to check on the welfare of the child. The case worker from the charity assigned to regularly visit and support Ms Boleyn was not a qualified professional. Nevertheless, the practice dilemmas she faced and her reluctance to address issues of concern through asking 'challenging questions' of Ms Boleyn are equally pertinent to trained social workers. Being unsure of your rights results in:

- being uncertain whether your rights have been violated or not;
- being hesitant to raise a matter that concerns your rights;
- being uncertain of the grounds for asserting your rights, but bluffing through in an attempt to justify your rights; and
- having chosen to raise a matter concerning a right, then being unsure about how insistent to be on obtaining a satisfactory response.

In the circumstances confronting the case worker, her entitlements could at a minimum have consisted of the following rights to:

- ask Ms Boleyn about the presence of Mr Taylor in the flat and his contact with Ryan;
- ask Ms Boleyn to explain the care arrangements she had entered into with Ms Hancox;
- ask Ms Boleyn to explain how she was caring for Ryan;
- observe Ms Boleyn's care of Ryan;
- interact with Ryan;
- express concern that as a vulnerable care-leaver herself, Ms Boleyn was providing care for a young and needy child; and
- express concern that Ms Boleyn was in a relationship with a man known to be violent.

These rights consist of three requests for information, two requests to do something and two expressions of opinion. It is important to reiterate that none of these are legal rights. None of them are enforceable by the police. Nevertheless, they are essential points of reference for any interaction with Ms Boleyn. They constitute professional entitlements in a situation where a child is at potential risk of harm. Attempting to impose these rights at any cost on others would be aggression, predicated on the belief that others have no right to refuse. An aggressive imposition of rights could include: walking into the child's bedroom without asking permission from the caregiver; using covert or explicit threats to withdraw services from the caregiver; speaking loudly; or using quick-fire questions to extract information. Alternatively, professional non-assertion, as demonstrated by Ms Boleyn's case worker, involves either not fielding exacting questions or requests, or else not pursuing these as soon as a caregiver indicates opposition or becomes unsettled. The possibility of encountering resistance from a caregiver in divulging information, acceding to a request or acknowledging a safeguarding concern means that it is not sufficient to merely identify what your professional rights are in a given situation.

Personal lifelong and established patterns of non-assertive behaviour in day-to-day interactions can be accentuated by the demands of professional practice.

Like most practitioners, Ms Boleyn's caseworker found herself in circumstances where she needed to be both mindful of a child's welfare and to assist a caregiver. Partnership-working with parents and other caregivers requires professionals to build and sustain ongoing relationships founded on trust, understanding and support through a commitment of time, effort and dedication to the task. This can make some front-line workers reluctant to jeopardise their positive working relationship with a caregiver by challenging them. This behaviour is also perpetuated through beliefs such as 'My opinions are less important than those of others' or 'Others will dislike or reject me if I say what I think'. A worker who is unsure of their professional rights, holds beliefs that perpetuate non-assertion and typically deals with conflict through acts of 'flight' will cease to pursue a question or request at any sign of a caregiver's annoyance or distress. Such a worker is unlikely to persist in articulating or elaborating upon their own opinion if a caregiver deprecates it or simply ignores it by changing the subject. While social workers cannot force caregivers to provide information, agree to requests or listen to advice, they can refuse to acquiesce when confronted by an uncooperative and resistant caregiver. Beliefs that bolster assertive behaviour can also be undermined by sympathy for the caregiver and *role ambiguity*. Ofsted's (2010, para 99) analysis of serious case reviews tackles the issue of partiality:

> [There] was the need for practitioners to maintain a dispassionate view. One executive summary illustrated this: 'The parents were very young and had some very troubled personal family histories. This meant that some workers in some agencies tended to over-empathise with the parents and believe what they said, rather than checking their statements out thoroughly. This was particularly true in terms of believing what these young people said about where they were living and with whom they were living. Some agencies were too optimistic about how this family could manage their difficulties and lost sight of the risks that they posed'.

Most social care workers enter the profession out of compassion for others and a wish to assist and support them in times of personal crisis or difficulty. This entirely laudable impulse can prove a personal challenge for some social workers when confronted with child protection concerns where caregivers are struggling with material disadvantage, prejudice and discrimination. Nevertheless, it is incumbent upon all practitioners to reflect on their perceptions of parents, their partners or substitute carers and to consider if their own sympathies are clouding their professional judgement. This process may be made all the harder by *role ambiguity* in a situation where, like that involving Ms Boleyn, it is not immediately clear whether the role of the worker is to support a care-leaver or protect an infant. While child protection always trumps other social work tasks, when practitioners are performing a portfolio of roles in relation to a family, it may sometimes be more difficult to discern and act in relation to child protection issues.

REFLECTIVE EXERCISE ON PERSISTING WITH ASSERTIVE RESPONSES

Recall three difference instances of working with resistant or reluctant caregivers. Ask yourself the following questions:

- Do you persist in assertive responses or retreat into non-assertiveness when the caregiver raises objections?
- Do you feel guilty or wonder if you were right when you behave assertively with caregivers?
- List the rights you think you had in each situation and consider which ones you claimed and which ones you retreated from claiming and account for these reactions. Do any patterns in your behaviour emerge?
- Write a Describe, Express, Specify, Consequence (DESC) script (see Chapter Four) to assert a right that you failed to claim in each situation.

Points for practice

- Conflict with some caregivers can arise because they do not carry out or complete agreed tasks or activities. In these instances, social workers need to assertively challenge inconsistencies in the stated intentions and behaviour of some caregivers.
- Practitioners should be astute to the ways in which some caregivers can undermine or sidestep their challenges, and devise strategies to ensure that challenges are heard and addressed by caregivers.
- Social workers need to examine their own thoughts and feelings about *making demands for work* on caregivers and to explore any reluctance they experience to make appropriate challenges when caregivers fail to undertake or complete agreed tasks.
- Some caregivers use hostile alliances with others to exert power and leverage over social workers and their agencies. It is important for practitioners in consultation with their supervisors to devise a range of strategies for dealing with this occurrence.
- Practitioners should be aware of their own levels of self esteem and cognisant of how this impacts on their ability to behave assertively with caregivers. Assistance should be sought from mangers if low self-esteem undermines practitioners' confidence and assertiveness.
- Prolonged aggressive behaviour by a caregiver can induce hostage-like responses in social workers, making them compliant with a caregiver's wishes.
- Practitioners need to develop a range of strategies for work with reluctant and resistant caregivers in order to engage them with social work interventions.

CHAPTER SEVEN

Managing conflict with mothers

Conflict with parents

Social workers predominantly interact with mothers in their child protection work, as they are usually the primary caregiver. Mothers confronted by intrusive safeguarding activities can react in angry and aggressive ways. Sometimes, this is out of indignation and anxiety; sometimes, it is a deliberate attempt to prevent discovery or defend against changes to family life intended to reduce risk to a child. Regardless of the source of a mother's aggressive behaviour, it can obstruct child protection investigations, together with assessment, care planning and the implementation of a child protection plan. For social workers, verbal aggression and intimidation by a parent can increase their stress, undermine their willingness to challenge parents and leave them unsupported by multidisciplinary colleagues or their front-line manager. In this chapter, the events surrounding the deaths of Peter Connelly and Ajit Singh are considered in two case studies, which each examine how aggression by a mother towards social workers can impair good practice in child protection.

Case Study 7.1: Peter Connelly

Haringey Local Safeguarding Children Board (2010) *Serious case review 'Child A'*

This case study returns to the evidence that emerged from the serious case review of Peter Connelly, as previously discussed in Case Study 3.2. Rather than returning to an analysis of the agency context, it examines the interactions between social workers and Peter's mother instead. It considers the challenges that working with Ms Connelly presented to practitioners and how they responded.

Parental background and aggression scripts

As a child, Ms Connelly witnessed domestic violence between her mother and father. Her mother received a police caution for physically assaulting Ms Connelly's brother. In addition, Ms Connelly was subject to physical attacks by her brother. At the age of 10 years old, Ms Connelly was placed on the Child Protection Register under the category of neglect, as the parenting provided by her mother was deemed inadequate and thought to be abusive. A year later, she was removed from the Register. In adulthood and certainly at the time of the events surrounding the death of her infant son Peter, Ms Connelly drank heavily. For some years, she had been seeing her GP and Primary Care Mental Health Worker in relation to depression and anxiety, which manifested as irritability and crying (para 3.310). According to Haringey Local Safeguarding Children Board (2010, para 3.8.4), Ms Connelly 'intimidated the staff with her volatile emotional states so much so that they were reluctant to approach her with concerns about the children or her own anti-social behaviour'. Both Brandon et al (2009) and Ofsted (2010), in their analysis of serious case reviews, have noted the pervasiveness of domestic violence and alcohol abuse among parents and other carers drawn into the child protection system. Alcoholism and childhood experiences of domestic violence are, therefore, not particular to Ms Connelly, nor are the aggressive behaviours associated with them.

Social learning theory posits that children model their behaviour based on their observation of others. If, during their formative years, they witness domestic violence in which physical and verbal aggression are rewarded by compliance from other family members, it is possible that they will reproduce these behaviours. Ms Connelly both witnessed and was the victim of aggression within her family. As she began to imitate some of these behaviours, to discover that they enabled her to dominate other people and achieve her goals would have acted as reinforcement, leading to the maintenance of such behaviours over time. The low threshold for aggression within Ms Connelly's early home environment undoubtedly shaped her own understanding of when it was appropriate to engage in physically or verbally abusive acts. Her cognitive schemata, derived from her own violent childhood experiences, may have vindicated aggressive responses towards anyone who sought to interfere with her own desires and goals. Social workers were therefore faced with someone who had already developed a propensity for aggressive responses to any frustration of her goals. This *aggressive script* may have predisposed Ms Connelly to engage in verbal abuse and intimidation in a wide variety of circumstances.

The second serious case review described Ms Connelly as a heavy drinker. The effects of alcohol would have made her liable to misconstrue other people's behaviour, since intoxicated individuals often overlook the conciliatory words and gestures of others or else interpret neutral behaviour as hostile. Alcohol disinhibits aggressive responses because they interfere with judgement and weaken individuals' normal reluctance to engage in behaviour likely to result in rejection from others. Yet, despite her exposure to violence during childhood and her high alcohol consumption, Ms Connelly tended to intimidate others through her explosive anger and threats rather than through direct physical attack. This may be attributable to a number of factors not explored by the second serious case review; it is possible that her expression of aggression was influenced by her gender. Research reveals that while women are no less aggressive than men, the majority of women, in contrast to men, tend to enact aggression through damage to relationships rather than through physical assaults (Wright and Craig, 2010). The wider societal structures that influence how femininity is performed among the white majority population in Britain would have shaped Ms Connelly's behaviour, as it does that of other women. Emotionality is usually socially rewarded while violence is generally penalised when performed by women. Ms Connelly's expression of anger through verbal aggression rather than physical aggression to some degree reflects gendered expectations.

Social workers frequently blame themselves when confronted by verbally or physically aggressive caregivers and assume that either they have somehow precipitated the aggression or are incompetent for not effectively de-escalating it (*Community Care*, 2011a, pp 4–5). Taking account of the past experiences of parents or their partners and how these influence their responses to frustration are pertinent to appreciating the degree to which *aggressive scripts* predispose caregivers to particular kinds of hostile reactions. Regardless of the personality, behaviour or decisions of social workers, they are likely to face very challenging responses from a proportion of caregivers who were victims of domestic violence. These aggressive responses are not the fault of the practitioner; nor can they simply be dispelled by practitioners' commitment to empathy and transparency in their work with caregivers, as this case study will demonstrate. *Aggressive scripts*, and the hostile intimidating behaviours they engender, constitute entrenched lifelong formats for dealing with interpersonal conflict. This is not to deny that there are courses of action available to social workers (discussed later in this book) that offer some means of managing the aggressive behaviour of parents, their partners or other family members. Such techniques are predicated on the recognition that a small, but significant, number of caregivers involved in the child protection system are exceptionally aggressive. They deploy aggressive behaviours, often consciously, but sometimes unconsciously, to resist change or impose their will on others, including professionals charged to safeguard children.

Lying to professionals

On 11 December 2006, Ms Connelly took Peter, then nine months old, to the GP with a swelling to his head. The GP referred the child to Whittington Hospital, where he was found to have many older bruises to his buttocks, chest and face, together with a number of scratches. Ms Connelly claimed she did not know how the injury to Peter's head had occurred and maintained that the other bruises were caused during play. She told hospital staff that he bruised easily. She also insisted that their two dogs had caused the abrasions found on Peter's body during medical examination. Tests showed that Peter was not suffering from any condition that would make him susceptible to bruising. The consultant paediatrician at Whittington Hospital concluded that the bruising was 'very suggestive of non-accidental injury' and a referral was made to Haringey's Children and Young People's Service that same day. Ms Connelly and her mother were arrested and questioned by police about the injuries to Peter. Both denied hurting the infant and suggested that he had injured himself during play, falling off the settee or due to the dogs (para 3.5.12). The two women also indicated that only Ms Connelly and her children lived in the home. They were released on bail pending further investigations.

Social workers insisted that Peter could not return home while they pursued a statutory inquiry into the circumstances resulting in his injury. However, rather than accommodate Peter in local authority care, they readily agreed to Ms Connelly's suggestion that he could stay with a family friend, whom they knew little about. This meant Peter moving to live with a close friend of Ms Connelly's who would most probably have a keen loyalty to her. Social workers also unquestioningly accepted Ms Connelly's assertion that Peter's father would be an unsuitable carer as he had slapped the children in the past, even though it was generally accepted by children's services that he had a positive relationship with Peter. Ms Connelly's allegation that Peter's father was an unsuitable carer because he hit the children was never investigated. Instead, Ms Connelly was taken at her word by social workers and, as a consequence, Peter's father was excluded from partnership-working in relation to his son. It may or may not be the case that Peter's father was an appropriate carer; the point is that Ms Connelly's assertion that he was not was apparently never subjected to interrogation. Estranged spouses can sometimes have ulterior motives for alleging child abuse by the other parent.

At the initial child protection conference convened on 22 December 2006, the social worker tasked to report on Peter actually based her positive account of his behaviour in the home and his relationship with Ms Connelly on Ms Connelly's own account (para 3.7.13). Once again, a practitioner took Ms Connelly at her word without substantiating her assertions through closer observation or further inquiry. As the second serious case review was to observe: 'there was too ready a willingness to believe [Ms Connelly's] accounts of herself, her care of the children, the composition of the household and the nature of her friendship network' (para 3.6.3). The review argued that given the fact that Ms Connelly was plainly lying about the cause of the injuries to her son, this ought to have alerted social workers to the possibility of her lying about other aspects of her situation. A sceptical stance by social workers would have encouraged them to question, observe and test her statements of fact through further investigations. These should have been pursued to corroborate or disprove Ms Connelly's assertions.

The second serious case review suggested that at the initial child protection conference held on 22 December 2006, 'it could have been stated unequivocally to [Ms Connelly] that she was not believed and until a more believable account was given a very serious view would be taken of the risk to [Peter] and other children' (para 3.8.2). The review also speculated that:

> [Ms Connelly's] presence in the meeting will have had an influence on the agency representatives who may have felt that they needed to protect their relationship with her as they have to work with her in the future. The impact of her presence would be compounded by the fact that she was accompanied by a solicitor. [Ms Connelly] was apparently a dominating and forceful personality who may have intimidated people in the meeting and certainly had done so outside of it. (para 3.8.26)

There is provision for parents and their supporters to be asked to leave a case conference so that multi-agency colleagues can deliberate without the inhibiting presence of a parent or carer. This option was not effectively availed of at the initial case conference. The failure to challenge Ms Connelly's statements about her circumstances or her explanation for events by individual professionals became a prominent feature of the events leading up to Peter Connelly's death.

Investigative interviewing

Ofsted (2010, para 98) quoted from one serious case review, which summed up the conclusions of many that:

> professionals must be prepared to challenge information, whether from a parent, carer, relative or other professional in order to establish the difference between facts, hearsay and opinion. Records should state clearly what the evidence is for any statement or assessment.

Demonstrably, there is a need to rigorously pursue inconsistencies in the version of events presented by caregivers and to forthrightly challenge them by informing a caregiver when a social worker has reason to believe that they are lying. It is also clear from the description of the initial case conference that professionals can be greatly inhibited from explicitly accusing a caregiver of lying for fear of undermining partnership-working or due to intimidation by the caregiver. Effective challenge requires that social workers have both the skills to identify inconsistencies that need further probing and the confidence to do so without undue fear of a retaliatory response by the caregiver. Social workers are not police officers; nevertheless, as child protection agents, they have the legal duty to conduct enquiries into child maltreatment. Current investigative interviewing techniques developed by the police, based on conversation management approaches rather than methods of interrogation, can assist social workers to clue into anomalies in caregivers' versions of events. They can also guide well-judged challenges to evasive answers.

It is vital to formulate an interview plan that includes: the aim of the interview in terms of the information to be gathered; the topics or matters that require exploration; and the key questions designed to elicit specific information from the interviewee. It is by introducing a comprehensive knowledge of the circumstances and concerns about a child's maltreatment into a well-planned and structured interview that social workers can best identify inconsistencies. Where appropriate, these can be challenged during the interview as they occur, or, if indicated at a later date by the practitioner, after debriefing with a supervisor or discussion at a multidisciplinary meeting. Alternatively, it may be decided after consultation that the contradictions evidenced in the interviewee's account should be pursued through a formal police investigation. Regardless of how the issue is handled, only if the practitioner is astute to the possibility of a caregiver lying in the first instance, can concerns be raised and dealt with, either by further social work enquiry or police investigation. Shepherd (2007, pp 79–80) identifies the telltale signs of lying during an interview, which are outlined in Box 7.1, and uses the analogy of a basket to illustrate how lies are constructed:

> Lying is rather like filling a basket with scraps of paper bearing information. Typically the liar will put into the basket some, perhaps even many, scraps bearing truthful detail. The liar also places in the basket scraps bearing two types of deceptive information: untrue details represented as the truth, and non-specific detail. The third way in which a liar deceives is evasion: not putting particular information in the basket at all.

Box 7.1: Common anomalies in accounts of events

- *Thin story* – The narrative description of events lacks detail throughout the account.
- *Missing detail* – There are significant omissions in the recollection of an incident.
- *Gaps* – Where the usual steps from one thing to another are missing.
- *Jumps* – An abrupt shift in geographic location or jump in time.
- *Absence of reasonably expected detail* – There is a lack of detail that would be anticipated.
- *Vagueness* – Lack of specificity about an event.
- *Ambiguity* – The information given has several different meanings.
- *Sidestepping* – Answering a question with a question, avoiding giving details of an event, changing the topic or giving minimal evasive responses.
- *Pat* – The account is told entirely chronologically without any normal narrative reversal of the sequence of events or too many adverbs and adjectives are used when most people just use a few descriptive words when recounting an action or describing a scene.
- *Inconsistency* – Anomalies between different things the individual has said or between what they have said and the account given by another person regarding the same event.
- *Contradiction* – The individual gives more than one version of the same happenstance.
- *Narrative contrast* – There is greater detail about the circumstances preceding or following the significant event than the event itself or there is much more detail about the significant event compared to what led up to or followed on from it.

The professionals who came into contact with Ms Connelly were aware of the anomalies in her version of events and some may have suspected that she was deceiving them during subsequent interactions with her. However, her angry and hostile manner appears to have discouraged most practitioners from pursuing their concerns with her, probing her information or challenging inconsistencies in her version of events. This happened for a range of reasons, some of which are explored later in this case study. One important factor accounting for the reluctance of social workers to persist in questioning Ms Connelly was her angry verbal retorts to attempts by them to interrogate her assertions. Shepherd (2007, p 239) explains the Describe, Explain, Action required, Likely consequences (DEAL) approach to managing disruptive behaviour during an interview, which is reproduced in Table 7.1. The DEAL approach could be employed by a social worker confronted by an angry caregiver such as Ms Connelly, who either repeatedly interrupts their attempts at exploration of an issue or explodes with anger when asked further questions. Equally, it can be deployed to counter other inappropriate behaviours during an interview or discussion.

Table 7.1: The DEAL approach to a disruptive interviewee

Step		Objective	Example
Qualify your assertion		Give him/her the benefit of the doubt = he/she is unaware of the behaviour.	I need to tell you about something that you may not be aware of.
D	Describe	Describe the behaviour.	I need to point out that every time that I ask a question, you interrupt me.
E	Explain	Explain the actual or potential effects of the behaviour.	This makes it difficult to progress matters. It will take even longer to cover the issues that I must cover.
A	Action required	Spell out the action needed to correct the behaviour.	Please do not interrupt me when I am talking. Allow me to finish what I am saying. I will pay you the same courtesy.
L	Likely consequence	Spell out what will happen if the requested action does not occur.	If you persist in this behaviour after my repeated requests, I will have no option other than to [specify consequence].

Source: Reproduced from Shepherd (2007, p 239).

A short set of guidelines for the use of the DEAL approach is as follows:

1. Initially ignore the disruptive behaviour, as taking notice of it can reward it.
2. If the same disruptive behaviour is repeated three times, this indicates that there is a pattern that needs to be addressed by the interviewer.
3. Deliver the first three steps – D, E and A.
4. If the behaviour continues, again deliver steps D, E and A, but drawing the interviewee's attention to the fact that he or she has already been told about the disruptive effect of their behaviour.
5. If the behaviour still continues, repeat the first three steps for a third time, but once again drawing the interviewee's attention to the fact that he or she

has already been told on several occasions about the disruptive effect of their behaviour. Add step L.

6. If the behaviour still persists despite being brought to the interviewee's attention on three previous occasions, implement the consequence stated in step L.

Social workers pursuing child protection enquiries will encounter resistance from caregivers, their partners, relatives or friends acted out through a variety of responses, including: verbal abuse; belligerence; unwillingness to relate to the practitioner; or conduct that sabotages the gathering of information. Such behaviours can induce fear, anxiety, frustration or anger and can be intensely stressful for a practitioner. Strong emotion usually clouds professional judgement and runs the risk of important information not being obtained or else of being overlooked in the heat of the moment. Remaining calm and collected in provocative or intimidating circumstances is a major test for most child protection social workers. Throughout any interview or discussion, it is important not to permit the caregiver to provoke you into an immediate response to his or her statement. Always pause and breathe slowly to give yourself sufficient time to make a considered reply to the caregiver. Shepherd (2007, pp 243–4) offers advice to interviewers for responding to different forms of resistance during an interview. These might equally inform social work practice when conducting child protection enquiries with a caregiver who is plainly being evasive. They are outlined in Box 7.2. These techniques are only for use when a social worker is convinced that the caregiver is deliberately being evasive during discussions that concern the protection of a child. Throughout, the practitioner should strive to remain courteous and considerate towards the caregiver.

> ## Box 7.2: Responses to caregiver evasions
>
> - *Answering a question with a question* – Do not respond to the caregiver's question and restate your own question.
> - *Changing the topic* – Disregard the caregiver's attempt to change the topic and restate your question.
> - *Passing the buck* – If the caregiver suggests that you should speak to someone else instead of him or her about the matter, either ignore this or agree to speak to the other person later. Then restate your question.
> - *Giving measured responses* – If the caregiver gives minimal replies or only 'yes/no' responses, remind him or her of the purpose of the interview or the question and ask for more detail.
> - *Putting down* – If the caregiver attempts to provoke you with offensive remarks, ignore these and repeat your question.
> - *Arguing* – The caregiver tries to start an argument to prevent you pursuing a question. Do not get drawn in, wait for him or her to finish speaking and then repeat your question.

> • *Becoming emotional* – Caregivers may feel indignant, upset or angered by some of your questions. Identify what triggers any of these feelings and use empathy to acknowledge them. Allow a caregiver to vent any pent up feelings before returning to your question.

REFLECTIVE EXERCISE ON CHALLENGING A CAREGIVER WHO LIES

Recall three different interactions with caregivers when you believed that they were lying about a matter that concerned a child at risk. Ask yourself the following questions:

- How did you deal with this?
- What were the strengths and weaknesses of your approach?
- Were you able to uncover the truth and, if not, how might you use investigative interviewing techniques to support your enquiries in the future?
- What are the challenges for you of using the DEAL approach to disruptive behaviour by a caregiver during an interaction, and how might you overcome these?

Disguised compliance by a parent

At the initial child protection conference attended by Ms Connelly and her solicitor, professionals expressed concern regarding: poor hygiene in her house; inadequate physical care of her children; the lack of supervision of her children; and the presence of two dogs in the home. Ms Connelly agreed that she needed to 'take more control of the children' and admitted that 'as much as she tried to supervise the children … she may miss things', she also agreed to remove the dogs from the house (paras 3.7.13, 3.7.19). At the initial child protection conference, the allocated social worker reported that Ms Connelly was cooperative. This observation appeared to be based on Ms Connelly's engagement with the mental health worker with whom she had regular sessions and Haringey Tenancy Support for Families, which was assisting her to secure better accommodation (para 3.7.21). In practice, nothing in fact changed over the period leading up to Peter's death. Ms Connelly continued to be a grossly neglectful mother whose house was filthy and whose children were unkempt and dirty. In fact, Ms Connelly was selective in the services she chose to avail of, for example, her sessions with the mental health worker focused on her, rather than her children. Similarly, Haringey Tenancy Support for Families was assisting her to obtain a larger dwelling, which Ms Connelly was very keen to move to, and so she tended to cooperate with professionals from this agency. By contrast, Haringey's Children and Young People's Service was requiring Ms Connelly to make changes to her preferred mode of living and focusing on her children's needs rather than her own. A parent can, therefore, give the impression of compliance by a selective commitment to some services, but not others.

A parent may also act out their reluctance and resistance towards a service by only engaging with it minimally, such as Ms Connelly's attendance at Mellow Parenting for nine out of 13 sessions and lack of any change in her parenting as a result. Brandon et al (2009, p 100) emphasise the vital importance of distinguishing between active and passive cooperation by a caregiver in order to develop an effective child protection plan. Within their taxonomy of cooperation, Ms Connelly's conduct fits that of 'low cooperation'. Caregivers falling into this category evidence both missed and kept appointments alongside work with some agencies but the evasion of others. It is this partial compliance with child protection plans and uneven engagement with services that can make such caregivers appear cooperative when, in fact, they are employing tactics, not necessarily consciously, to frustrate social work interventions. Deliberating on this issue, the serious case review on Baby Peter opines:

> The uncooperative, anti-social and even dangerous parent/carer is the most difficult remaining challenge for safeguarding and child protection services. The parents/carers may not immediately present as such, and may be superficially compliant, evasive, deceitful, manipulative and untruthful. Practitioners had the difficult job of identifying them among the majority of parents who are merely dysfunctional, anxious and ambivalent. The interventions were not sufficiently authoritative by almost every agency. The authoritative intervention is urgent, thorough, challenging, with a low threshold of concern, keeping the focus on the child, and with high expectations of parenting. (para 4.3)

Social workers can be ill at ease with the use of authority in child protection contexts. Many who enter the profession do so primarily to help and support the disadvantaged. It can feel profoundly uncomfortable to use authority, make demands, set boundaries, draw their attention to negative consequences and insist that caregivers change. A proportion of social workers may feel much more at ease listening sympathetically to the caregiver's perspective, talking through their difficulties, employing empathic skills and providing support to them. Of course, good child protection practice includes both these sets of skills, but if a practitioner feels more comfortable exercising one set of skills than another, children are likely to be left at greater risk of significant harm. Practitioners can create their own inner sense of *role incompatibility* if they construe the social work task as essentially one of assisting parents in safeguarding situations, which actually require them to use their authority to reduce the risk of harm to children. Ferguson (2011, p 203) speaks of the necessity for practitioners to develop a 'child protection skin' which involves: acknowledging and working through their own resistance to using authority; to ask often intrusive questions about family life; to move around a home to inspect various rooms; and to insist on being permitted to interact with the child. According to Ferguson (2011, p 203), a social worker who successfully inhabits a 'child protection skin', is able to undertake these kinds of tasks without experiencing guilt, shame or undue anxiety (without feeling fearful could also be added to this list). This does not imply that social workers should be devoid of sensitivity to the impact that their use of authority is having on a caregiver. They must, of course, be attentive to the mix of worry, anger and indignation felt by many caregivers, but it is important not to permit this awareness and the empathic responses it rightly elicits to undermine an authoritative approach by the social worker.

REFLECTIVE EXERCISE ON POSSESSING A CHILD PROTECTION SKIN

Recall work with three different parents in relation to child protection concerns and identify what you found the most challenging aspects of your interactions with them. Ask yourself the following questions:

- Do any of these relate to the use of authority and, if so, which tasks did you feel most uncomfortable with?
- How did this discomfort influence your interaction with the parent in terms of behaving non-assertively, assertively or aggressively?
- What are your beliefs about what you, as a social worker, should be doing in your work with parents?
- How might these beliefs shape your behaviour in terms of non-assertive, assertive or aggressive responses when undertaking child protection tasks with caregivers?
- Do you possess an effective child protection skin and, if not, how might you use supervision or other opportunities to develop one?

Negotiating in bad faith

Even when social workers are proficient in their use of authority, they will still be confronted by some caregivers who may either be too frightened of their authority to openly contest it, or who intentionally deceive the practitioner in order to avoid making any changes. Ms Connelly was insincere in the agreements she reached with social workers regarding changes in the home environment and her treatment of her children. Her behaviour is not unique; social workers are occasionally confronted by caregivers intent on winning a contest of strength, rather than negotiating a genuine agreement. Isenhart and Spangle (2000, p 57) identify a set of strategies deployed by unscrupulous negotiators who struggle for dominance in a zero-sum game and the achievement of goals that nullify those of the other negotiator. Practitioners may encounter a number of these strategies when working with caregivers who are determined to pursue their own goals rather than reach mutually acceptable settlements to protect children. The set of strategies is as follows:

- *Good guy/bad guy* – There are several negotiators, one presents as collaborative and friendly, while the other is adversarial and makes extreme demands. This tactic is aimed at unbalancing the social worker and extracting more concessions from him or her by the apparently friendlier person. Couples can engage in this behaviour when one appears conciliatory and the other aggressive. Social workers intimidated by the aggressive partner can be tempted to make risky concessions to the conciliatory one.

- *Bad faith negotiating* – The caregiver expresses a commitment to collaborate but is simply playing for time or else agrees on an issue only to later renege on the agreement. This approach is designed to extract greater concessions. For example, a caregiver initially agrees to undertake intensive drug rehabilitation, but fails to turn up for the necessary sessions. The social worker then arranges for the caregiver to participate in a less demanding programme.

- *Lack of authority* – The caregiver claims that he or she lacks the authority to make agreements and shuttles backwards and forwards to confer with a third party. This can lead to constant changes and renegotiation of different aspects of any agreement. For instance, a caregiver insists that he or she has to gain the approval of a partner or other family member before agreeing to the social worker's proposal.

- *Inaccurate data* – The caregiver engages in deception by conveying misleading information, either through lying or the omission of certain facts or details. This tactic was effectively used by Ms Connelly.

- *Many for one* – The caregiver makes several minor concessions early on in the negotiation with the social worker and then insists on larger concessions in return. For example, a mother agrees to attend a parenting skills course and in return insists that the social worker should reduce demands on her regarding standards of hygiene in the home.

- *Information overload* – The caregiver produces masses of information with the intention of hiding facts or of stalling the negotiation. For example, when the social worker tries to reach agreement on a particular issue, he or she is bombarded with facts and figures about other issues by the caregiver. This tactic was successfully used by the foster carers in Case Study 6.1 to stall agreement on matters of concern to the social worker.

REFLECTIVE EXERCISE ON MANAGING AGGRESSIVE NEGOTIATION TACTICS

Examine the tactics used by disingenuous negotiators. Ask yourself the following questions:

- Which of these have you encountered in your work with caregivers and how have you dealt with them?

- What have been the strengths and weaknesses of your approaches to these different tactics?
- How might you improve your responses to these types of tactics by drawing on the work of Ury (1991), who suggests a number of constructive steps to managing the aggressive negotiation tactics of others (see Box 7.3)?

Box 7.3: The breakthrough approach

- *Step 1: Don't react – go to the balcony.* It assists to avoid impulsive retaliatory or acquiescent responses to aggressive tactics. This technique involves psychologically removing oneself from the ongoing interaction and looking at it as if from the perspective of a detached observer on a balcony. Such a position opens up space for social workers to gain distance from their swirling emotions and to refocus on the purpose of the discussion with the caregiver and the goals of any negotiation.

- *Step 2: Disarm them – step to their side.* It serves to prevent the escalation of negative emotions. When confronted with aggressive tactics, social workers must act in opposition to their own aggressive impulses by responding with 'positive constructive communication'. This means using active listening to acknowledge the caregiver's points without necessarily conceding them, demonstrating respect for them and emphasising shared understandings or goals.

- *Step 3: Change the game – don't reject, reframe.* This seeks to frame the negotiation positively. Social workers need to reframe the negative tactics of a caregiver by reformulating a personal attack as a difficulty the caregiver is experiencing with tackling the problem at the core of the negotiation. Or social workers can reinterpret a caregiver's aggressive interjection in less confrontational terms. At the same time, a social worker should continue to draw a caregiver's attention to their shared interests and goals.

- *Step 4: Make it easy to say yes – build them a golden bridge.* This is designed to reduce resistance to reaching agreement. Common reasons for negotiators being unwilling to agree a settlement are that it: did not originate with them; does not satisfy their goals; causes them to lose face; or requires them to make a major adjustment. Persuading resistant caregivers therefore necessitates: involving them in formulating the agreement; addressing their needs; taking account of their constraints; assisting them to save face with others; and pacing the adjustments that the caregiver needs to make.

- *Step 5: Make it hard to say no – bring them to their senses, not their knees.* It avoids confronting power plays by a negotiator with counter-power plays. This step entails: drawing caregivers' attention to the adverse consequences for them of not reaching an agreement; stressing the alternatives to a negotiated agreement open to the social worker; and assisting caregivers to see the advantages to them of reaching an agreement.

Aggression towards professionals

Mr Connelly, when interviewed by a social worker in March 2007, claimed that Ms Connelly had a boyfriend who spent time at her home. When the social worker put this to Ms Connelly during a telephone conversation, she angrily denied it. However, she did admit to having a male friend she was interested in dating as a boyfriend, but claimed he neither lived in the house nor had contact with her children. The angry reaction of Ms Connelly on the telephone with the social worker, combined with the established tendency of practitioners to take her at her word, meant that the social worker simply backed off. The social worker neither inquired about the identity of Ms Connelly's male friend, nor asked to meet him. An interview with him had the potential to confirm or disconfirm Ms Connelly's version of events. As the second serious case review commented, such a request to meet the man, had it been refused by Ms Connelly, would have revealed more about her mindset; but she was never asked (para 3.12.3). The anonymous friend was, in fact, Mr Barker, who actually lived with Ms Connelly and was subsequently convicted of causing or allowing Peter to die. Ms Connelly's insistence that she lived alone with her children was not subjected to any further scrutiny, either by the police or children's services.

Ms Connelly's volatile temperament and angry responses to challenge by professionals undoubtedly cowed some practitioners and often made it unpleasant and difficult to work with her. As her early childhood experiences reveal, Ms Connelly was herself subject to an abusive and neglectful childhood in a home where she witnessed domestic violence between her parents. It is therefore unsurprising that Ms Connelly should have developed an *aggressive script*, which led her to attempt to resolve conflict with practitioners through angry outbursts and intimidation rather than negotiation. Ms Connelly's aggression appears predominantly *reactive*. She likely perceived social workers as intruding upon her private life and making demands of her that she deemed unnecessary and unreasonable. In particular, she may have viewed the regular home visits being conducted by social workers at the time as a violation of the social norm that places family life within the private sphere. From Ms Connelly's standpoint, and given her *aggressive script*, such a norm violation would have constituted a provocation and, therefore, to her thinking, justified a verbally abusive response.

During the social worker's telephone conversation with Ms Connelly, which broached the subject of her male partner, her angry verbal riposte may well have been driven by her indignation at a professional questioning her about her intimate relationships. Certainly, it was another social norm violation, however necessary in the course of safeguarding a child. Possibly, Ms Connelly's response during the telephone discussion was *displaced aggression* relating to her ex-partner, whom she regarded as stirring up trouble for her, but who she felt unable to confront directly and so took out her annoyance on the social worker. Howsoever these factors contributed to Ms Connelly's aggression, she certainly thought that social workers were frustrating her own goal-oriented behaviour. It is salient that at around the time of the initial child protection conference in December 2006, the mental health worker involved with Ms Connelly reported that she 'was angry and upset with the social work service because the high frequency of visits she was receiving prevented her relaxing and enjoying her children' (para 3.13.2). In other words, Ms Connelly was becoming progressively more resentful of, and resistant to, social work intrusion into her life. She wanted to relax and not be troubled by professional expectations of domestic hygiene or attention to her children's welfare. As Geen (2001, p 22) observes from his compilation of the research literature, 'curtailment of freedom' is a major source of frustration. Ms Connelly conveys the impression that she regarded social workers as doing just that.

Social workers, for their part, were discouraged from pursuing disagreements with Ms Connelly because of her angry objections to their enquiries, advice or criticism. The verbal aggression of Ms Connelly constituted a source of stress for those interacting with her. In response, many practitioners understandably sought to manage their anxiety by 'flight' reactions, such as dropping a subject of discussion if Ms Connelly became irate, or being unobtrusive when making home visits. These reactions were designed to reduce the scope for angry confrontations by Ms Connelly. Unfortunately, such 'flight' responses would have reinforced Ms Connelly's aggressive behaviour by rewarding it. It was exceptionally difficult for individual professionals to stand up to Ms Connelly without an agreed multidisciplinary strategy to manage her aggression.

The uneven cooperation of Ms Connelly with agencies, depending on the degree to which they met her needs or challenged her, also meant that while Ms Connelly appeared to have a good working relationship with the mental health worker, she was uncooperative with child protection social workers. This type of caregiver behaviour can divide the multidisciplinary team, as it lends credence to the assumption that it is an individual practitioner who is at fault for failing to establish good partnership-working with the parent, rather than a parent's sometimes judicious use of anger as *proactive aggression* to deter social work safeguarding activity. Division of the multidisciplinary team was played out during the initial child protection conference in December 2006, as many professionals in attendance did not challenge Ms Connelly in order to avoid jeopardising partnership-working with her. Even as early as the first case conference, a number of agencies and their staff had already concluded that the less challenging the professional, the more likely would be Ms Connelly's cooperation. But it was partnership-working and cooperation by Ms Connelly of a superficial nature. Protecting Peter Connelly demanded the willingness of social workers to challenge his mother, even when confronted with her *reactive* and *proactive* aggression.

The failure to challenge

The general failure by practitioners to challenge Ms Connelly was, in the opinion of the serious case review, compounded by the piloting of Solution Focused Brief Therapy (SFBT) in child protection in Haringey Children and Young People's

Service. This model aims to improve parents' care of their children by focusing on parental strengths and was being used by the Safeguarding Team working with Ms Connelly. Indeed, some senior managers within Haringey Children and Young People's Service believed that it could be extended to statutory child protection enquiries and child protection conferences. The professional culture created by the widespread use of this model of intervention within the Safeguarding Team meant that it 'did create an ethos which above all emphasised the importance of supporting parents' (para 3.16.5). In its findings, the serious case review noted that:

> this approach may have a place in family work, and emphasising the strengths of parents is important. But it is not compatible with the authoritative approach to parents in the protective phase of enquiries, assessment and the child protection conference if children are to be protected. (para 3.16.7)

Reiterating the conclusion of the Baby Peter second serious case review, Brandon et al (2009, p 47), in their analysis of serious case review reports, expressed concern that:

> the recent emphasis on strengths based approaches and the positive aspects of families (for example in the Common Assessment Framework) arguably discourages workers from making professional judgements about deficits in parents' behaviour which might be endangering their children. A determination to follow a strengths based approach without at the same time weighing up any risks of harm to the child, was apparent in a number of reviews.

Practitioners working with Ms Connelly probably experienced *role incompatibility*. On the one hand, their agency promoted support for parents using solution-focused approaches, yet, at the same time, social workers were required to protect children. As the second serious case review concluded, these were incompatible objectives in a safeguarding context. Endeavouring to pursue them simultaneously caused confusion and indisputably heightened the stress of social workers involved with the family. It may have added to the irritability of social workers already coping with heavy workloads and the frequent turnover of staff, as described in Case Study 3.2, and, in so doing, probably contributed to aggressive responses in their work with colleagues and caregivers.

Dealing with verbal detours and distractions

This serves to illustrate that a successful challenge involves more than just a good Describe, Express, Specify, Consequence (DESC) script, as discussed in Case Study 4.1, even if it is well-rehearsed and delivered with assertive non-verbal behaviours. People, such as Ms Connelly, who perceive negotiation as a contest with only one possible winner or who habitually use verbal aggression to attain their goals, are unlikely to acquiesce after the first assertive statement by a practitioner. Many social workers will encounter a plethora of responses designed to ignore, distract, insult or threaten them when challenging caregivers over their attitudes, opinions or behaviours.

Bower and Bower (2004, pp 144–63) identify 15 distinct verbal strategies commonly used by individuals when they do not wish to address issues raised about their standpoint or conduct. These strategies are not confined to people who habitually engage in aggressive manoeuvres to attain their goals, but are deployed from time to time by virtually everyone when confronted by dispute. Table 7.2 outlines these defensive verbal moves, which Bower and Bower (2004) characterise as 'detours', and elaborates on them in relation to social work. These need to be

Table 7.2: Common detours to assertive challenges

Type of detour	Explanation of detour	Illustration of detour	Basic counter-strategy
Put-off	Avoids discussing the issue by putting you off.	'I'm too busy now', 'Let's discuss it another time', 'I'm too upset to deal with this'.	Insist that your concern is discussed now, but keep it brief. Alternatively, agree a specific time when it will be discussed in the future.
Distracting	Reponses designed to sidetrack you onto an irrelevant issue.	'My problem is ...', 'I don't like the way you're talking to me', 'Shouldn't you be assessing the children'.	Refuse to respond to the distraction and continue to focus on your concern.
Denying	Denial of your description of the problem or that there is any problem.	'I don't know what you're talking about', 'You're lying', 'That's nonsense'.	Briefly disagree with the denial and/or restate your concern. Do not engage in an argument as to whose perspective is correct.
Blaming	Blaming you or someone else for the problem and thereby resisting any change to behaviour.	'I shout because you're not listening', 'I don't go to the meetings because you frighten me', 'The house is dirty because the children are messy'.	Disagree quickly and return to a focus on your concern. Do not let yourself be diverted into a discussion about who is to blame.
Verbal-abusing	Use of abusive language, sarcasm, personal attacks or attempts to belittle and humiliate you.	'Are you completely stupid?', 'You're the worst social worker I've ever had', 'I can tell you're new to this job'.	Ignore the verbal abuse and stay focused on your concern. Alternatively, briefly acknowledge the emotion behind the abusive language.
Joking	Ridiculing or mocking the issue you have raised.	'Are you on commission for taking kids off parents?', 'If I tidied up, I'd never find everything again', 'My eyes would wear out keeping an eye on that boy'.	Ignore or quickly disagree with the jocular behaviour and focus on your concern.

Table 7.2: continued

Type of detour	Explanation of detour	Illustration of detour	Basic counter-strategy
Reinterpreting	Giving a positive meaning to objectionable behaviour, such as good intentions.	'It was only a joke, lighten up', 'I was trying to be helpful', 'I was just giving you information'.	Emphasise that you can only see what someone does, not their motives and restate your concern.
Psychoanalysing	Interpreting your motives and character and presuming to read your mind.	'You're angry because you didn't get that job', 'You're saying that because you think men can't be good fathers', 'You're just worried about looking bad'.	Quickly disagree with the interpretation and restate your perspective or feelings regarding the issue in dispute.
Poor me	Drawing attention to feeling hurt, offended or upset by your statement.	'You've upset me so much, I can't think straight', 'I've been worried for days on end and can't sleep'. Non-verbal behaviour such as crying or sulking. Minor ailments such as a headache, which repeatedly occur during a disagreement.	Do not feel guilty. Wait until the person has stopped crying if it is completely impeding discussion of your concern. Otherwise, continue with your DESC statement. If crying prevents discussion, get an agreement to discuss the concern at a specific future time. Alternatively, state your opinion that the person is using crying to inhibit discussion about the issue you have raised.
Negative body language	Use of posture, gesture and tone of voice to convey being hurt, upset or angered.	Non-verbal behaviour such as glaring, covering face with hands, looking into the distance or silence.	Use an empathetic statement that acknowledges the emotion being non-verbally expressed before returning to your concern. Alternatively, ignore the negative body language and state your DESC.
Apologising	Excessive apologies and self-abasement designed to make the other person feel guilty and back off.	'I'm really sorry, I didn't realise', 'I'm so sorry, it won't happen again', 'Sorry, I'm just so stupid'.	Avoid feeling guilty or softening your position or articulation of the problem.
Threatening	Threat of excessive retribution.	'I'm going to the newspapers about this', 'Don't talk to me like that or I'll complain to your manager', 'If you keep pushing me, I'll fall apart'.	If the threat appears empty, ignore it or make clear that you know it is a bluff. If the threat is realistic, try not to reward it, as this will reinforce the behaviour. Respond by criticising the use of threats, point out their self-defeating effects or indicate the negative consequences of refusing to negotiate over your concern.

Table 7.2: continued

Type of detour	Explanation of detour	Illustration of detour	Basic counter-strategy
Debating	Debates issue by asking many questions or putting up numerous counter-arguments.	'Why are you asking me this question?', 'Why do you assume it's all my fault?', 'You're just saying I can't look after my children because I'm depressed'.	Elaborate briefly and then restate your concern. Do not get sidetracked into having to justify every point of your DESC statement. Avoid going into detail on issues, as this provides more material for debate and disagreement.
Procrastinating	Deceptively appears to listen and agree, but does not change behaviour.	'I'll do it next week', 'I'm thinking about it'. 'Seems fine to me, but I need to speak to my husband about that'.	Insist that an agreement to change is reached now or set a deadline for agreement and behaviour change. Alternatively, agree that if behaviour change does not occur by a specific date, then negative consequences will automatically ensue.
Non-negotiating	Rejects the notion that there is any problem with behaviour or refuses to change because the positive or negative consequences are not great enough.	'That's nonsense'. Non-verbal behaviour includes leaving the room or engaging in another activity that ignores the other person.	Restate your concern, insisting that there is a problem. Increase the attractiveness of the reward for behaviour change. Emphasise the negative consequences of a refusal to negotiate.

understood as manipulative stratagems designed to forestall social workers from addressing crucial issues with caregivers, be they foster carers, guardians, parents or their partners. Some stratagems may be deliberative, while others are unconscious and habitual ways of defending against unpleasant and stress-provoking realities. Regardless of whether the detour is a conscious or unconscious one, practitioners must challenge it through an assertive riposte that enables them to maintain both their own focus and that of the caregiver on the safeguarding concern.

Great caution must be exercised in identifying defensive stratagems. It would be entirely wrong to assume that a caregiver who cries when confronted with a social worker's query about a child's injury is being manipulative and attempting to impede the enquiry. Equally, it would be erroneous to suppose that a parent who ridicules a practitioner's expressed concern is trying to insult or sidetrack that professional; the caregiver may simply be shocked and confused by the gravity of the situation. Likewise, a parent may ask many questions because they feel overwhelmed and are simply trying to comprehend the problem. The stratagems set out in Table 7.2 are exactly that; meaning that they are a habitual mode of interacting with a social worker, which results in the practitioner being repeatedly diverted away from a child protection concern. Establishing that a caregiver is using one or more of these detours does not mean alighting upon a few instances when they attempt to psychoanalyse the social worker or make an insulting comment. It requires the social worker to reflect on his or her interaction with a particular caregiver and to identify a pattern of verbal or non-verbal behaviour which indicates that a detour is being deployed. Moving on from the detours people use to avoid addressing issues they would prefer to ignore, Bower and Bower (2004, pp 144–5) identify a range of responses that can be used to engage a reluctant individual in discussing aspects of the disagreement. These are described in Table 7.3.

Table 7.3: Counter-responses to detours

Counter-response	Explanation of counter-response
Persist	Repeat your key point.
Disagree	Disagree using a short direct statement and return to your key point.
Emphasise feelings/thoughts	Draw attention to your feelings or thoughts about the issue.
Agree ... but	Accept that the other person is entitled to different feelings or views, but return to your point of disagreement.
Dismiss	Ignore the detour or dismiss it quickly as irrelevant, then return to your key point.
Redefine	Do not accept the other person's negative interpretation of your behaviour and reframe it in positive terms.
Answer quickly	Respond with a 'yes' or 'no' answer or other brief reply, then return to your key point.
Ask a question	Ask for clarification of a derogatory or accusatory statement.
Stipulate consequences	Offer realistic rewards for behaviour change. State realistic negative consequences if the problem attitude or behaviour continues.

The following examples illustrate how a combination of different strategies can be used to combat a range of verbal detours by caregivers or, indeed, colleagues and managers:

- *Non-negotiation detour:* 'That's nonsense'. *Counter-response:* 'No, it's not [disagree], failing to clear cutlery away into a drawer out of reach is putting your toddler at risk of hurting himself [persist]'.
- *Debating detour:* 'Why are you asking me this question?'. *Counter-response:* 'I am concerned about your child's safety [answer quickly]. I am worried [emphasise feelings] about your seven-year-old daughter being left alone all day [persist]'.
- *Procrastinating detour:* 'I'm thinking about it'. *Counter-response:* 'You have been thinking about this issue for the last week, I suggest that if you have not decided to attend the course by next Wednesday, that we cancel your place on it [stipulate consequences]'.
- *Poor me detour:* 'You've upset me so much, I can't think straight'. *Counter-response:* 'I appreciate this is upsetting for you, but your foster child is distressed by being excluded from organised activities with your own children [agree ... but]'.
- *Verbal-abusing detour:* 'I can tell you're new to this job'. *Counter-response:* 'Please explain what you mean by that [ask a question]'.

REFLECTIVE EXERCISE ON VERBAL DETOURS

Recall interactions with some of the most challenging caregivers you have worked with. Ask yourself the following questions:

- Which of the above detours did they use and how did you respond to these?
- Which detours did you effectively counteract and which detours did you go on with the caregiver, resulting in distraction from the matters you set out to address with him or her?
- Employ some of the counter-strategies to detours suggested earlier in your work with challenging caregivers. Appraise their effectiveness in keeping both you and the caregiver focused on activity related to reducing the risk of harm to a child.

Case Study 7.2: Ajit Singh

Barking and Dagenham Safeguarding Children Board (2010)
Serious case review: services provided for Child T and Child R
August 1997–February 2010

Satpal Kaur-Singh was of Indian heritage and a Sikh. She was born and grew up in the UK. Her husband was born in India and was also a Sikh. He first came to Britain in 1995 and married Satpal a year later. The relationship between the couple was characterised by domestic abuse, frequent calls to the police by Mrs Singh, followed by a refusal to give evidence against her husband, who drank heavily and was violent. Their first child, Ajit, was born in 1997. He was born 10 weeks premature, which resulted in severe learning difficulties. In August 1998, Ajit was admitted to an Accident & Emergency Unit with a head injury allegedly caused by his father. He was placed on the Child Protection Register in September 1998. The parents refused offers of support and it became difficult to monitor Ajit's progress. In January 1999, the couple's second son was born and, in June 1999, he was also placed on the Register due to the high levels of domestic violence within the household. Ajit was identified by a health visitor as having a 'global developmental delay', which resulted in the offer of assessments and support services. But Mrs Singh refused to cooperate, despite the fact that both children were subject to child protection plans. This became a pervasive dynamic, with social workers unable to progress assessments due to Mrs Singh's refusal to permit access to her children, bolstered by her numerous complaints against professionals.

Court proceedings were not initiated because local authority lawyers maintained that the threshold for a Care Order had not been met. In 2002, both children were removed from the Register and treated as *children in need*, as the father had left the home. Thereafter, the children were moved between a succession of schools by their mother and both missed years of education. Ajit attended school for the last time in May 2007, when he was permanently withdrawn from formal education as Mrs Singh stated that she would tutor her son at home. Both children were again made the subject of child protection plans, which were later lifted and then reinstated. A number of child protection plans were drawn up, but Mrs Singh consistently refused to comply with them and the children's education continued to suffer. In January 2010, legal advice from the local authority lawyers changed, partly because of the father's renewed involvement with his family, and social workers decided to apply for Interim Care Orders on the children. Satpal Kaur-Singh was informed by letter of the intention to remove the children from her care. She came to a meeting with the Children's Disability Team Manager and the social worker on 9 February 2010, when she again refused to comply with the child protection plans for the children. That evening, Mrs Singh telephoned the police to inform them that she had forced Ajit to drink bleach and intended to kill herself as well. Ajit was pronounced dead on arrival at hospital. He was 12 years old. His mother, who had drunk a little bleach, was discharged from hospital into police custody the same day.

Satpal Kaur-Singh pleaded guilty at the Old Bailey to the manslaughter of Ajit on the grounds of diminished responsibility and was given a seven-year custodial sentence.

Non-cooperation with child protection plans

The local authority's lawyers indicated that there were no grounds for legal proceedings in relation to the children, which continued to be their position up until January 2010. This legal advice contributed to an ongoing state of affairs whereby no matter how outrageously Mrs Singh flouted the stipulations laid down in child protection plans, no legal recourse by social workers appeared available. During the period 1998–2010, the two children were the subject of child protection plans for three separate periods, amounting to over six years in total (p 7). Throughout a decade of social services involvement, only occasionally did Mrs Singh participate at child protection conferences, despite requests for her to attend. Each inception of a child protection plan requiring the completion of assessments and school attendance was followed by Mrs Singh's non-compliance. Indeed, Mrs Singh even refused to sign her agreement to child protection plans on several occasions, apparently with impunity. Even during her final meeting with social workers at the offices of the Children's Disability Team with a pending application for an Interim Care Order, Mrs Singh resolutely maintained that 'she had no difficulties with her parenting ability and only she understood her child' (*The Telegraph*, 2010).

Often, her non-cooperation escalated when education or social services appeared to threaten or interfere in her relationship with the children. Immediately after social workers held yet another legal planning meeting with local authority lawyers in 2007, Mrs Singh refused them entry to her home or any access to the children. Similarly, in January 2010, a social worker was refused entry to the home by Mrs Singh, who reluctantly only agreed to bring the two children to the front door. This seemed to be on the grounds that she suspected the social worker had met with Mr Singh to discuss matters, which the latter refused to confirm (p 35). There was clearly an emergent pattern to Mrs Singh's behaviour of non-cooperation. Its effect would have tended to discourage professionals, who wanted to preserve contact with the children, from challenging her.

The sense that social workers were impeded in taking concerted action by legal advice was further exacerbated by conflicting views of the mother. From 2000 onwards, differences of opinion emerged between the professionals involved with the family. Some viewed Mrs Singh as a single mother doing her best to care for a severely disabled son, while others believed that Mrs Singh's failure to engage with services was aggravating Ajit's developmental delay (p 13). The serious case review highlighted this underlying disagreement and criticised those who 'showed an unjustified level of sympathy for the mother because she was perceived as a victim of abuse' (p 44). As a consequence of making allowances for Mrs Singh, 'the criteria for making judgements became the stated good intentions of the mother rather than on how she was actually parenting the children and the outcomes that the children were achieving' (p 14). This led some professionals to excuse Mrs Singh's non-compliance and to, instead, commend her diligence in caring for a severely disabled son. According to the categorisation devised by Brandon et al (2009, p 63), Mrs Singh's behaviour was classifiable as 'not cooperative' on the basis that she missed many appointments and was actively hostile towards professionals from numerous agencies.

Effective intervention by practitioners was hampered by a compassionate and benign view of Mrs Singh as a victim of domestic abuse striving to parent a severely disabled son. The serious case review opined that the sympathetic view taken of Mrs Satpal Kaur-Singh by a number of professionals 'led them to lose their focus on the children and to underestimate the level of risk' (p 44). Substantiating this criticism, Brandon et al (2009, p 47), in their biennial analysis of serious case reviews, expressed concern that:

> there was reluctance among many practitioners (including among health and social work staff working with children) to make negative professional judgements about a parent. Workers, including those in adult-led mental health services, domestic violence projects and substance misuse services, were keen to acknowledge the successes of the often disadvantaged, socially excluded parents who were using their services. This could even occur when the child was the subject of a child protection plan.

Similar disquiet emerges from Ofsted's (2010, paras 96–8) analysis of serious case reviews.

Games people play

Both Mrs Singh and the professionals seem to have been involved in a collusive, if unconscious, set of interactions that led to the predominating perception that she was a well-intentioned, struggling mother disadvantaged by domestic violence and single parenthood. Her non-compliance was consequently excused rather than confronted. This was despite the existence of child protection plans and the consideration given by social workers to seeking a Care Order. One possible reading of this state of affairs was that those involved were caught in a psychosocial game created by their own life scripts. Berne (1968) and Steiner (1990) analyse common patterned interactions between people in which both are seeking a pay-off at a psychological level, which is not immediately apparent from their social exchange. Games are structured by the players to achieve this pay-off at the end. The particular games people play are determined by their life script, which is shaped predominantly by parental influences during childhood. Typically, these games are subconscious and the players are not fully aware of their own patterned interactions and the pay-offs they are endeavouring to gain. Berne (1968) and Steiner (1990) argue that these games, and the pay-offs they generate, are necessary to maintain the mental equilibrium and functioning of the people playing them. Drawing attention to the games caregivers are playing, refusing to play the game with them and depriving them of its pay-off will cause caregivers to feel anxious, confused, despairing and angry. It is this psychological discomfort and the loss of perceived social or material benefits that lead many people to resist moves by a social worker to halt their game. Nevertheless, explicitly challenging the manoeuvres of a game is the only way to stop the game and open up the possibility of replacing it with more satisfying social interactions. But during this challenge, it is vital for a social worker to recognise that the caregiver may be oblivious to the game they are playing.

Social workers also have life scripts that have led them to enter the caring professions, and these too can produce games. When caregivers and social workers are playing complementary games, they can collude in their behaviour to the detriment of protecting a child at risk. For example, the caregiver plays 'wooden leg', which is a game whereby the person claims he or she cannot do something because of a disadvantage, such as domestic violence, and the professional plays 'nurse', by perpetually trying to rescue the caregiver who is perceived to be a victim (see Table 7.4). The professional accepts the caregiver's excuse for being unable to change and makes few demands of him or her. Instead, the professional provides excessive support in an attempt to do for the caregiver what he or she ought to take responsibility for doing (albeit with some assistance). Such complementary games may have been played between Mrs Singh and some of the professionals involved with her. Practitioners should therefore be alert to their own predisposition to play certain games. Based on the work of Berne (1968) and Steiner (1990), the typical games of caregivers and practitioners are outlined in Table 7.4.

REFLECTIVE EXERCISE ON GAME PLAYING

Read through the patterned interactions that people commonly engage in. Recall interactions with three different caregivers you found challenging to work with. Ask yourself the following questions:

- Do any of the games mentioned in Table 7.4 seem to explain recurring patterns of behaviour?
- Have you engaged in any patterned interactions typical of people who assume a helping role?
- How might some of your own inadvertent game-playing have colluded with that of the caregivers you have worked with?
- How might you monitor and resist colluding in playing these games in future?
- Utilising guidance on how to craft an effective challenge presented in Case Study 6.1 and advice elsewhere on assertion, formulate and write down several challenges to draw a caregiver's attention to a particular game he or she is playing. Decide how you would avoid giving him or her the pay-offs that maintain the game?

Table 7.4: Common psychosocial interpersonal games

Common games	Explanation	Pay-off
Why don't you ... yes but	The caregiver asks for help, but regardless of the suggestions made by the social worker, always has a reason for rejecting each one in turn or demonstrating why each will not work.	By not providing the caregiver with a workable suggestion, the caregiver can blame the social worker for inadequacy rather than him or herself for not trying to change and, thus, for sustaining their unsatisfactory situation.
Wooden leg	The caregiver repeatedly cites the same real or imaginary disability, such as depression, headaches, stress or alcoholism, as the reason why they cannot do something.	The social worker treats the caregiver as incapacitated, lowers his or her expectation of what the caregiver can achieve, and does not *make a demand for work*.
Look how hard I've tried	The caregiver apparently tries, but repeatedly fails, to complete a required task.	The social worker accepts that the caregiver is trying their best, so the caregiver is either helpless or blameless. Either way they cannot be justifiably penalised by the social worker.
If it weren't for you	The caregiver complains that it is a partner, children, other family member or the social worker who is restraining him or her from making positive changes.	The social worker accepts that the caregiver is hindered from making changes and either lowers expectations of change or does not make an appropriate *demand for work*.
Got you	The caregiver sets the social worker up to fail, for example, by not giving him or her all the necessary information, or having unreasonable expectations, or misinterpreting an agreement in relation to a task being undertaken by the practitioner.	The caregiver blames the social worker for failure and feels justified in venting intense anger and severely criticising the social worker. The caregiver also gets to feel superior to the social worker, who appears inadequate by comparison.

Table 7.4: continued

Common games	Explanation	Pay-off
See what you made me do	The caregiver lets the social worker make the decisions and goes along with them. When matters go well, the caregiver is satisfied, but when matters go badly for the caregiver, he or she blames the social worker. Caregivers may also play this game in relation to other members of their family.	The caregiver can absolve him or herself of responsibility for adverse events or consequences and places this on the social worker or another family member who made the decision.
Schlemiel	The caregiver repeatedly makes mistakes or causes accidents, resulting in difficulty and distress for others, including the social worker. But the caregiver is extremely apologetic after each episode.	The caregiver derives satisfaction from their carelessness. However, they are not held accountable or penalised because they express much regret. The caregiver is forgiven by the social worker.
You're a wonderful professor	The caregiver constantly tells the social worker that he or she is right or wonderful. However, the caregiver makes no or little change as a result.	The social worker is beguiled by an appreciative caregiver who boosts their self-esteem. Consequently, the social worker is less perceptive about the lack of work being done by the caregiver and reduces a *demand for work* on him or her to change.
I'm only trying to help you	This is a game played by social workers and other helping professionals. The social worker makes a number of suggestions and offers support only to find the caregiver failing to make the changes required.	The social worker feels angry and frustrated by the caregiver's failure to make changes. This reinforces the social worker's belief that caregivers are ultimately ungrateful and disappointing. The social worker blames the caregiver, takes little responsibility for the failure and makes no effort to improve their own practice, convinced that they have applied the correct procedures.
Nurse (compulsive helper)	This game is played by many people in the caring professions, but women are particularly susceptible to it. The social worker's motivation is to help others and she consistently puts the needs of others before her own. The social worker is perpetually trying to rescue caregivers by providing them with excessive support.	Social workers engaged in this game are perceived by themselves, colleagues and caregivers to be generous, selfless and caring. They receive positive evaluations by others, which affirm their commitment to tireless work on behalf of caregivers.
Big daddy	This game is played predominantly, but by no means exclusively, by men and sometimes by male social workers. The practitioner works hard and takes on considerable responsibility for others. He worries about the welfare of caregivers. The social worker believes that he knows best and due to his expertise and responsibility, feels justified in dictating to caregivers and expecting their deference.	Social workers playing this game have the satisfaction of believing that they are always right and of not admitting to any weaknesses in their practice. Like the 'nurse', this social worker also receives positive evaluations from others for selfless and tireless work.

Use of complaints to obstruct intervention

After a history of sporadic attendance, Mrs Singh withdrew Ajit from his special school in January 2003 on the grounds 'that the school nurses had removed stitches from an operation scar without consent and that school staff had attempted to undertake experiments on him' (p 17). The serious case review could find no evidence to support these allegations and concluded that they were a defensive reaction to staff insisting that Ajit attend school regularly and requests that the mother change her management of Ajit in order to introduce greater consistency between his home and school life (p 17). At this juncture, Mrs Singh also sent letters of complaint to each of the agencies involved with the family, including social care services. These accused professionals of 'racism, lack of cultural sensitivity and unnecessary interference in family life' (p 17). Social work management responded to Mrs Singh's complaint about the social worker by reallocating the family to a different social worker, who was on the Children's Disabilities Team.

In 2005, Mrs Singh took her children to India, returning in 2006, when a social worker was again allocated to the family. In April 2006, he met with Mrs Singh to engage her in planning for the education of her children, who were once again not in school. She made a complaint about him. At a subsequent case conference held on 26 April 2006, the social worker detailed his concerns about the children, including the mother's failure to cooperate with the core assessment he was endeavouring to complete. Thereafter, Mrs Singh complained about him again. As the social worker was also of Indian heritage, Mrs Singh did not pursue her objection to him on the grounds of cultural insensitivity, but, instead, on that of gender. Management removed him from further work with the family and he was replaced by a female social worker (p 20). A number of GPs declined to attend child protection conferences 'because they feared that this would provoke complaints from the mother' (p 66).

In November 2008, Mrs Singh wrote numerous letters of complaint about individual teachers at a Redbridge Primary School, where Ajit's younger brother was enrolled. By January 2009, the principal felt compelled to take legal advice because the mother was coming up to the school and 'shouting at teachers and other parents and pupils, reducing members of staff to tears' (p 27). When the mother complained about the 'unprofessional' behaviour of school staff at a child in need meeting convened to discuss the principal's concerns, teachers then withdrew from further meetings for some months (p 27). In January 2010, the social worker attempted to make a home visit to see the children, during which the mother suspected her of having met with the father. The next day, the mother arrived at the offices of Children's Disability Services with the father to pursue a number of complaints against the social worker (p 35).

In short, the complaints procedure became the recourse of default for Mrs Singh whenever she felt pressured or confronted by social workers or teachers. The serious case review recorded that 'she continued to refuse to cooperate with professionals and frequently complained about anyone who challenged her approach to the care of the children' (p 13). When challenged, Mrs Singh escalated her non-cooperation, engaged in aggressive behaviour or made complaints. The combination of these behaviours led professionals to avoid conflicting with her, evade interactions with her or to withdraw from multiagency forums concerned with the family. On receiving complaints about the allocated social worker, social work managers sought to placate Mrs Singh by changing the practitioner or reallocating the case to another team entirely. According to the serious case review, 'some professionals were intimidated by her hostile behaviour', while 'agencies responded to repeated complaints by making concessions that were not in the interests of the children' (p 44). At the same time, 'managers and supervisors in all agencies failed to recognise the impact of this behaviour and to provide adequate guidance and support to staff dealing with the mother' (p 44). As the serious case review concluded:

> her aggressive and difficult behaviour led professionals in a number of different agencies to avoid challenging her which had a profound bearing on the assessment of risk to the children, the services that the children received and the overall management of the case. (p 44)

Examining the same issue in relation to practice more generally, Brandon et al (2009, pp 100–1) quote a research participant who neatly conveys one of their key findings:

> The last frontier in my view, in respect of child protection, is the hostile, uncooperative, dangerous family. So far we have demonstrated only too well that we do not know how to deal with this kind of family. We do not know how to be authoritative and helpful and we back off them so they run circles around services.

REFLECTIVE EXERCISE ON THE IMPACT OF COMPLAINTS MADE BY CAREGIVERS

- Have you ever been threatened with a complaint or had a complaint made against you by a caregiver and, if so, how did this make you feel?
- How did these feeling affect your capacity or willingness to offer challenges to the caregiver or to other caregivers you worked with subsequently?
- Did it change what you challenged, how frequently you challenged or the way in which you made your challenges?
- Were your challenges in the wake of a complaint or threatened complaint more or less assertive, non-assertive or aggressive?
- Did the complaint change any other aspects of your professional behaviour with caregivers, colleagues or managers and, if so, how?

- What kind of support would have been helpful to you at the time of the complaint or threatened complaint and if it was not available, what could you do to ensure this support is accessible in the future?

Complaints as aggression

Local government agencies delivering services to children are required by law to have a complaints procedure in place that can be availed of by caregivers and children who are dissatisfied with the performance of professionals or disagree with their decisions. Complaints procedures are designed to drive up care standards by providing critical learning for agencies and their employees. They ensure that caregivers and children in receipt of inadequate services or who encounter poor social work practice have their grievance heard, addressed and rectified. Indisputably, they provide a vital mechanism for righting wrongs. Complaints procedures are also open to abuse by a small number of parents or guardians. Caregivers can seek to hide their cruelty to a child by misusing the complaints procedure to block or delay effective intervention. Alternatively, some caregivers may employ the complaints procedure to retaliate against social workers for what they perceive to be an unjustified interference in family life.

The local government complaints procedure is comprised of three distinct stages at which attempts are made to resolve the problem with the caregiver or child. A failure to satisfactorily address the grievance to the complainant's satisfaction results in it being referred upwards to a further stage involving more formality and senior personnel. If pursued through all three stages, the progress of a complaint can take up to four months and still be within the prescribed timescales for resolution. This means that if the complaint is made about a service, decision or practitioner, it has the potential to delay vital interventions or leave a social worker anxious for a substantial length of time as to the outcome of the investigation into it. Laird (2011, p 17) draws attention to the abuse of the complaints procedure by a number of caregivers in an effort to deflect scrutiny away from their treatment of children, as evidenced in other serious case reviews and inquiries. Mrs Singh's case is, therefore, not exceptional.

As Geen's (2001, p 3) definition of aggression indicates, it can comprise intimidating behaviour that involves neither physical violence nor verbal abuse. Indeed, it can be the very absence of these elements that makes it difficult to detect and recognise as aggression. Moreover, in a situation where complaints procedures legitimise, although they may not substantiate, a caregiver's grievance, it is remarkably difficult for a social worker to voice the suspicion that the process is being subverted to malicious ends. In the case of Mrs Singh, this common hesitation to discredit a complaint by a caregiver was intensified by the fact that several of the complaints related to issues of race and gender. Training in anti-discriminatory practice stresses the responsibility of social workers to challenge negative stereotypes, counteract disadvantage and empower service-users from oppressed social groups, including women and those from black and minority ethnic communities (Dominelli, 1997; Thompson, 2006, pp 68–9, 92–5). Social work training and practice requires students and qualified professionals to examine their own prejudiced attitudes and discriminatory behaviour towards people from disadvantaged groups. Recognising, addressing and counteracting one's own sexism and racism is a major endeavour for all those aspiring to be good social workers.

The exclusive focus on this aspect of anti-oppressive practice can make it dissonant for professionals to then consider how someone from an oppressed group might rely on that disadvantaged status to obstruct safeguarding activities. In such circumstances, a white social worker becomes vulnerable to a malicious complaint of racism by a black caregiver or a male social worker becomes vulnerable to an unfounded complaint of sexism. Resistant or angry caregivers can resort to the unjustified use of complaints procedures when they feel controlled, trapped or threatened with discovery. Other caregivers can use unjustified complaints as a form of *reactive aggression*, provoked by social work interference in their lives. For some, this may be a conscious choice; for others, it is an expression of subconscious *hostile attribution biases* formed by abusive experiences in childhood or discrimination in later life. For yet others, their reluctance is expressed through ambivalence towards social work interventions that can manifest as one-to-one accusations or escalate into more formal complaints. This is not to deny that sometimes social workers are indeed racist or sexist and many caregivers' complaints are entirely warranted. Nevertheless, as a number of serious case reviews and inquiries now reveal, it would be a mistake to assume that caregivers who are black, female, disabled, aged or homosexual are by virtue of their minority status incapable of abusing it through unfounded allegations of discrimination against social workers.

The capitulation of practitioners and their front-line managers to the stream of complaints by Mrs Singh simply reinforced her aggressive behaviour. She was being rewarded for aggression by a change of social worker, by fewer home visits and by the drop in attention of professionals. In short, she perceived that intimidation worked. It became for her a highly adaptive behaviour, which generated a relentless succession of formal complaints. As Case Study 7.2 demonstrates, if the complaints procedure is treated as sacrosanct, with no consideration given as to how it can be refashioned by angry or unscrupulous caregivers, it is highly problematic for safeguarding activity.

Social workers who are the subject of complaints by caregivers or children and are peremptorily removed from involvement with that family also suffer unduly. When front-line managers act in this way, as in Mrs Singh's case, they imply that the practitioner concerned is, indeed, guilty of discrimination. Such decisions pay little heed to proper procedure or the welfare of the social worker, particularly in relation to self-esteem and stress. For the genuinely anti-racist and anti-sexist social worker, it creates doubt about his or her own attitudes and behaviour, in turn, undermining good practice in the future as he or she becomes inhibited from challenging female or black caregivers. The removal of a social worker in these circumstances also sets up the next practitioner for more of the same treatment from the caregiver, who perceives that a baseless allegation is quickly rewarded. It also undermines safeguarding activity by failing to allow for the fact that the caregiver may be attempting to avoid anxiety caused by the entirely appropriate challenges posed by a self-assured practitioner. Making a complaint may actually be an endeavour by a caregiver to replace one perspicacious social worker with a much less exacting one. The important point here is that both social workers and front-line managers should be alive to the possibility that a complaint can be a weapon for some caregivers in a battle of wills between them and children's services. The serious case review into the death of Ajit recommended that agencies should be 'alert to the potential misuse of complaints as a means of diverting attention away from concerns about children' and concluded that Mrs Singh:

> complained that services were being 'insensitive' or that white workers did not 'understand her culture' and then withdrew from the service or demanded to have the worker changed. These complaints and comments were not valid or justified but professionals and agencies frequently failed to question or challenge these views. Overall professionals attributed too much weight to the mother's ethnicity and religion in explaining her behaviour and insufficient attention to her individual psychology and personal history. They lacked confidence in dealing with a service user from a minority ethnic group. (para 157)

Giving constructive feedback

Mrs Satpal Kaur-Singh frightened most professionals from across a variety of agencies with her explosive anger, verbal aggression and persistent complaints against anyone who challenged her. As a result, many professionals either minimised their interactions with her or muted their criticisms when in her presence. In safeguarding situations where caregivers are engaging in conduct that puts themselves or children at risk, social workers need to assertively: state their view; disagree; offer criticism; give unwelcome news; or communicate unpalatable decisions by professionals to caregivers. Assertively disagreeing means not only stating one's views and explaining how they differ from someone else's, but permitting space for others to also articulate their views. It also entails statements that highlight points of agreement, thus reducing the possibility of the caregiver experiencing the exchange as a personal attack. Approaching conflict in this way ensures that disputed issues are not fudged, information is not lost and ideas are not excluded from discussion.

Criticising the attitudes or behaviour of a caregiver, who could be a foster carer, parent or guardian, may be necessary to effect positive change and reduce risk of harm to a child. However, criticising in a fashion that humiliates, ridicules or insults a caregiver is a form of aggression that concentrates on admonishing a caregiver instead of assisting them to improve their performance. Aggressive forms of criticism rest upon beliefs such as 'I know best' and 'Things are always black and white'. Non-assertive criticism involves: failing to articulate it at all; hinting or vaguely alluding to it; diluting the criticism down so much that it becomes innocuous; or hedging the criticism with apologies. Non-assertive criticisms are underpinned by inhibiting beliefs such as 'The other person will become upset and it is wrong to upset other people' or 'The other person will become angry and it will be my fault'. All criticism should be constructive and focused on improving a caregiver's abilities rather than simply faulting him or her for, say, the inadequate supervision of an infant. To make criticisms in a constructive and assertive way, it is necessary to believe that, as a social worker, you are entitled to require caregivers to improve their performance when the safety of a child is at stake. Constructive criticism should be: very specific; deal with one issue at a time; and focus on observed behaviour, not suppositions about a caregiver's motivation for their actions. It should also be concise and to the point. But it must encourage the caregiver to engage with the criticism and to suggest ways in which they can make positive changes. Social workers should also be open to the possibility that caregivers may have justifiable reasons for their aggressive behaviours, which are related to either the practitioner or children's services. This implies that practitioners must also consider making changes in their behaviour where indicated in order to improve partnership-working with parents and their partners. The problem raised for professionals working with Mrs Singh, was that she wanted changes to their behaviour that increased the risk of harm to her children.

REFLECTIVE EXERCISE ON PROVIDING CRITICAL FEEDBACK

Recall work with a caregiver that required you to provide critical feedback on his or her behaviour that was putting a child at risk of harm. Applying the guidelines on delivering criticism set out earlier and using the DESC technique, write down several different statements constructively criticising the caregiver's behaviours.

Mental health of the mother

It needs to be acknowledged that even the best-framed criticisms can still founder when met by outright opposition and denial from caregivers. Professional interactions with Mrs Satpal Kaur-Singh illustrate precisely this situation. She was utterly intolerant of criticism and reacted aggressively towards those who offered it. There was an emerging pattern of behaviour that led to concerns among professionals from 2000 onwards regarding the mother's mental health. In part, these were occasioned by her innumerable complaints about professionals, which included a number of extreme and unfounded allegations against them, for example, accusing school staff of experimenting on her son. Even more pronounced was her aggressive and verbally abusive behaviour towards all those around her, encompassing professionals, neighbours and members of the public alike. The serious case review identified very many such incidents. In March 2004, a family of Pakistani origin moved to live in the house adjoining Mrs Singh's. This resulted in a series of disputes, involving abusive language and violent behaviour towards her neighbours, which culminated in her conviction for common assault and harassment in June 2005. She was made the subject of an indefinite Restraining Order and Community Punishment Order. Nevertheless, conflict between the mother and her neighbours continued, resulting in further police involvement due to her anti-social behaviour.

All the schools that the children attended reported poor or difficult relations with their mother. In 2005, the head of an infant school came close to banning Mrs Singh from its premises because of her verbally abusive behaviour towards staff and parents alike. During this period, the school made a referral to social care because of concerns about the mother's mental health. The referral achieved little, as Mrs Singh did not accept that she had a mental health problem. In 2007, at the children's primary school, Mrs Singh became involved in a dispute with the head teacher within six weeks of Ajit attending and withdrew him completely from schooling. While Ajit's younger brother continued to attend school, albeit intermittently, staff became unwilling to approach the mother for fear of being verbally abused by her. In March 2009, the head teacher of the primary school attended by Ajit's older brother wrote to Mrs Singh threatening her with police involvement due to her behaviour on the school premises. This included shouting at other parents, using abusive language and gestures, and causing distress to children. The head teacher described the mother's language and behaviour as 'very threatening to parents' (p 28). A neighbour, speaking to a journalist after the trial, characterised Mrs Singh as 'blowing everything out of proportion and not being capable of talking reasonably with anybody' (*The Telegraph*, 2010).

Mrs Singh rejected repeated requests by social workers for her to undergo a mental health assessment. Only in September 2009 did Mrs Singh self-refer to the Mental Health Brief Intervention and Assessment Service, but after a screening interview by telephone, she failed to take up any of the offered services or referrals. At the time, Mrs Singh insisted that she could see no point in availing of support in relation to domestic violence. At trial, she was not diagnosed with any mental illness, although one psychiatrist assessed her as suffering from a 'paranoid personality disorder' (*The Telegraph*, 2010). Evidence received by the serious case review during its deliberations led to the conclusion that she most likely had a personality disorder that, according to the review, constituted 'an enduring impairment of her ability to make and sustain normal relationships' (p 44). To some extent, this would have accounted for her aggressive behaviour towards virtually everyone in her life.

Mrs Singh's unreasonable and contradictory behaviour, her physical aggression, and her often indiscriminate verbal abuse of others, in conjunction with her relentless pursuit of complaints against professionals, led many practitioners to suspect that she had mental health problems. But Mrs Singh refused to acknowledge that she had any mental health problems, instead blaming social workers for her feelings of distress. Without the mother's agreement to a mental health assessment, professionals were unable to establish what her care needs might be or, indeed, the risk she might pose to her children as a result of her state of mind. As the serious case review noted: 'the signs and symptoms were not linked to any obviously recognisable mental illness. No one recognised that the mother might have a personality disorder and the potential impact of this on her ability to parent the children' (p 45). Brandon et al (2009), in their analysis of serious case reviews, concluded that the mental health problems of parents were a contributory factor in the abuse or neglect of a child in a significant number of families.

As already discussed in Chapter Two, there are a number of mental health conditions that increase the risk of aggressive behaviour. In Mrs Singh's case, it seems probable that she had a paranoid personality disorder, which would have made her profoundly distrustful of others. She would have misinterpreted neutral verbal responses as personal attacks or been suspicious of even the benign actions of others. The contentious and highly charged atmosphere created by child protection enquiries and the implementation of a child protection plan would have heightened Mrs Singh's predisposition to suspicion and her tendency to easily take offence. All the evidence from professionals and neighbours points to her being quick-tempered, reacting with disproportionate anger to events and given to recurrent verbally aggressive outbursts. Faced with such deep-seated behaviour, no social worker could have constructively engaged with Mrs Singh. She would not suffer criticism or contemplate change, and it was this trenchant refusal that made her a danger to her children. In such situations, effective partnership-working with caregivers may not be feasible and social workers must deal with regular verbal abuse while they pursue measures to protect children.

Points for practice

- The *aggression scripts* of some caregivers mean that they quickly resort to aggressive behaviour when thwarted in any way. This can result in high levels of anger and aggression being directed at child protection social workers.
- In situations where caregivers lie to social workers, investigative interviewing techniques can assist practitioners to identify and challenge inconsistencies in their assertions. These can also be used to counter disruptive responses by caregivers during interactions.
- Low or non-cooperation, disingenuous negotiation, and overt aggression towards professionals are all means by which some parents, their partners or substitute carers seek to avoid a *demand for work*. These evasions require challenge by social workers.
- Assertive challenges by social workers can be frustrated by the psychosocial games and verbal detours of caregivers. Therefore, practitioners need to be aware of common games and detours and their own susceptibility to collusive game-playing with caregivers.

- The ethos and imperatives of agencies can create role incompatibilities for social workers, which inhibit the use of their authority to *make a demand for work* on parents, their partners or substitute carers.
- Some caregivers can resort to using the complaints procedure to pursue groundless accusations against child protection social workers. Practitioners should be aware of how such complaints affect their practice and discuss any detriment to it with a supervisor.
- A caregiver's mental state may contribute to their feelings of anger and their expressions of aggression. Social workers who think that the aggression of a parent, partner or substitute carer is linked to a mental health problem must pursue this with involved professionals.

CHAPTER EIGHT

Managing conflict with fathers

Conflict with fathers

Much criticism has been directed at the social work profession for failing to engage with fathers or the male partners of mothers in child protection interventions (Featherstone, 2003, 2009; Brown et al, 2009). A number of serious case reviews, including those concerning Baby Peter and the two Doncaster brothers, both analysed in this book, have also identified inadequacies in the approach of practitioners to fathers. As this chapter reveals, there is anxiety attaching to men as fathers, which results in their being largely excluded from child protection work, avoided during interventions or insufficiently challenged. The circumstances surrounding the deaths of Richard Fraser, aged five, in 1974 and Ainlee Labonte, aged two, in 2002 are explored in this chapter through the public inquiry and serious case review, respectively, which investigated failings in the child protection system. Consideration is then given to the skills practitioners need to develop if they are to better work with male caregivers who are aggressive.

Case Study 8.1: Richard Fraser

London Borough of Lambeth (1982) *Richard Fraser: 1972–1977. The report of the independent inquiry*

Richard was born in May 1972 to a mother of Nigerian heritage, aged 17, and a Guyanese father, aged 21. By October of the same year, the health visitor was concerned that Richard was not receiving adequate nurture. He was received into the care of the local authority in November and released back to his parents in April 1973. The mother was known to be regularly physically assaulted by the father. By August 1974, the mother had moved to another area and the father had entirely taken over caring for his son Richard at the Effra Road Reception Centre, where he was joined by his new female partner and her two infants, aged three-and-a-half and four-and-a-half years old, respectively. This meant that two adults and three young children were all living in one room at the Reception Centre. The reconstituted family now became the responsibility of Lambeth Social Services and a social worker was allocated.

In February 1975, the father was sentenced to four months in prison for assault. During this period, Richard was left in the care of his stepmother. At the day nursery that Richard attended, he was discovered to have scratches and bruises, which a paediatric registrar reckoned to be non-accidental. A Place of Safety Order (now called an Emergency Protection Order) was obtained and social workers removed Richard from his home and into temporary residential care. A Care Order was obtained in May 1975, but Richard was immediately permitted home on trial. At a case conference on 1 September 1975 it was known that the father had violently assaulted Richard's stepmother on several occasions. Professionals at this meeting concluded that the stepmother was unfit to care for either her own children or Richard and consideration was given to taking the stepmother's birth children into care. All children were now on the 'At Risk' register.

The stepmother had another child in October 1976 and was again subject to beatings by Richard's father. The family were rehoused in a three-bedroom dwelling in Brixton, with a transfer of responsibility from Lambeth Council to Brixton Council and the appointment of a new social worker in November 1976. In March 1977, Richard was discovered with multiple skin lesions and in June of that year, with a bruise to his arm. No decisive action was taken on either occasion and he remained in the care of his father and stepmother. In June 1977, assessments of the children by an educational psychologist concluded that they were 'grossly retarded' and that Richard was a 'very damaged child' (para 34). A case conference held on 1 July 1977 agreed that the children should remain on the 'At Risk' register. Neither social workers nor health visitors were to see Richard alive again despite attempts to visit him at home. Richard was taken to hospital unconscious and with severe head injuries on 11 September 1977. He was pronounced dead aged just five years old.

The father was given a life sentence for Richard's murder, while his stepmother received a two-year prison term for assault, ill-treatment and neglect.

The threat of violence

Richard's father was known to regularly assault both Richard's mother and, later, his stepmother. He had also physically assaulted a female neighbour during August 1974 as she intervened to prevent him from removing Richard from his birth mother, for which the father was to serve a four-month prison term. In March and April 1975, scratches and cuts to Richard's face were seen by nursery staff and on 21 April, he was taken to hospital by the social worker and examined by a paediatric registrar who concluded that these were non-accidental. As Richard's father was in prison at the time, the conclusion drawn was that the injuries had been inflicted by his stepmother. On 1 May 1975, shortly after the release of the father from prison, he forcibly removed Richard from hospital despite protests by medical staff. When social workers and police sought to enforce a Place of Safety Order (now an Emergency Protection Order) to recover Richard from his home, the father reacted violently, physically injuring a female police officer. This was an assault for which Richard's father was given a further three-month custodial sentence. Nevertheless, when a Care Order was obtained on 28 May

1975, Richard was immediately permitted to return home on trial with his father and stepmother.

A number of physical assaults committed by Richard's father occurred when it appeared that his son was being separated from him, either by the birth mother, hospital staff or police officers. A social interactionist interpretation of the father's behaviour construes it as a form of *instrumental aggression* aimed at rectifying an injustice. On this interpretation of events, the father's behaviour becomes a deliberative strategy to regain custody of his son and enforce a right being violated by others. Individuals who engage in aggressive acts often perceive these to be vindicated by the transgression they think has been committed against them. Felson and Tedeschi (1993, p 3) claim that aggression is constituted 'of punitive actions that attempt to redress some grievance or injustice'. In this instance, the father might have deemed custody of Richard as his inherent right as the child's father. His behaviour is an attempt to restore justice by gaining back his son, whether from the birth mother, the hospital or the police.

The father's behaviour could also have partly been motivated by a desire to shore up his positive self-identity as a caring father or potent man and certainly one able to control events in relation to his son. Richard's father may have felt that he was not being treated with the respect, honesty and fairness due to him. Indeed, as a young black man in his 20s, confronted by predominantly white professionals, he may have sensed or imagined racist attitudes and behaviours, which also led him to react violently in an attempt to reassert a positive notion of his own black identity. Precisely because aggression is an act bound up with maintaining a positive identity, the presence of others during an altercation can increase the likelihood of verbal or physical abuse as the aggressor attempts to save face. In this case, Richard's father was confronted with an audience on each occasion, a neighbour intervened, hospital staff looked on and police officers and social workers subsequently arrived at his home to wrest Richard from him.

According to Tedeschi and Nesler (1993, p 31), once aggrieved, Richard's father had a number of options before him as to how he reacted. These included: doing nothing; forgiving or removing blame from the harm-doer; disputing the harm-doer; or punishing him or her. The father may have initially argued his viewpoint with those trying to remove his son from him. When they refused to give way, it seems that Richard's father quickly chose to resort to punishment in an effort to restore justice. From a social interaction theoretical perspective, the physical assaults perpetrated by the father on neighbours and professionals were extreme coercive strategies aimed at ensuring his son remained with him. Given his frequent physical attacks on both Richard's mother and, later, his stepmother, it is likely that the father had developed a *coercive script*, making him liable to choose physical force over other forms of coercion such as threats or social penalties.

Often, the aggressive acts of caregivers are forms of *proactive aggression* driven by a perception that their rights or accepted social norms are being violated. However, these causes of belligerence do not exclude the possibility that the offensive or violent behaviour of a parent or their partner is also the consequence of being frustrated by social workers or of *displaced aggression* caused by environmental stressors. In the case of Richard Fraser, his father, stepmother and three other children were living in one room at the Effra Road Reception Centre. Overcrowding is known to be a major source of stress and interpersonal aggression. It is perhaps significant that all of the assaults perpetrated by Richard's father against professionals took place while he was living in one room with his family from August 1974 onwards. Only in July 1976 were the family rehoused in a three-bedroom dwelling in Brixton, although, as the independent inquiry pointed out, the dwelling was located in a 'decaying Inner City Area' where many houses were in disrepair and there was a high level of unemployment (paras 41–3). The disadvantaged, and usually poverty-stricken, circumstances of the majority of families who come to the attention of the child protection system are sources of frustration and stress for caregivers. With long waiting lists for social housing, limited employment opportunities and restricted welfare benefits, caregivers unable to change these realities may well displace their aggression onto social workers. It is quite possible that some of the verbal and physical aggression exhibited by Richard's father stemmed from his living conditions and was actually *displaced aggression* redirected at social workers and other professionals. Regardless of the sources of the father's aggressive behaviour, its impact on practitioners seriously undermined their safeguarding activity.

By early 1976, the social worker was making home visits twice a week. This coincided with a period of extremely poor school attendance by the children. At a case conference on 13 April 1976, the social worker explained that she felt 'uneasy because of an atmosphere of antagonism towards her' and 'felt herself to be at risk'. She requested not to work with the family and that the case be transferred, as she was fearful of the parents. However, it was agreed at the meeting that 'she would continue on the case, but would undertake only *low profile* visits of a routine nature'. Yet this reduction in contact with the family occurred at a time when the parents were refusing to ensure that the children attended school regularly. By September 1976, nursery staff at Hill Mead Infant School were reporting that Richard rarely spoke or played with other children, but 'that he ate voraciously'. At the time, the health visitor reported that he appeared thin and quiet (para 22).

In October 1976, when the family was transferred from Lambeth to Brixton Social Services where they had obtained a three-bedroom house on Barnwell Road, the social worker from Lambeth wrote in her final report: 'whoever takes on this case should be aware that there is potential violence especially when pressure on family from other agencies' (para 25). The inquiry concluded that 'during 1976 and through no fault of her own the relationships between this social worker and the family declined alarmingly, and the family's frustrations were vented on her' (para 20). The reduction in the number of social work visits to the home was attributed to the 'aggressive attitude of the parents' by the inquiry. It also highlighted the fact that after the adoption of *low-profile* visiting, the social worker's file records deteriorated from being 'clear, informative and concise' notes to ones that were 'generalised and vague' (para 62). The inquiry could find no discernible reason as to why the social worker at Lambeth experienced such intense antagonism from the parents and noted that she had previously had a good working relationship with them. Indeed, the inquiry praised the social worker, acknowledging that she had 'worked tirelessly for the benefit of Richard, and the improved family life after the move to Barnwell Road was to a large degree the result of her efforts' (para 62). The inquiry also observed that 'on more than one occasion the father had expressed his appreciation of the support she was giving' (para 62). It would appear that, however supportive the social worker was and however good her practice, she was confronted by intimidating behaviour by Richard's father.

The social worker's request to cease work with the family was patently an act of 'flight' designed to remove the stressor constituted by the intimidating behaviour and constant threat of physical violence posed by Richard's father. The multidisciplinary team, rather than develop a 'fight' response, which would have sought to challenge and contain the father's aggressive behaviour, instead colluded with a 'flight' reaction. The social worker in question can hardly be blamed for seeking to avoid the persistent threat of violence emanating from intervention with the family when she was being inadequately supported to deal with it by front-line management and the multidisciplinary team. It is clear from the investigation of the independent inquiry that her practice was extremely good, yet she faced an inexplicable antagonism from the caregivers. Her frequent home visits, perceptive questioning and appropriate challenges may ultimately have been the cause of the father's belligerence towards her.

Aggressive Incident Model

The Aggressive Incident Model, widely used to inform the understanding of violent episodes, comprises five distinct stages with *reactive aggression* only occurring at the final stage of the sequence (Davies and Frude, 2004). This model lacks explanatory power for *proactive aggression*, which is predicated on different intrapersonal and interpersonal interactions. The successive stages leading up to an act of reactive aggression are elucidated in Table 8.1. This model posits that intervention to prevent or reduce the risk of violence can be attempted at any of the five stages.

Once generated, anger is a form of mental and physical energy that needs to be discharged. Often, this is directly through aggression against the person regarded as the cause of the service-user's anger, such as the social worker. Alternatively, it can be displaced onto someone or something else, as when a father or mother hits an infant after a home visit by a practitioner or smashes the windscreen of a social worker's car. However, it can be released safely through a process known as catharsis, for example, hitting a punchbag or finding a private space alone to scream. Anger can also be gradually reduced through a variety of relaxation techniques (Greenberg, 2008). These last two modes of expressing anger rely on some form of training and for a number of caregivers or children, arranging attendance at anger management sessions may be appropriate.

Table 8.1: The five stages of the Aggressive Incident Model

Situation	The trigger for the individual's initial anger, anxiety or fear, which can be associated with environmental stressors, suffering a detriment or a transgression.
	Intervention: knowledge about the service-user in relation to what triggers his or her anger, when and where, alongside any patterns of drug or alcohol use.
Appraisal	The individual's interpretation of the objectionable situation as attributable to a deliberate or unintentional act. This will be influenced by character traits such as a hostile attribution bias and proximate experiences, including the occurrence of other frustrations or stressors at around the time the situation arose.
	Intervention: Identify any misunderstandings, acknowledge any blame, initiate action or offer remedies to resolve the situation. Avoid ambiguous communication, which could be interpreted as hostile.
Anger	If the individual interprets the objectionable situation as due to the intentional or careless behaviour of another person, then he or she will become angry. This emotional state induces physiological arousal and behavioural changes indicating agitation. Unless discharged, this anger is likely to intensify.
	Intervention: Use of empathy to acknowledge the service-user's feelings and perspective and convey that he or she is being listened to and taken seriously.
Inhibition	Individuals are inhibited to a greater or lesser extent from expressing anger through aggressive behaviour by fear of the consequences, their moral values or the desire for social approval. However, inhibition may be selective, with, for example, the individual perhaps resorting to verbal abuse, but not physical assault when angered.
	Intervention: Appeal to the known value base of the service-user, praise positive behaviours in the past or encourage in the present. If indicated, allude to the possible adverse consequences of aggression.
Aggression	Individuals tend to evolve characteristic ways of expressing aggression related to social learning, their beliefs, the intensity of their anger and the opportunity to express aggression that is presented. In sustained social or professional relationships, the mode of aggression may be directed at the vulnerabilities of the individual's partner, child or key worker.
	Intervention: Influence the form of aggressive expression by removing objects that can be used as weapons or removing the person from their proximity.

REFLECTIVE EXERCISE ON MANAGING AN ANGRY PARENT OR THEIR PARTNER

Recall an interaction with a caregiver during which you have felt physically threatened. Consider the five different stages in the Aggression Incident Model and the proposed interventions to try and prevent an angry person progressing to the next stage. How might you have better intervened to reduce the likelihood of the caregiver moving up through the stages to the point of physical violence?

The risk management of aggression

Sometimes, practitioners can be required to work with caregivers or their partners who have a history of violence. Despite good intervention by social workers to reduce the likelihood of anger becoming translated into physical aggression, they can still be at considerable risk of attack from caregivers such as Richard's father. Davies and Frude (2004, p 35) compiled a Risk Assessment Inventory (reproduced in Box 8.1) to assist practitioners to evaluate the level of risk posed to them by a particular service-user. The risk assessment should be completed before the social worker leaves his or her base to encounter the service-user, regardless of whether this is at the office, home or a family centre. The Risk Assessment Inventory is based on an appraisal of risk along three dimensions, comprising: the personal characteristics and circumstances of the service-user; the purpose or task of the practitioner during interaction with him or her; and the setting in which the encounter is to take place.

Box 8.1: Risk Assessment Inventory

The more questions that can be answered 'yes', the more risky we should judge the situation to be.

1. The person
Relatively permanent aspects
- Has the person a previous record of threats, anger or aggression?
- Does the person's physical appearance indicate membership of an intentionally aggressive subgroup?
- Does the person have negative attitudes to our profession?
- Has he or she got unrealistic expectations?

Temporary aspects of the person
- Are they currently agitated or in a bad mood?
- Are they drunk or under the influence of drugs?
- Are they currently in an acute psychiatric condition?
- Are they likely to be carrying a weapon?
- Have they come with a complaint or grudge?
- Are they abusive or threatening?
- Are they feeling 'trapped'?
- Have other people been winding him/her up?

2. The task
- Are we having to give bad news?
- Are we refusing to give something the person wants?
- Is there a mismatch between what is expected and what we can provide?

---

3. The environment/setting
- Are we alone with the person?
- Are our colleagues unaware of the fact that we may be in a particularly threatening situation?
- Are we out of our normal workplace?
- Are there potential weapons around?

Reducing the likelihood of an aggressive incident depends upon the individual practitioner and their organisation adopting a set of precautions. Davies and Frude (2004) identify a variety of safety measures that practitioners should observe in their preparation before and during encounters with service-users. These are each considered in turn, supplemented by advice from Linsley (2006, pp 95–9). However, as the two authors point out, precautions are only effective if an accurate risk assessment has already been completed. Precautions related to interviewing or assessing service-users in the office and at home are also discussed.

Personal precautions

- *Clothes* – Social workers are often intervening with people in low-income groups and wearing designer attire can irritate service-users, as can dressing down, which can convey a lack of respect for them. Revealing clothes worn by female practitioners may be perceived as sexual invitations, as can a male social worker's open shirt. Clothing should also be culturally sensitive. Dressing modestly and blandly is generally prudent. Avoid wearing expensive jewellery, together with necklaces, bracelets or earrings that can be grabbed by a service-user. Long hair should be worn up to prevent it being taken hold of by a violent service-user. Shoes that the social worker can run in are also advisable.
- *Information* – Be as well informed as possible about the service-user before meeting them. This will not only contribute to an accurate risk assessment, but will also reduce irritating the service-user by asking them to repeat information that they have previously shared with other professionals.
- *Workload management* – Social workers should schedule encounters with potentially aggressive service-users at a time when they have the highest energy levels to manage the risk. The temptation is to procrastinate and put off such meetings to later in the day or week and delay unpleasant interactions for as long as possible. Schedule the meeting at a time when the social worker is least likely to be hassled by other calls upon their time. Already stressed social workers are less able to manage the strong emotions and impulses evoked in them by service-users' anger and aggression. Timing the meeting when passers-by will be around, such as at the start or end of the school day, or when the service-user is least likely to have taken substances or alcohol, can also help to reduce risk to the practitioner.
- *Personal alarm* – Personal alarms may be supplied by an employer or carried at the discretion of the individual practitioner. Colleagues need to be made

aware of the sound it makes when set off. These may be affixed in an office, day centre or residential facility, or carried by the individual practitioner. They can be used to distract an aggressive service-user by the social worker throwing it away from themselves, which often leads the aggressive person to focus attention on trying to silence the alarm while the worker escapes.

- *Personal details* – Consider an ex-directory landline to prevent service-users from being able to identify a social worker's home address. Avoid posting any information on social networking sites that could be abused by a service-user to identify personal vulnerabilities or locate the social worker's home and, thus, facilitate aggression.
- *Immunisation* – A practitioner working with high-risk service-users or those who abuse substances may need to ensure that all their vaccinations are up to date to provide protection against infectious diseases. These may be available through the agency.
- *Training opportunities* – These include short courses in: anger management; managing challenging behaviour; first aid; or breakaway techniques that can be deployed if grabbed by a service-user.

Additional precautions for work in offices

1. Do not meet potentially violent service-users when alone in an office suite or building.
2. Ensure the service-user is aware that there are other people in the office.
3. Inform colleagues when about to interview a high-risk service-user.
4. Have an agreed protocol for checking on and coming to the aid of anyone interviewing a high-risk service-user.
5. Minimise waiting time for a high-risk service-user, as this can increase frustration and, thus, his or her irritability. Ensure the service-user is given a full explanation if a delay in seeing them is beyond the control of the practitioner.
6. Prevent interruptions while meeting with the service-user, as this can increase his or her frustration and irritability.
7. Arrange office furniture to ensure that it does not obstruct the practitioner or service-user from leaving the room. The practitioner should take up a position that provides easy access to an exit in case of violence. The service-user should not be between the practitioner and the exit. Ideally, there should be an alarm, telephone or window to another office to make contact with colleagues in an emergency.
8. Remove dangerous objects or anything else that could be used as a weapon or missile, for example, a vase of flowers or a cup of tea.

Additional precautions for home visits

1. When making home visits, practitioners should ensure that colleagues are aware of their whereabouts and the time of their return to the office.

2. Observe any agency checking-in system for home visits at the end of the day.
3. If indicated, negotiate a joint home visit with a colleague to reduce risk, but assign the colleague a purposeful task that facilitates discussion with the service-user.
4. When in the service-user's home, immediately observe where the exits are, plan escape routes and avoid these being cut off by the service-user.
5. If the service-user or other people in the home become angry and cannot be calmed down, a reassessment of the task may be necessary if pursuing it would place the social worker in danger of an attack.
6. Practitioners should aim to park their cars within easy reach of the home and positioned to facilitate a speedy exit.
7. When walking to or while in the home, practitioners can be confronted by unruly or ferocious dogs. It may be sensible to carry a commercially available 'dog repellent'.

Additional precautions if escorting service-users

1. Ensure that the service-user understands the purpose of the journey and travel on main routes that are well populated and lit.
2. If indicated, request another colleague to jointly help to escort the service-user.
3. If escorting a high-risk service-user in a car, ensure that a colleague sits beside them in the back seat.
4. Inform colleagues about any journey involving the escorting of a service-user.

REFLECTIVE EXERCISE ON RISK MANAGEMENT

Recall work with a caregiver who (or whose partner) was known to have engaged in violent behaviour previously. Ask yourself the following questions:

- What risk management strategy or precautions did you adopt?
- Did you feel that this was adequate and, if not, why not?
- Having read the preceding section, how might you improve your risk assessment of a violent incident occurring with a caregiver and how might you reduce the risk in a future encounter?

Organisations and risk management

Evidence from the independent inquiry into Richard Fraser's death indicates that the allocated social worker for Richard received inadequate support and guidance from her agency in relation to potential violence by Richard's father. The response of both the multidisciplinary team and front-line management was to reduce her contact with the father. There is no evidence of effective risk management or engagement with Richard's father about his threatening behaviour towards the social worker. To generalise, Brockman and McLean (2000, p 5), in their review of the research, and a survey of child protection social workers reported by *Community Care* (2011a, pp 4–5) found that the majority of practitioners regard their agencies as unresponsive to problems associated with the aggressive behaviour of caregivers or their partners. This lack of responsiveness encompasses: failure to provide clear protocols for managing risk; poor training opportunities; unsympathetic attitudes; and lack of support for front-line social workers who experience verbal aggression or suffer physical attack from service-users. Based on the feedback from professionals who attend their risk management training courses, Davies and Frude (2004, pp 31–2) speculate on the reasons why this is so. These include denial that there is a problem and a widespread belief that adopting precautions is an admission of failure. This can be compounded by the failure of front-line staff to report incidents of aggression due to fear of being judged incompetent and management expectations that they tolerate aggression as part of the job, as evident in the studies by Brockman and McLean (2000) and *Community Care* (2011a, pp 4–5).

In Britain, the health and safety of social workers, whether in residential, day care or fieldwork settings, is protected by section 2 of the Health and Safety at Work etc Act 1974, which places a legal duty on all employers to design 'safe systems of work' for their employees. The Health and Safety at Work etc Act 1974 obliges employers to conduct risk assessments of the dangers posed to the health and safety of employees and to design procedures and practices that prevent or reduce these risks. They are also responsible for instituting workplace policies for reporting injuries sustained in the course of work and procedures for dealing with serious dangers. These duties are elaborated in *Essentials of health and safety at work*, produced by the Health and Safety Executive (2006), which provides practical guidance to management. The instructions from the Health and Safety Executive (2006, pp 79, 81) to employers regarding safe working and work-related violence, and highlighting the legal obligations of managers towards practitioners, are reproduced in Box 8.2.

Box 8.2: Management obligations towards front-line social workers

Safe systems and procedures

- Make sure employees are well-trained or skilled and understand the hazards and risks of the work they have to do.
- Make sure there are safe systems and procedures for routine work.
- Make sure there are written procedures for work that is done less often or is high in risk.
- Make sure you consider issues such as workload or job design if you want the procedures to be followed properly.
- Do not forget to consider emergencies.
- Supervise to make sure people are actually following the safe systems and procedures, especially for work which is high in risk.
- Take action when instructions, rules or procedures are not being followed.

Violence at work

- Ask your employees whether they ever feel threatened and encourage them to report incidents.
- Keep detailed records, including of verbal abuse and threats.
- Try to predict what might happen – there may be a known pattern of violence linked to certain work situations.
- Train your employees so that they can spot the early signs of aggression and avoid or cope with it.
- Consider physical security measures, for example, video cameras or alarm systems and coded security locks on doors.
- Support victims, for example, with debriefing or specialist counselling and time off work to recover.

REFLECTIVE EXERCISE ON HEALTH AND SAFETY AT WORK

- What systems or procedures does your agency or an agency you have worked for have in place to manage risk and protect the health and safety of social workers in relation to violent caregivers or their partners?
- Do you think these are adequate and, if not, why?
- How might they be improved and how might you bring your suggestions to the attention of your agency?

Non-compliance with school attendance requirement

To return to the events surrounding the death of Richard Fraser, the attendance of all three children at infant schools was poor to the point where, in February 1976, Coldharbour Lane Day Nursery actually discharged the two younger children for scanty attendance. This occurred during a period when the social worker was making home visits twice a week. The situation was discussed at a case conference held on 13 April 1976. The decision was made to reduce social work contact due to parental antagonism and there was little challenge to the parents regarding poor school attendance. Instead, the education welfare service secured two alternative nursery school places for the two children. However, these were not taken up during the summer term and when questioned about this by the social worker, the stepmother replied that the children stayed at home 'so they could play together' (para 20). No further action followed. Richard was enrolled at Hill Mead Infants School in September 1976, but his attendance was extremely irregular. During his first term at the infant school, he attended only 43 out of 99 half-days. In the following spring term, he attended just 20 out of 104 half-days prior to removal from that school mid-term by his father (para 86).

In November 1976, when the case was transferred to a new social worker at Brixton Social Services, school attendance continued to be poor. The new social worker meeting the family on 10 November was more focused on practical issues connected with the repair of the property and the payment of utility bills than school attendance (para 26). Despite the head teacher of Hill Mead Infants School telephoning the social worker to express concern that Richard had only attended 10 out of 70 half-days, the social worker appeared not to have tackled this issue with the father or stepmother. At this stage, the social worker was making home visits once a week, which he reported the family as willing to accept. He accounted for the failure of the parents to send the three children to school as due to two reasons: first, that one school was not prepared to accept Richard's father as the guardian of the stepmother's children; and, second, that the father stated that he was afraid the staff at Hill Mead Infants School would accuse one or other parent of physical abuse because of the marks on Richard's body. The social worker appears to have accepted this explanation at face value.

The inquiry concluded that within a short space of time, the social worker from Brixton Social Services was only visiting monthly, with little sight of or interaction with Richard on the occasions when he did make home visits, which were always by appointment (para 64). According to the inquiry:

> this social worker's prime objective was to maintain good relationships with the family. On occasions he was apparently content to meet the parents in the street, and to accept assurances that Richard and the other children were in good health. (para 65)

The social worker admitted to the inquiry that he experienced 'difficulty in building a relationship' with the parents. This may explain why, according to the inquiry, he tended 'to appear to agree with the parents whenever possible' (para 65). It is likely that the social worker believed that if he assisted the parents, they 'would become more amenable to authority' (para 65). This plainly did not happen. It simply meant that Richard's ongoing poor attendance at nursery school was never effectively tackled with his parents by the social worker. It is, of course, true that Richard was not of statutory school age, but he was on the 'At Risk' register and subject to a Care Order, which made his attendance at an infant school where he would be closely monitored and assessed imperative.

Within the Brandon et al (2009, p 63) taxonomy of family cooperation already detailed in Chapter One, the behaviour of Richard's caregivers would rank as 'not cooperative, actively avoiding involvement/hostile'. Although there was some initial engagement with the school, this quickly tailed off, with Richard being absent from nursery for the vast majority of the time. Brandon et al (2009, p 64) warn against a rigid categorisation of families that fails to allow for the way in which cooperation with children's services may fluctuate over time. The important point is to notice change, recognise when caregivers or children are becoming more or less cooperative, and to modify social work practice accordingly. Little, if any, challenge appeared to have been made to the father and stepmother as Richard's attendance at nursery declined. Quite to the contrary, the explanations of the parents are actually accepted by the social worker, perhaps even espoused by him during supervision and multidisciplinary forums as he adopts the perspective of the caregivers. Here was a new social worker who had taken a handover from the previously allocated one with a file note that read: 'there is potential violence especially when pressure on family from other agencies' (para 25). In the absence of any strategy devised and backed up by his supervisor or the multidisciplinary team, the social worker became essentially an isolated lone worker. As such, he was vulnerable to the reactions occasioned with Stockholm Syndrome, such as compliance with a threatening caregiver, already discussed in relation to hostage theory in Case Study 6.1. This would have led him to comply with the father's requests, such as arranging repairs to the home and assisting with the payment of utility bills. Alongside this demonstration of manifest compliance, the social worker also plainly refrained from challenging the parents over their care of Richard.

The new social worker was trapped in circumstances of immense stress. Faced with the constant threat of violence, unable to 'fight' or escape through 'flight', the new social worker appeased the parents. Rationalising this behaviour to himself and others, he intimated to the independent inquiry that he believed this would make Richard's father amenable to his authority. In fact, it was the social worker who became amenable to the father's authority. Attempts by social workers to ingratiate themselves with caregivers in order to avoid aggressive responses or preserve partnership-working are not unique to the case of Richard Fraser. Ofsted (2010, p 100), in its collation of learning from serious case reviews, alighted on one in particular that:

> gave a revealing explanation of why parents' statements and actions had not been challenged sufficiently often and why, as a result, the abuse had continued over two generations, affecting three children who were now adults and their seven children. The executive summary expressed the view that: 'Professionals worked hard to be accepted by the family and to stay on the right side of them in the belief that only by doing so would they gain access to the children to be able to provide the necessary services to them'.

Egan (1990, p 169) opines that resistance is the caregivers' way of 'fighting back' and is the acting out of opposition to coercion by a professional. It can take the form of sabotaging social work interventions, such as failing to turn up for an appointment or, as in the case of Richard, removing a child from a setting in which he or she can be observed or assessed. Caregivers who are resistant commonly exhibit an unwillingness to establish partnership-working and seek to terminate social work intervention at the earliest opportunity. The temptation, as in Richard's case, can be for practitioners to fabricate partnership-working by avoiding challenges that antagonise the caregiver and might lead to their withdrawal from contact with a service or the practitioner. For many social workers, the prospect of a caregiver refusing to engage with them can of itself be a source of intense stress. As such, it can cause 'flight' from appropriate challenge of the caregiver and contribute to irritability in practitioners, which may manifest in angry or abrasive responses to colleagues and caregivers alike.

REFLECTIVE EXERCISE ON CHALLENGING A CAREGIVER

Recall work with a caregiver you felt intimidated by. Ask yourself the following questions:

- What feelings and thoughts did you have and how did these affect whether you challenged, what you challenged and how assertive these challenges were?
- What questions, requests, critical feedback or challenges do you think you ought to have made but did not?
- What action might you take in the future to assist you to follow through on these with this caregiver or another caregiver who behaves aggressively?

Case Study 8.2: Ainlee Labonte

Newham Area Child Protection Committee (2002) *Ainlee Labonte: Chapter 8 Review*

Dennis Henry, of black British heritage, was in his mid-30s in June 1998 when he first met Leanne Labonte, who, aged 16 years old, already had one infant son. Leanne's baby son was accommodated by the local authority shortly after birth, as he was being left unattended for long periods of time. At the time of embarking on his relationship with Leanne, Dennis Henry was known to be violent. Leanne, like Dennis Henry, was hostile to authority, broke rules and could be aggressive towards people. Not long after starting their relationship, Leanne became pregnant by Dennis. At around the same time, she was undergoing a formal assessment of her parenting skills with the prospect of reuniting her with her infant son, who was on the Child Protection Register for neglect. Dennis joined Leanne at the Amber Project where she had a residential placement with her son and both of them became the subject of a joint parenting assessment. From the outset, Dennis encouraged Leanne's non-cooperation with the assessment and both he and Leanne persistently obstructed access by practitioners to Leanne's son at the Amber Project.

When Ainlee Labonte was born, Dennis and Leanne moved from the Amber Project into a flat, where they continued to prevent social workers or health visitors from assessing the welfare of the two babies by refusing them access to the flat. The Amber Project closed the case as they were unable to pursue an assessment. During this period, Ainlee was admitted to Accident and Emergency with, variously: breathing difficulties; rigid limbs; rashes; and shaking. There was continuing concern about Ainlee's low weight, but she was treated as a 'failure to thrive' infant. Throughout this period, both Dennis and Leanne were aggressive towards professionals, with the result that agencies began to reduce contact with the couple.

The parents continued to miss appointments in connection with their children's health and frequently changed hospitals, GPs, health visitors and their own names, making it difficult to track what was happening to the children. In May 2000, Leanne gave birth to Dennis's second child and refused any further social work contact. Ainlee was found to have a small weight gain and Leanne promised to attend health-related appointments for her children in the future. The case was closed by social services and, thereafter, a few home visits were conducted by social workers in response to concerns expressed by health visitors. The police were called to the flat several times due to domestic disturbances but there was minimal interaction with the children on these occasions and there were no further visits by social workers or health professionals in the six weeks prior to Ainlee's death. On 7 January 2002, paramedics arrived at the flat after a phone call from the couple to find Ainlee already dead. She was aged two years old and at post-mortem was found to be half the normal weight for her age and covered in 64 scars, scabs and bruises caused by scalding, burning and pinching.

In 2002, the Crown Count found Dennis Henry and Leanne Labonte guilty of cruelty to Ainlee and of her manslaughter. Dennis Henry was given a 12-year custodial sentence for manslaughter to run concurrently with a nine-year sentence for cruelty. Leanne Labonte was handed a 10-year jail term for manslaughter to run concurrently with an eight-year custodial sentence for cruelty.

Verbal aggression and physical violence

When Dennis Henry met Leanne for the first time, he already had convictions for acts of criminal damage, causing actual bodily harm and carrying a bladed weapon. His criminal record was known to social services at an early stage in his relationship with Leanne. He was also a drug-user. Concomitantly, Leanne came from a background of domestic violence and had a history of non–cooperation and hostility, which appeared to be exacerbated by Dennis's presence in her life. The couple were verbally aggressive towards all professional staff and physically aggressive towards a number of them. In a defensive response, agencies limited their contact with the couple. Housing officers and health visitors refused to make home visits due to intimidation and fears for their personal safety. Hospital-based professionals would only meet with the couple if accompanied by another member of staff. Health clinic staff were abused and threatened by the couple, and one health visitor was assaulted at the clinic by Leanne. Both Dennis and Leanne were banned from the offices of the housing department due to their aggressive and violent behaviour (p 10). A doctor making home visits to the couple's flat was given police protection on each occasion due to the threat of violence from them (p 16).

At one hospital, Dennis and Leanne snatched notes about Ainlee from the consultant and later stole other medical records relating to Ainlee's 'failure to thrive'. Dennis was removed from a GP's list for abusive behaviour and Leanne physically assaulted another patient at a surgery (pp 14, 16). When a series of child protection conferences were held to consider the situation, Dennis and Leanne subsequently confronted individual professionals about their contributions to these meetings (p 11). Throughout, police were frequently called by Leanne to attend incidents of domestic violence at the couple's flat, but after initial intervention, she quickly rejected any further assistance and, consequently, charges were not pressed against Dennis Henry. Neighbours also complained to the housing authority and police about the aggressive behaviour exhibited by Dennis and Leanne (pp 11, 14). Indeed, in their evidence to the review, the police described Dennis and Leanne as 'a violent, aggressive, obstructive, devious and dishonest couple' (p 22).

The constant violence and aggression exhibited by Dennis and Leanne culminated in the withdrawal of multiple agencies from engagement with the couple. Even when professionals no longer visited the home for reasons of personal safety, meetings with the couple at clinics, surgeries, hospitals or departmental offices proved to be forums where Dennis and Leanne still abused or assaulted staff. The feelings of fear and intimidation were widespread among professionals who came into contact with the couple and led to distortions of their practice. Health visitors became understandably worried for their own physical safety and stopped visiting the flat, although they knew that there were developmental and health concerns about Ainlee and the other children. Disputes arose between agencies as to who was responsible for working with this dangerous family. For instance, when Leanne failed to take Ainlee for a developmental check-up in October 2001, the health visitor refused to make a home visit and insisted during her discussion with the duty social worker that, given the circumstances, this was a social work task. The duty social worker proposed a joint visit, although this never actually took place.

Accounting for the reactions of professionals, the Chapter 8 Review (now known as a Serious Case Review) conjectured that 'this couple became so powerful through their manipulation, aggression and refusal to co-operate that the focus on the needs of the children became lost' (p 20). Dennis and Leanne were extremely manipulative. They freely approached health professionals, social workers and housing officers when seeking to further their own desire to be rehoused, while simultaneously blocking access to their children or thwarting discussion about them by those same professionals (p 22). Often, their aggressive behaviour towards social workers, health visitors and doctors took the focus away from the children and onto the parents, as professionals struggled to cope with the couple's uncooperative and threatening behaviour (p 23). Dennis and Leanne successfully diverted attention away from their children, as professionals found their energies absorbed in trying to physically protect themselves while struggling with the couple's non-compliance.

Leanne was a victim of domestic violence both in her childhood and, as a teenager still in her formative years, when she met Dennis Henry, who assaulted both her and others. These experiences probably led Leanne to model her behaviour on the aggression she witnessed around her. As she observed verbal and physical aggression being rewarded by other people's compliance, over time she acquired an *aggressive script*, which normalised her precipitous resort to aggression when faced with even minor frustrations of her goals. It is also probable that she grew up in a household where alternative approaches to conflict were rarely used. She may have developed a skills deficit characterised by poor information exchange abilities, inadequate behaviour management and unfamiliarity with problem-solving techniques for conflict resolution. These skills deficits would have considerably undermined her ability to draw on a repertoire of pro-social behaviours to assist her in coping with disagreement. Given her grossly limited range of potential responses to conflict, much of Leanne's reaction was confined to verbal and physical aggression. As a young person frequently subjected to abuse, Leanne was more liable than most to attribute hostile intentions to those around her. This *hostile attribution bias* would have led her to interpret the innocuous responses of social workers as antagonistic, and to construe expressed professional concern about her care of Ainlee as a malicious attack. The high levels of anger Leanne felt most likely impaired her ability to process social information, leaving her to alight upon imagined slights and criticisms while ignoring kindness and conciliatory responses.

Dennis Henry abused drugs and, although these are not specified in the Chapter 8 Review, it is probable that, in common with many users, he took several different substances. Research indicates that combinations of drugs elevate aggressive behaviour by addicts beyond that of those engaged in mono-drug usage. The domestic violence between Dennis Henry and Leanne may have related to arguments over the acquisition of drugs or were caused by his irritability during periods of withdrawal or craving for another fix. His aggression towards professionals was at least in part attributable to the psychopharmacological effects of the drugs he was taking. As studies of substance users reveal, these effects include impairment of cognitive processes, which result in a greater *hostile attribution bias*. Intoxication with drugs is known to break down normal inhibitions around displays of aggression based on fear of ostracism or punishment. Doubtless the causes of Dennis Henry's aggression were multiple, but they were also associated with his drug habit.

Both Dennis and Leanne engaged in verbal and physical aggression towards professionals, neighbours, each other and, ultimately, their child. There appears to be little differentiation in the types of behaviour either of them exhibited in this respect. While research on gender differences in the expression of aggression by males and females consistently shows that men tend to express this more directly and physically than women, these findings need to be set against those from studies on individual differences. Gender is only one dimension in accounting for how people express aggression. Most men and women do not verbally abuse and attack others. While gendered expectations of how Leanne should behave as a female may have led to some repression of aggressive impulses, her individual biography of domestic violence as a child and adult, together with her male partner's approval and encouragement of her violent behaviour, are also salient factors. Likewise, Dennis was a drug-user and while men are more predisposed than women to use physical forms of aggression, most men do not assault others. Dennis did, not because he was a man, but because of the conjunction of drug use and masculine gender roles, which reward demonstrations of physical strength. The *hostile attribution biases* and *aggressive scripts* that Dennis and Leanne developed reflect individual differences, which interact with gender differences in the expression of aggression. Neither parent evidenced control of their aggressive impulses and seemed to lack the fear of social disapproval, rejection and retaliation that commonly restrains violent acts in most others. This made them unpredictable, volatile and physically dangerous people to work with.

Dealing with verbal aggression

Verbal aggression refers to comments, sometimes accompanied by gestures, designed to frighten, offend, hurt or provoke a fight with the social worker. Some caregivers may not be fully aware that they are engaging in these behaviours and may need it brought to their attention. Others are only occasionally verbally aggressive and this conveys important information about their state of mind. Not every instance of verbal abuse should be addressed. Sometimes, trying to deal with it becomes a distraction from a crucial discussion with a parent about a child at risk of significant harm. Nevertheless, as the case studies in this chapter testify, verbal aggression can have a devastating impact on good practice in child protection and the well-being of practitioners. Therefore, it needs to be assertively confronted. This means first recognising the different forms that verbal aggression can take. These are outlined in the Box 8.3.

Box 8.3: Common forms of verbal aggression

- Personal attacks, consisting of negative stereotyping, derogatory generalisations about the practitioner, disparaging remarks, questioning of professional competence or criticism of values and beliefs.
- Accusations of telling lies or insinuations that the social worker holds ulterior motives or is acting unprofessionally.
- Harassing the social worker, which includes repeatedly demanding material or financial assistance or that particular actions are executed, or nagging a social worker continuously about a matter already in hand.
- Being patronising, using sarcasm or describing the social worker's actions and decisions in very emotive language.
- Dismissing the perspective of the social worker.
- Constantly interrupting, frequently shouting or talking over the social worker.
- Blaming the social worker for circumstances and outcomes that are consequences of the caregivers' behaviour.

> • Using threats in order to coerce the social worker, such as to: withdraw cooperation; prevent access to children; complain to management; contact the newspapers; or instigate a physical attack on the social worker, their family or property.

Social workers confronted by any of these verbally aggressive behaviours need to develop effective ways of responding that do not: undermine the possibility of partnership-working; permit the caregiver to continue being abusive; or misuse the social worker's power to punish a caregiver. Individuals often experience emotional and psychological blocks to responding assertively when confronted by verbal aggression. For this reason, it is imperative that social workers examine the emotions that particular kinds of verbal abuse have on them. An unscrupulous caregiver who identifies the vulnerabilities of a practitioner is likely to exploit that information. Social workers who fail to acknowledge the extent to which a sexist or racist comment angers them are liable to act out their annoyance with the caregiver through an aggressive retort. If confronted by a parent who calls into question their professional competence, social workers uncertain of their abilities may feel foolish or embarrassed, leading to a non-assertive reply. When evoked in practitioners, strong emotion often clouds judgement and blocks effective responses to caregiver aggression. As already explored in Case Studies 4.1 and 5.1, personal beliefs also interfere with assertive interactions with others, and social workers need to reflect on these and how they hamper their verbal interactions with caregivers, children and colleagues. The primary aim of an assertive response by the social worker should be to defuse aggression, create assertive–assertive interactions between themselves and caregivers, and move towards the explicit discussion of disagreements.

Developing personal beliefs that facilitate a sound inner dialogue enabling assertive responses is a prerequisite for apt responses to verbal aggression. So, as previously examined in Chapter Four, a belief such as 'I am in control, I can choose how to behave' supports a confident inner dialogue such as 'I know Mr Smith is trying to draw me into an argument, but I'm not going to be wound up by him or distracted from addressing the harsh punishments he metes out to his son'. Conversely, a social worker lacking in self-esteem might hold a belief such as 'Other people will not like me if I say what I think', making them liable to sustain an inner dialogue along the lines of 'Mr Smith will become even more aggressive if I challenge his behaviour and I need to keep him on board'. Finally, practitioner beliefs such as 'I must give as good as I get' facilitate inner dialogues such as 'I'll show Mr Smith he can't insult me and get away with it'. Social workers need to examine their emotions, beliefs and the different dialogues that run through their minds when confronted by a variety of verbally aggressive statements by caregivers. They need to reflect on what their vulnerabilities are and what kinds of verbal abuse are likely to upset, frighten or anger them. Back and Back (2005, p 144) advise that when confronted by a verbally aggressive statement, individuals should follow the ensuing six steps adapted for social workers and employ the forms of assertion that have already been explained in Chapter Four:

1. Take a breath and get a sound inner dialogue before responding – Often verbal aggression can be unexpected and can catch a social worker entirely off-guard. Pausing before replying gains time to both recover composure and buy some thinking time to formulate an assertive response.
2. *Responsive assertion* asking for clarification – People who are angry can be muddled in their expression or speak very fast and it is important to understand what the issue is for them. Asking for information at this point conveys attention to the issue that is prompting their aggression. Speaking calmly and with good pacing can help to reduce the building tension. It may be necessary to permit the caregiver to vent emotion before replying at this point.
3. *Basic* and *responsive assertion* or *discrepancy assertion* if the aggression is maintained – At this point, the social worker can continue to explore the caregiver's feelings and viewpoint, but he or she needs to articulate the social worker's perspective. The response at this point conveys both continued interest in the caregiver's feelings and opinions, but makes explicit the differences that exist between the two parties.
4. *Basic assertion* or *discrepancy assertion* can be repeated if aggression is maintained – This should not be merely a repetition of the social worker's statements during Step 3, but should provide added emphasis to his or her rights, feelings or opinions. However, it should acknowledge and reflect any new relevant information provided by the caregiver in reply to the social worker's *responsive assertions*. Speaking slowly in a calm deliberative tone of voice, with emphasis on key words and using brief, to-the-point sentences, is important during this step.
5. *Negative feelings assertion* and/or a *consequence assertion* if aggression is maintained – A social worker still on the receiving end of verbal aggression from a caregiver may start to experience strong feelings of anxiety or anger and it can be important to make the caregiver aware of the hurt or offence their behaviour is causing. It may also be necessary to state a negative consequence if the caregiver continues to be abusive. This should be done in a neutral tone and without rancour.
6. Cut off interaction by meeting again latter or returning to the issue that sparked aggression at a later point in the discussion, or examine the underlying processes leading to the verbal aggression – Time out may assist the caregiver to calm down or consider the adverse consequences of continuing with their verbally aggressive behaviour. It can also de-escalate the rising tension between the social worker and caregiver as they both become increasingly influenced by strong emotion. A shift away from dealing with a particular aggressive comment to examining the underlying issues precipitating the aggression may also be a productive approach.

Later steps in this sequence are only completed if the verbal aggression continues. Social workers who complete all the steps without any abatement of the aggression may be stymied from progressing child protection activities, as occurred in the case of Dennis and Leanne. If this happens, social workers should bring the matter to the attention of their supervisor or front-line manager and possibly the multidisciplinary team. This provides an opportunity for a supervisor or line manager to help the social worker consider whether her response to the verbal aggression could be improved upon or whether the sustained verbal abuse of the caregiver is indicative of a refusal to engage with child protection concerns and is evidence of increased risk to a child. The following example employs this six-step approach to dealing with verbal aggression from a parent who repeatedly shouts 'You're complete bloody rubbish, you never bloody listen, the last social worker was far better' at you:

1. Inner dialogue: 'I can learn from feedback. I can stay calm when provoked', pause for a count of five.
2. 'Can you explain what you mean by that?'
3. 'I have listened to your view on this. What makes you think that I have not?'
4. 'You say that I never listen, but last week you thanked me for arranging a playgroup placement for your son.'
5. 'I feel annoyed when you accuse me of not listening to you. When you are rude to me I find it difficult to concentrate on what you are saying.' Alternatively: 'If you do not stop insulting me, I will have to discuss your behaviour with my manager, as it is making it hard for us to work together on this problem.'
6. 'I think it is better for us to leave this matter for now and to return to it later.' Alternatively: 'I notice that you get angry each time I bring up the subject of your son's father, can you please tell me why this upsets you?'

REFLECTIVE EXERCISE ON RESPONDING TO VERBAL AGGRESSION

Recall a specific interaction with a caregiver when he or she behaved aggressively towards you and about which you feel dissatisfaction in relation to your own responses. Drawing on the guidance set out earlier, consider how you might improve on your responses to the verbal aggression of this caregiver. Try out your improved revised responses the next time this or another caregiver is verbally aggressive towards you.

Preventing access to children

Throughout the period of Ainlee's short life, Dennis Henry and Leanne failed to attend numerous health-related appointments for their children, were aggressive towards professionals and actively prevented social workers and health visitors from seeing or assessing any of the children. As early as the Amber Project's assessment of the couple's parenting skills in April 1999, Dennis had refused entry to a social worker who sought access to Leanne's child at their residential placement. At the time, Dennis alleged 'that social services did nothing for them and they did not need to co-operate' (p 28). The review found that, around this time, out of 10 home visits made by professionals over a 12-day period, only one was successful in gaining admission to the couple's home (p 29). The Amber Project soon closed the case on the grounds that it was unworkable and they were unable to proceed with an assessment of the couple's parenting skills. Thereafter, Dennis and Leanne moved to their recently allocated flat with two babies, even though Leanne's son was placed on the Child Protection Register. The review was to conclude that 'the assessment was incomplete because of the failure of Leanne and Dennis to co-operate. The boundaries were not enforced nor were the couple confronted with their behaviour' (p 19).

Even on those few occasions when social workers did manage to gain access to the couple's flat, their interaction with the children was usually fleeting or curtailed. For instance, in 2001, a health visitor expressed concern to social services that the parents were refusing to have their children immunised and denying her access to them. A duty social worker then made a home visit and saw all the children asleep. In August 2001, a social worker made another home visit to assess the family's needs. The discussion with the parents focused on support networks, respite for the child and the state of repair of the dwelling. In other words, the interaction was firmly focused on practical matters of interest to the parents, who were seeking to be rehoused at the time. Throughout this home visit, the children were in another room. The social worker then asked to see the children and was shown Ainlee and her older brother in their bedroom. However, Ainlee was strapped into a high chair that was facing the wall and no eye contact was made with her and her condition could not be gauged. The social worker was told by the couple that Ainlee was being punished because she 'kept flicking food around' (p 33). The visit was intended to assess the children's needs, but it appeared that direct work with the children was either not attempted or not permitted (p 34). In effect, as the Chapter 8 Review was to conclude, 'the fear with which the family are regarded leads to almost paralysis in terms of action. The theory being that there are social work visits and the children are "seen but not engaged"' (p 18). As the pathology report later revealed, most of Ainlee's injuries would have been hidden from sight by her clothing (p 23). This meant that discovering any of her injuries would have necessitated some degree of physical engagement with her. Reflecting on why social workers failed to interact with children at risk of significant harm during family visits in a string of serious case reviews, Brandon et al (2009, p 44) speculate:

> Where families are hostile or hard to engage practitioners can have low expectations of what can be achieved. Sometimes just getting through the door feels like a major achievement and there is little energy left to use the time with the child or family productively. From

the family's point of view, there may be similar low expectations and lack of trust with most agencies. This issue has to be addressed jointly by the professionals working with the family.

Intimate child protection practice

Ferguson (2011) examines what he terms 'intimate child protection practice', which focuses on the moment-to-moment experiencing of social workers as they: travel to an address; negotiate entry; walk around the rooms of a home; interact with parents and children during their visit; and journey back to the office. Dennis and Leanne repeatedly prevented social workers and other professionals from entering their home, and Ferguson (2011, pp 47–51) describes the doorstep conflicts that often arise as social workers endeavour to gain permission to enter the homes of caregivers to assess the circumstances of their children. The doorstep is the demarcation that separates off private and public space and is a major site of interaction between parents or their partners and social workers. It is also a place of transition from a public area into a private one and, as such, a place of normlessness and uncertainty (Ferguson, 2011, p 49). This can cause social workers to feel unsure of their professional right to insist on entry or, indeed, to what extent they should persist in attempts to gain permission to enter the family's dwelling.

The necessary violation of the social norms that make family life a private affair is a further inhibitor for practitioners made to wait on the doorstep by resistant parents. For many social workers, whose training and codes of practice demand that they respect the rights, feelings and perspectives of service-users, trying to enter the home of resistant parents may be experienced as deeply counterintuitive and uncomfortable. Struggling with this apparent *role incompatibility* can be a significant source of stress. When caregivers are intimidating or physically aggressive, as in the case of Dennis and Leanne, this can compound the inhibition or hesitation a practitioner already feels about pressing for access to the home. The blend of emotions and cognitions evoked by confusion over professional rights, inhibitions surrounding the breach of social norms, hesitancy to contradict parental views or contravene parental wishes, fear of aggression from caregivers, and the sheer stress of engaging in conflict evidence the huge inner and outer barriers social workers must overcome simply to get over the threshold into a hallway. Dennis and Leanne consistently used aggressive doorstep encounters with professionals to deny them access to their home. Confronted by intimidation and beset by inhibition, social workers' self-assertion was most likely compromised, resulting in many calls being made to the couple's address, but few resulting in actual home visits. The serious case review states that the couple were not challenged over their behaviour. It may be that professionals, concerned for their personal safety, found it too dangerous to effectively confront these highly aggressive parents.

Once inside the home, practitioners are in a space controlled and presented by the caregivers. As respectful professionals, mindful of the rights, feelings and perspective of resistant or reluctant parents, practitioners may continue to experience inhibition. Sometimes, like those who encountered Dennis and Leanne, they may also be subject to continuing intimidation. Ferguson (2011) examines how social workers move around the home after they have gained access. He describes the ability of caregivers to conceal children's injuries by choosing their clothes or how they are positioned in a room or by blocking the social worker's access to interaction with them. A parent may permit the practitioner to have sight of the child in the bedroom, but actually be standing in the doorway barring the way into the child's room. A dog penned up in another room of the dwelling may actually be a ploy by the parent to impede a practitioner's access to that room. Indeed, an unruly or fierce dog running free in a living room can effectively confine a social worker to a couch and make them dependent on close escort around the dwelling by the caregiver. It is often crucial for a social worker to check the condition of a child's bedroom, to speak to the child alone or to touch him or her in the course of assessing his or her well-being. All of these activities require movement from one place to another within the home and proximity to the child. In reality, such movements are actually mediated by the ability of caregivers to restrict the mobility of social workers within their home, while the personal anxieties of practitioners can act to cause further forms of immobility (Ferguson, 2011, p 62).

When social workers do manage to gain access to Dennis and Leanne's home, they *see*, but do not *engage* with, the children. A duty social worker *sees* the children asleep. Another social worker who visits with the purpose of assessing the children's needs actually spends the whole time discussing only practical matters relating to building repairs and rehousing with the parents. On asking to meet the children, the social worker is shown them from the bedroom door and *sees* no more than Ainlee's back. These all appear to be examples of immobility, of inhibited or blocked motion. If these social workers had already encountered considerable opposition and intimidation on the doorstep from the parents, by the time they actually entered the home they may well have been in a state of heightened stress and fearful of precipitating violence from one or other of the parents. Perhaps *seeing* the child was the most these social workers thought they could obtain permission for without abruptly being told to leave the house or incurring verbal abuse or physical attack. Possibly, just getting into the house had exhausted their reserves of energy to cope with yet further confrontation. Maybe they self-censured, immobilising themselves, by not walking into the bedroom and moving towards Ainlee for fear of triggering another episode of threatening behaviour from Dennis and Leanne. Perhaps, as Ferguson (2011, pp 103–10) contends, their movement was impaired by inner constraints, which rendered them, like many other social workers, afraid to touch children for fear of: an accusation of abuse; attracting a complaint from a parent; or contravening a social prohibition on touching other people's children.

In some contexts, intimate child protection practice can be a fearful and anxiety-provoking experience. These overwhelming emotions can cause social workers to engage in 'flight' responses from sources of stress. In Case Study 8.1, these were acted out by avoiding discussion with parents about child protection concerns and, instead, focusing on their own needs and priorities for rehousing. It was also evident in the willingness of the social workers to acquiesce to the limited view they were permitted of the children and in a failure to either move towards the child to engage in interaction or to ask for explicit permission from Dennis or Leanne to touch the child. The hazard created by these forms of 'flight' is that the degree of acknowledgement by parents of a problem, their motivation to make positive changes or the measure of cooperation forthcoming from them is never properly tested. This means that accurate information is not gained and fed back into the child protection process.

Caregivers can justifiably feel reticent about permitting professionals to interact with their children, as it can be experienced as intrusive or infringing their parental rights. Such initial opposition demands sensitive negotiation by practitioners. But implacable opposition should raise child protection concerns. Identifying blatant obstruction can only occur if social workers engage in attempts to access different rooms and speak to or touch children in the first instance. Self-censorship, which causes practitioners to confine themselves to safe practical issues in conversation with parents, to discuss parent-centred rather than child-centred priorities and not ask to see other rooms in the house or request interaction with a child, generates no information. It is no coincidence that the serious case review sums up professional behaviour in relation to Dennis and Leanne as 'paralysis in terms of action'. Social workers lacking in self-assertion, inhibited by social norms, confused by apparent *role incompatibilities* and scared by the aggression of caregivers, are, indeed, paralysed if they fail to: walk into a kitchen to check food cupboards; enter a bedroom; amble towards a youngster in the lounge; or reach out to touch a child.

Dennis and Leanne were exceptional in their verbal and physical aggression towards professionals. Their threatened or actual violence was a prime factor in preventing social work access to Ainlee. However, as Ferguson (2011, pp 168–9) points out, resistant caregivers can engage in *passive-aggressive* behaviours, which while not overtly intimidating, can nevertheless convey hostile subliminal messages. These inhibit social workers from asking challenging questions, moving into other rooms of the house or interacting with a child just a metre away from them. A father who arranges to be out of his flat for pre-announced home visits shortly after a social worker has spoken to him about his inadequate care of a child is probably acting out anger and indignation through refusing entry to the practitioner. This may inhibit the practitioner from challenging the father in future interactions, as partnership-working with parents and professional competence are premised on maintaining contact and building a relationship. Recently qualified or unconfident social workers may feel reliant on the goodwill of caregivers to permit home visits or allow access to children in order to demonstrate their professional competence to themselves and front-line managers. Like overtly aggressive behaviour, *passive-aggressive* responses by caregivers can have a devastating impact on practice, unless social workers are alert to the coercive pressures being brought to bear upon them by parents or their partners and take note of the information this conveys about the safety of children.

REFLECTIVE EXERCISE ON EXPERIENCES OF ANXIETY

- What sort of interactions with caregivers makes you feel anxious?
- Which social work tasks make you feel most anxious?
- How do you manage your feelings of anxiety?
- How does your anxiety affect your interactions with caregivers or how you perform social work tasks in relation to child protection?
- Do any of your ways of reacting to or managing anxiety hinder good practice and, if so, how?

Anxiety management

The fear, worry and dread that caregivers such as Dennis Henry and Leanne Labonte evoke in social workers can be extreme and, as the inquiry in relation to them illustrates, these feelings can greatly hinder good practice. The behaviour of caregivers does not have to be as extreme and violent as that of Dennis and Leanne to elicit intense feelings of apprehension. As Ferguson (2011) indicates, anxiety pervades child protection practice as social workers knock on the door of a previously unknown family or attend a difficult multidisciplinary meeting. Such feelings have to be successfully managed by social workers if they are to overcome their own inhibitions to pursue searching enquiries and offer appropriate challenges in relation to caregivers. Anxiety has been defined as 'a subjective feeling of tension, apprehension, nervousness, and worry accompanied by activation or arousal of the autonomic nervous system' (Greenberg, 2008, p 131). Anxiety can be triggered by particular people, places, tasks or events, either in anticipation of the happening or as it occurs. It can take the form of mild unease or an intense sense of dread and trepidation.

For some individuals, even contemplating an upcoming interaction or situation can induce anxiety or a panic attack. People who feel anxious about a happening tend to ruminate on it and are often preoccupied by thoughts related to past, present and future associations with that person or situation. These thoughts further intensify the feelings of anxiety. They can escalate into *catastrophising*, a well-recognised psychological response to a perceived threat or challenge in which the individual predicts the worst-possible outcome, immobilising them from taking any action or engendering avoidance strategies. Thought processes associated with anxiety states act to amplify feelings of stress and fear, sometimes precipitating irritability, which is, of course, a common symptom of stress. Loss of concentration or inability to concentrate and forgetfulness are also typical during anxiety states. Physiological arousal accompanies these cognitive and affective changes, as the body prepares itself for a 'fight' or 'flight' response to a perceived threat.

Anxiety management techniques aim to break the vicious cycle created by interrelated thoughts, feelings, physical symptoms and avoidance behaviour. Social workers need to take care of their longer-term welfare by giving consideration to lifestyle choices such as alcohol consumption or late nights, which can play into anxiety states. Outside of this, practitioners should develop a set of techniques that can variously be deployed as they are confronted by uncooperative, avoidant, hostile or aggressive behaviour: in their office; in their car; on a train or bus journey; walking to a venue to meet family members; as they stand on the doorstep of a dwelling; and during actual interactions with caregivers, their partners and children. There are innumerable self-help guides available, offering advice and promoting a range of anxiety management strategies (see the Appendix). Social workers need to take responsibility for learning about some of these techniques and integrating them into their day-to-day practice.

REFLECTIVE EXERCISE ON MANAGING ANXIETY

How do you typically manage anxiety in your work with caregivers? Read a self-help guide on anxiety management and identify what practical steps you can take to improve your management of anxiety in child protection work.

Points for practice

- Verbal and physical aggression or threats of assault by caregivers can undermine good practice by making social workers hesitant to challenge parents or their partners. Practitioners may become susceptible to compliant behaviours in relation to caregivers.
- A small minority of fathers and mothers or their partners may physically threaten or attack social workers involved in child protection activities. Where there is a history or potential for violence from family members, risk assessment and risk management is vital.
- Familiarity with anger de-escalation techniques is essential for social workers operating in the emotionally charged context of child protection with families. Without intervention, feelings of anger can quickly escalate into aggressive behaviour.
- Some agencies may be reluctant to admit that aggressive behaviour by some service-users is a problem and social workers may need to remind management of their own legal rights and the obligations of employers under health and safety legislation in these instances.
- Social workers need to respond assertively to verbal aggression by parents or their partners in an endeavour to achieve assertive–assertive interactions with them and to build partnership-working.

- Some caregivers use highly aggressive behaviour to discourage or obstruct social workers from accessing children. Practitioners may feel intimidated or exhausted by these tactics and fail to engage with children at risk. Such situations require the active involvement of line management and the multidisciplinary team.
- Child protection social workers routinely confront a myriad of anxiety-provoking circumstances and they need to learn and practise anxiety management techniques in order to effectively intervene where children are at risk of significant harm.

CHAPTER NINE

Managing conflict with children

Conflict with children

Serious case reviews and inquiry reports commonly focus on incidences where non–cooperation or intimidation by caregivers or their partners has resulted in social workers and allied professionals withdrawing from the family or failing to offer sufficient challenge to parents. Practitioners can also find themselves in conflict with children as they endeavour to protect them from harm or care for them within foster or residential placements away from their family. It can be difficult for practitioners to admit to their own anxieties or lack of expertise in work with children who have been traumatised by abusive experiences, are uncooperative and present with a range of challenging behaviours. In this chapter, the serious case review investigating the assault on other children by two young brothers and a public inquiry into the use of a punitive form of behaviour modification at a number of children's homes are analysed to expose the complexity of the interaction of fear and anger that social workers experience. Such fear and anger can sometimes be acted out to the detriment of their professional relationships with children.

Case Study 9.1: Doncaster brothers

Doncaster Local Safeguarding Board (2009, 2010) *Serious case review 'J' Children*

A large white British family of seven children aged between nine and 19 lived with their mother and father in a suburb of Doncaster. The police were regularly called to the house in connection with domestic violence or incidents of anti-social behaviour. Neighbours and friends repeatedly contacted Doncaster Children's Social Care Services to express concerns about the children's care and behaviour. Social workers were aware that the father drank heavily and was violent, while the mother, who abused drugs, suffered from depression. Although the family had first come to the attention of social services in 1995, and despite repeated referrals from multiple agencies, there was virtually no engagement by Doncaster Children's Social Care Services until an initial child protection conference in early 2009. Two of the younger brothers became notorious in the locality for their acts of vandalism, harassment and verbal abuse of neighbours and passers-by. In 2006, at the age of eight, one of the brothers threatened a member of staff at his school with a baseball bat, which resulted in his exclusion. Although there was a multiagency meeting after this incident, which included education and children's services, no further action was taken. Subsequently, alternative arrangements for his education were not effectively implemented or monitored. In 2007, the brothers were suspected of involvement in arson and killing ducks at a park, but no action was taken. By late 2008, the brothers were evidencing an escalating pattern of aggressive behaviour, which included violence towards adults and children alike. They were described by neighbours as out of control. At the beginning of 2009, both were made the subject of a child protection plan and placed on the Child Protection Register.

In early 2009, within months of the father leaving the home, the mother contacted children's social care services and asked for the two brothers to be accommodated by the local authority as she felt unable to cope with their behaviour. In March 2009, the two brothers, then aged 10 and 11 years old, were moved into foster care with a couple who lived in a village near Doncaster. Within two weeks of this placement, the brothers had physically assaulted an 11-year-old boy in a 20-minute attack that was only curtailed by the intervention of a passer-by, by which stage the boys had punched, kicked and stamped on their victim. The incident was reported to the police and they were due to be interviewed about the matter a week later on 4 April. On that date, the two brothers did not report to the local police station for the interview, but were instead involved in a second attack. The brothers lured two other boys, aged nine and 11, to a deserted parkland on the edge of the village. There, they subjected them to an exceptionally vicious assault lasting for an hour and a half, which included burning, stabbing, beating, sexual assault and pelting the two boys with bricks. The elder boy had a ceramic sink dropped on his head causing severe injuries and was found by paramedics half-naked at the bottom of a ravine and in a coma.

The two brothers pleaded guilty to grievous bodily harm at Sheffield Crown Court and were sentenced to indefinite detention with the requirement that they each serve at least five years in custody.

Sources: Doncaster Local Safeguarding Board (2009, 2010), court hearings and contemporaneous newspaper accounts in the *Guardian Online* (2010; Walker, 2010; Walker and Wainwright, 2010) and *BBC News* (2009a, 2009b).

Children's aggression scripts

At their trial, the Crown Court was told 'how the brothers regularly watched their father punch and kick their mother, sometimes while drunk but often when sober'. If any of the brothers attempted to intervene, then either their mother was struck harder or they were also beaten by their father (Walker, 2010). The mother was a heavy cannabis user and is believed to have frequently given cannabis to her children, often hidden in their food, in order to make them sleep and easier to manage. In court, the children's home life was described in terms of 'routine aggression, violence and chaos' (Guardian Online, 2010). The brothers habitually watched ultra-violent films, horror movies and pornographic DVDs from a young age. They frequently stayed up all night without hindrance and both of them drank spirits, smoked cigarettes and consumed their father's home-grown cannabis (BBC News, 2009b; Walker, 2010). The two brothers had a history of verbal and physical aggression towards both children and adults in the area where they lived. They were frequently involved in vandalism, which included breaking windows, uprooting trees in the local park and throwing stones at passing cars. Both boys had been excluded from school because of their aggressive behaviour.

The serious case review criticised social workers for not recognising the extent to which the brothers' anti-social behaviour was attributable to the impact of: witnessing and being the victims of domestic violence; neglectful care; substance misuse; and the lifestyles to which their parents exposed them. So damaged were the two boys by the years of physical and emotional abuse endured in their family environment that the Crown Court judge characterised them as intent on controlling others 'by domination, degradation and inflicting pain for the purpose of [their] own emotional pleasure'. In handing down an indeterminate sentence, he described them as exhibiting a 'chilling detachment' from their crime and reasoned that they both posed 'a serious risk of harm to others' (Walker and Wainwright, 2010). This view was based on the report of the child psychiatrist who examined the brothers at the time of the trial. She was of the opinion that they exhibited 'no apparent capacity for empathy or remorse' and that without treatment, at least one of the brothers was likely to become psychopathic in adulthood (Walker, 2010).

Social learning theory suggests that the two boys modelled their behaviour on that of their father after witnessing and being the victims of the domestic violence he regularly perpetrated against his family. The cognitive schemata the children developed would have included beliefs that normalised physical assault as a reaction to frustration or perceived provocation. The *aggressive script* they acquired as they grew older was also shaped by their father's abuse of alcohol and their own consumption of it. People who are inebriated are: less able to accurately interpret social clues; more liable to misconstrue the behaviour of others; less self-aware; and disinhibited from aggressive acts. As the children regularly imbibed alcohol, its effects would have lowered their threshold for aggressive responses yet further. Moreover, as males witnessing their father's performance of masculinity as violent control of others in an ultimate expression of strength, they were predisposed to exhibit their aggression in sex-typed ways, which meant using physical and direct means to resolve conflict (Wright and Craig, 2010, p 49).

Watching violent films on television and DVDs was another factor in the development of the boys' *aggressive scripts*. Research studies consistently reveal the aggression-enhancing effects induced by watching violent media content (Krahé, 2001, pp 94–6). Reviewing a series of experiments into this phenomenon, Wood et al (1991, p 380) concluded 'that media violence enhances children's and adolescents' aggression in interaction with strangers, classmates and friends'. Similar conclusions are drawn by Paik and Comstock (1994) and Hogben (1998), who undertook a meta-analysis of the burgeoning studies on media and aggression. Both concluded that there is a gender and age aspect to the subsequent expression of aggression after watching violent content. There was a stronger association between expressions of aggression and watching violent films or programmes for males than females, while children were more likely to exhibit aggression than adults after seeing the portrayal of violence. Longitudinal studies demonstrate that the aggression-enhancing effects for children of watching violent content are long-term and enduring (Krahé, 2001, pp 101–2). As young boys, this made the two brothers from Doncaster particularly susceptible to the aggression-enhancing affects of watching violence on television or DVDs. Individuals exhibiting high trait aggression (as the two brothers did, primarily due to their father's domestic violence and alcohol consumption) are also more likely to want to watch violent content and to behave more aggressively afterwards than are those low in trait aggression (Bushman, 1995). This suggests a vicious cycle within which highly aggressive individuals choose to watch aggression–enhancing media content. Of course, the brothers were young children and should have been prevented by their parents from accessing this kind of programming.

The combination of alcohol abuse and extreme *aggressive scripts* meant that the children behaved aggressively towards their peers, police officers, teachers, practitioners from a variety of agencies and their foster carers. The aggressive reactions of the brothers towards professionals were not attributable to poor practice, but to the brothers' childhood conditioning in a violent and chaotic household. They needed remedial programmes of treatment and support delivered by specialists. The serious case review intimated that work with the brothers was beyond the capability of even experienced social workers, who would have required advice and input from experts in the area of child mental health. Recognising when the expression of aggression by a child is indicative of grave disturbance, and not attributable to poor practice, is difficult in an organisational and professional ethos that tends to blame social workers for failing to prevent violence from service-users.

Aggression and anti-social behaviour

The family had been known to social services for 14 years and both brothers were subject to child protection plans. At the time of the attack on the two children, the younger brother had previously received reprimands for actual bodily harm and common assault and was on bail to appear at a Youth Court on two charges of actual bodily harm. Two months previously, the older brother had been given a one-year Supervision Order for battery (*BBC News*, 2009a). In addition, the police were known to have arrested the boys on a number of occasions in connection with incidents relating to anti-social behaviour and aggressiveness towards others. They had also been excluded from school because of their increasingly violent behaviour and there had been constant complaints from neighbours concerning their behaviour.

Despite the long litany of incidents, which were well known to professionals, much of the brothers' anti-social behaviour was dealt with through a series of agreements and warnings made by different agencies with the boys and their parents. The serious case review describes children's social care services as being reluctant to get fully involved with the family, and multiagency work between it, the Youth Offending Service and the police as inadequate. Even when social workers did become engaged with the brothers, enquiries and assessments were often not completed. Only when the father left home and the mother subsequently requested that the two brothers be accommodated by the local authority did social workers actually remove them from their home. Even then, and despite their known aggressive behaviour, there was no proper planning or supervision by social workers of the two boys' foster placement (*BBC News*, 2010b).

The serious case review describes some practitioners as treating the two brothers as 'naughty children' rather than as children exhibiting the deleterious effects of abusive and neglectful parenting or of constituting a risk of harm to others (para 8). As a result, practitioners resorted to reproof, warnings and voluntary contracts rather than statutory intervention. One of the reasons identified by the serious case review for this deficient approach was the lack of specialist input availed of by social workers at the time, especially from children's mental health services. Child and Adolescent Mental Health Services only became involved in early 2009, when there was liaison with Youth Offending Services, and even then a student social worker was sent to conduct an initial home visit with the brothers (Doncaster Local Safeguarding Board, 2009, para 290). There may also have been other reasons for the inadequate response to the needs of the children. Dr Vizard, the child psychiatrist who completed reports on the children for the Crown Court trial, described feeling 'intimidated' while interviewing the younger brother (Walker, 2010). During a core group meeting called after one of the brothers hit and kicked another child, he is described in the report of the meeting as showing 'no empathy for his peers and showing no respect for police or authority ... he has no fear of consequences and blocks people trying to help' (Doncaster Local Safeguarding Board, 2009, para 302). Arguably, a number of practitioners who came into contact with the two brothers found their behaviour intimidating and difficult to manage. They were overwhelmed by the extreme behaviours they encountered and, consequently, lacked 'the confidence to act with sufficient resolution and clarity', according to the serious case review (para 8). A weak authoritative approach also characterised much social work intervention with the children's parents, who could themselves be anti-social and uncooperative. Ultimately, a number of social workers floundered in their practice when working with two extremely aggressive children engaged in a plethora of anti-social behaviour. The serious case review found 'an insufficiently authoritative, consistent and assertive strategy in working with a family who were uncooperative and antisocial in attitude and behaviour' (para 7).

Both brothers were verbally and physically aggressive towards others, destroyed property, and had either been convicted for assault or were awaiting a court appearance in connection with one. They frequently engaged in threatening and violent behaviour and probably intimidated the social workers they came into contact with. The serious case review concluded that given the extreme behaviours of the two children, 'for many professionals the extent of their problems would be beyond their experience and training' (para 8). As Lazarus and Folkman (1984) established in their groundbreaking research on stress, a perception of a threat constitutes the *primary appraisal*, but it is the *secondary appraisal* of the individual, which assesses his or her resources to deal with the threat, that ultimately determines whether or not it becomes a stressor. While social workers allocated to the children would have made a *primary appraisal* and assumed that the boys' aggression presented a source of stress, it was most likely their *secondary appraisal* of their own knowledge and skills to deal effectively with the stressor that elevated levels of stress among involved practitioners. As the serious case review indicates, for a number of social workers, deficits in training meant that their expertise was lacking and they were actually overwhelmed by the needs and challenges presented by the brothers. According to the serious case review, what little outside specialist assistance was availed of occurred too late to improve work with the family before the attack perpetrated by the children (para 8). Perhaps practitioners felt reluctant to admit to more senior staff that they needed help to carry out social work tasks because of a belief that requesting support would be perceived as evidence of a professional failing. It is precisely this type of belief that inhibits social workers from being assertive with management when better supervision or the involvement of specialists is required.

The aggressive behaviour of the children, together with their anti-social and uncooperative parents, may account for the reluctance of children's social care services to become involved, as social workers engaged in 'flight' responses from an intimidating family and the intense stress they induced in those who came into contact with them. The failure of some practitioners to complete enquiries or assessments in relation to the children may be attributable to their avoidance of interactions with family members, who were often anti-social and intimidating. Avoidance is a key 'flight' response deployed to remove a stressor. Hostage theory could explain the apparent paradox of recorded high levels of violent behaviour exhibited by the brothers juxtaposed against the perception of many practitioners that they were merely 'naughty'. A major psychological defence utilised by individuals subject to inescapable life-threatening or physically hazardous situations is to deny or minimise the danger. A number of social workers may have subconsciously sought to reduce their feelings of stress by minimising the nature of the aggression displayed by the brothers. The reaction of social workers towards the violence of the two boys is important to note, as practitioners are, at times, required to work with young offenders who are aggressive, but also children in need or at risk of harm.

Stanley and Goddard (2002, pp 129–32), in their study of Australian child protection social workers subjected to intimidation or violence, discovered, as hostage theory predicts, that they engaged in distortions of reality. These included gross underestimates of: the levels of violence within the family; the amount of violence practitioners were exposed to; and the intensity of their own fearfulness during a violent or threatening incident. Social workers also greatly underestimated the prevalence of intimidation and violence against their own colleagues, despite being employed in the same organisation. In other words, social workers minimised the violence and intimidation they encountered during child protection activities as a subconscious coping strategy. In so doing, they were distorting reality and liable to miss or misinterpret vital information in their work with families. Practitioners who intervened with the two brothers in Doncaster, given the level of violence they displayed, may have engaged in the type of reality distortion found in the research conducted by Stanley and Goddard (2002). This would explain the perception of the children as 'naughty' held by a number of professionals, rather than as exhibiting levels of aggression indicative of profoundly damaged children who also posed a serious risk of harm to others. It is possibly also the reason why an insufficient causal connection was made between the abusive and neglectful care of the parents and the boys' violent behaviours.

REFLECTIVE EXERCISE ON WORKING WITH A CHILD EXHIBITING AGGRESSIVE BEHAVIOUR

Recall a child you found challenging to work with because of their aggressive or anti-social behaviour. Ask yourself the following questions:

- What did you think your strengths and weaknesses were in managing this behaviour in relation to safeguarding that child?
- Did you seek or receive support to undertake this work and, if not, why not?
- What kind of assistance might have been helpful to you and how might you avail of this in future?

Dealing with potential physical aggression

Since the perception of a stressor is dependent on an individual's *secondary appraisal* of their ability to successfully deal with a threat, the more relevant capabilities social workers possess, the less likely they are to engage in 'flight' responses. Knowing how to de-escalate a physically threatening situation or to take evasive action if attacked might have reduced the anxiety levels of the practitioners who interacted with the brothers. Basic principles governing the management of physical aggression from children or their caregivers ought to inform the responses of social workers when their personal safety is at risk. This requires knowledge of the different phases involved in an aggressive attack. The *assault cycle* was first proposed by Kaplan and Wheeler (1983), based on studies of violence, and has since been utilised by a number of trainers in aggression management (Breakwell, 1997; Paterson and Leadbetter, 1999; Faupel et al, 2011). The *assault cycle* consists of five distinct phases, commencing with the Trigger for anger and followed by the Escalation, Crisis, Plateau and Post-crisis Phases. These are represented diagrammatically in Figure 9.1.

Figure 9.1: The typical assault cycle

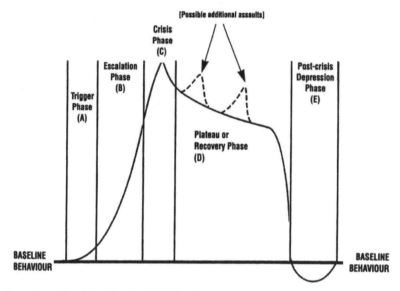

Source: Reproduced from Breakwell (1997, p 43).

The Trigger Phase is the initial event that provokes the aggressor's anger and can consist of an actual happening or be because of a private thought, for example, recalling a past incident. This is followed by the Escalation Phase, during which the individual becomes physiologically affected as their body prepares for a 'fight' or 'flight' response to the source of aggravation. Once the Crisis Phase is reached, automatic physiological defences take over and the aggressor's judgement is normally impaired due to a reduced capacity for empathy, rationality and social information processing. It can be exceptionally difficult for an individual to listen to others or exercise self-control once the Crisis Phase commences. At this point, the physical assault occurs. As the aggressor's body starts to recuperate after the release of energy through the assault and returns to a state of equilibrium, he or she is still highly sensitive to subsequent physiological arousal and further assaults can occur during this Recovery or Plateau Phase. As the aggressor moves into the final Post-crisis Depression Phase of the *assault cycle*, his or her body returns to rest and he or she can begin to feel confused, guilty and vulnerable, as the ability to process information and rationality are re-established. At this point, the aggressor may experience lowered self-esteem or engage in remedial behaviours such as apologising.

Research indicates that the adult body takes up to 90 minutes to fully return to its equilibrium state after the Crisis Phase, although this can be somewhat short for children. Further assaults can easily be sparked off during this period, while the aggressor will continue to be generally unreceptive to attempts at reasoning with him or her. It is precisely because automated physiological defence mechanisms become ascendant on entering the Crisis Phase that intervening before this stage is reached is crucial. Early intervention requires that social workers be attuned to the verbal and non-verbal clues that individuals commonly send out as they enter the Trigger and Escalation Phases, which include physical agitation such as pacing, drumming fingers, swinging legs, fiddling with hands or objects and generally quicker movements or restlessness. Overreaction to criticism or misinterpreting neutral comments as criticism, alongside more rapid speech, are also indicative of individuals entering the *assault cycle*. Social workers should be vigilant as to any movement by an aggressive individual to block their escape exits.

Davies and Frude (2004), in their training manual, introduce a range of verbal and non-verbal techniques that can be deployed to calm an increasingly aggressive person, be they a child, caregiver or another family member. These are adapted for application by social workers to practice situations in Table 9.1, which addresses non-verbal skills and then considers verbal skills. Many of these techniques draw on the repertoire of capabilities that social workers should already possess, while others require the development of new skills. Some of them may be appropriate for one situation or individual, but not for another. Such techniques take time to master and deploy appropriately. Precisely because individuals are unreceptive to appeals to their moral sense, logical problem-solving or even self-interest on entering the Crisis Phase, engaging in calming measures should take priority until the aggressor has returned to a state of physiological equilibrium.

Dealing with an imminent assault

All of the techniques just described are designed to forestall an individual from reaching the Crisis Phase, when their body will be fully physiologically prepared for a physical 'fight' response. Despite the best endeavours of practitioners, angry caregivers, their partners or children can lose control and present a direct danger to the social worker. In these circumstances, practitioners need to take evasive action to avoid a possible assault. The safest action to take is simply to leave the house, interview room or other location in which the interaction with the aggressor is taking place. In situations where social workers are at risk of imminent assault, they must not hesitate to make whatever excuse or devise whatever pretext is necessary to enable them to get away from the aggressor safely. Davies and Frude (2004) describe a number of strategies that can be deployed by social workers if an aggressor blocks their escape route. These are summarised in Table 9.2.

Table 9.1: Verbal and non-verbal de-escalation techniques

Non-verbal skill	Explanation
Mood matching and the vocal tone	Resonating with another person's mood is generally an automatic response, but leads to conflict escalation if the mood matched is one of anger. Appearing exceptionally calm in the face of mounting anger can convey to the aggressor that he or she is not being taken seriously and, thus, heighten rather than reduce feelings of anger. Rather than being calm, practitioners should strive to project being controlled and concerned.
Escaping from a confrontation	Avoid confrontational face-to-face stances with an aggressor and, if necessary, the practitioner should reposition to ensure his or her body is at a slight angle away from the aggressor.
Maintaining normal eye contact	If the aggressor breaks off eye contact or engages in staring, the practitioner should strive to maintain normal eye contact. But it is important to be aware of cultural differences.
Using calming gestures	The practitioner adopts slow patting movements using both hands palm down out in front of him or her at about chest or waist height. Alternatively, the practitioner holds both hands up in front of his or her face, which is turned slightly away, with open palms towards the aggressor.
Mirroring	Individuals speaking to each other tend to unconsciously mirror one another's posture. A practitioner subtly mirroring the posture of an aggressor, although not any aggressive positions, can convey a degree of empathy with him or her.
Body buffer zone	It is important for the practitioner to avoid violating the personal space of the aggressor by moving too close to him or her. This space can expand as an individual becomes more physiologically aroused. However, if the practitioner stands too far away from the aggressor, he or she can appear aloof and possibly play into the aggressor's anger. As a rough guide, if someone is aggressive, it is generally advisable to be positioned about two arm's lengths away. It is important to be aware of cultural and gender differences regarding what is normally considered personal space.
Height of seats	Ideally, the practitioner and aggressor should be seated on chairs or other furniture of the same height so that neither the aggressor nor the practitioner appears to be dominating over the other.
Verbal skill	Explanation
Allow the person time and space	The practitioner should give the aggressor permission to vent their feelings (not the aggressive behaviour) in an effort to assist him or her to ventilate. This also relies on conveying that the practitioner has time to listen and is interested in what the aggressor has to say.
Show concern and understanding	Practitioners should use active listing skills to convey their interest and concern about what the aggressor is thinking and feeling.
Communicate clearly	While practitioners are used to adopting clear communication strategies, these can be particularly important in a situation where the aggressor's heightened emotionality is interfering with their ability to accurately read social cues or comprehend what is being said to them.
Convey desire to reduce distress	If feasible, practitioners should endeavour to assure the person that some action will be taken to address the situation that is causing them distress, even if this is simply listening to their point of view and expressing concern.
Avoid escalating by confrontation	This can be difficult in practice, as aggressors can make deeply provocative comments that can trigger anger in practitioners. Nevertheless, it is crucial for the social worker to exercise self-control throughout the altercation and persist in trying to de-escalate the tension.

Table 9.1: continued

Verbal skill	Explanation
Avoid provocative phrases	This is obvious in theory but sometimes difficult to achieve in practice. A practitioner may be subjected to offensive or hurtful remarks by a child or their caregiver, causing the social worker to become angry in turn.
Be ruthless with the issue, gracious with people	This involves separating the social work task from the caregiver or child who is aggressive. The practitioner needs to make clear to the aggressor that tasks relating to child protection must be completed, while still acknowledging the effect this is having on a caregiver or child and treating them with respect.
Depersonalise the issue	It is vital that practitioners do not appear to be taking personal responsibility for actions that are the decisions of a multidisciplinary team, management or involve the implementation of policy. Otherwise, this sets the practitioner up as a target.
Personalise yourself	Often, aggression is directed at a social worker due to their child protection role. The judicious use of self-disclosure can help the aggressor to perceive the practitioner as a person and not an automaton. This needs to be relevant to the situation and appropriate.
Empower the person	This can be difficult in a situation of high emotional tension. It involves adopting a one-down position through the use of role-reversal, for example, asking the aggressor what he or she would do in the practitioner's position. Empowerment can also be attempted through shifting the focus onto the aggressor's strengths, which can assist him or her to feel more positive about the situation.
Make a token concession	This often consists of conceding one or more of the points made by the aggressor and is designed to break the stalemate created if neither party is prepared to acknowledge any fault. The practitioner should be careful not to appear to be simply giving in to the demands of the aggressor. However, it does involve considering whether the aggressor has some justified grievances.
Make a deliberate friendly gesture	The practitioner may be in a position to offer something tangible to the aggressor or it may be a token gesture such as agreeing to set aside time to listen to the aggressor's grievances or to carry out a small task to assist the aggressor.
Use of 'we'	The use of 'we' rather than 'I' and 'you' in conversation can convey a notion of shared endeavour rather than an adversarial situation. This requires the practitioner to invite the aggressor to work together with the social worker on the problem that angers him or her.
Using diversions	Diverting the attention of the aggressor onto a more appealing issue or activity can be an effective short-term measure. Used frequently, it can appear to reward aggressive behaviour.

Experiencing an assault

If, despite all the attempts at de-escalation and escape, a practitioner comes under physical attack from an aggressor, according to Davies and Frude (2004), there are a number of actions they should take. These include shouting at the aggressor to stop the attack and shouting or screaming for help, which can also deter the aggressor from pursuing his or her attack. Unfortunately, many people can feel inhibited about screaming, which can be counterproductive during an assault. If possible, social workers should press the button of a personal alarm, panic alarm system or, as a last resort, any fire alarm system. If a practitioner's life or bodily integrity is endangered, he or she must not hesitate to use whatever means are

Table 9.2: Escape strategies

Escape strategy	Explanation
Play for time	When a practitioner's bodily integrity or life is at risk, he or she may need to be willing to agree to whatever the aggressor's demands are simply to escape the situation without serious assault.
Keep talking	Ask highly relevant questions in a steady well-paced tone; avoid silences, which can be threatening to the aggressor.
Try diversionary tactics	These should be simple distracting activities that are likely to be pleasant and attractive to the aggressor and that can assist to reduce his or her physiological arousal.
Keep a distance	Keep between one to two metres away from the aggressor. This is out of reach of a punch and avoids violating the aggressor's personal space.
Stay controlled and concerned	Though difficult in a frightening situation, it is helpful for the social worker to use *negative feeling assertion*, indicating the effect that the aggressor is having on him or her.
Locate and move towards escape exits	As a matter of routine, practitioners should survey unfamiliar homes, offices, day centres or residential units to establish where the exits are before or during their interaction with a potentially aggressive individual.
Tell the person to put any weapon down	The practitioner should repeatedly ask the aggressor to put the weapon down and indicate that further negotiation cannot take place until they do so. Practitioners should not ask the aggressor to hand the weapon to them.
Delayed compliance	The practitioner asks the aggressor to do something within a specified time frame. This technique can be used to permit the aggressor to consider the request and to save face when complying with it.
Consider the use of physical restraint	This is a last resort and must only be used by social workers who have received specialist training in this technique and are normally employed in children's residential homes.

at hand to prevent the continuation of a physical assault. For social workers who have undergone training, breakaway or physical restraint techniques may be an appropriate response at this point.

If an assault does occur, victims will experience a multitude of feelings and, sometimes, changes in their attitudes towards their work, colleagues, caregivers and children. In the immediate aftermath of an attack, practitioners are likely to be relieved at having survived it, which may induce some euphoria. They may also feel angry, shocked, exhausted and tense (Breakwell, 1997; Davies and Frude, 2004). For some, psychological numbing and the determination to carry on with work as usual characterises their response. These initial reactions to the assault can be followed by longer-term effects. Rowett (1986), who conducted early research on violence against social workers in Britain, found that many felt guilt. This stemmed from the belief that both they and the service-user were at fault, resulting in self-blame. Many social workers in the study thought that if they had been competent, they would have been able to defuse the situation and prevent the attack.

Breakwell (1997, p 61) observes that self-blame can be exacerbated by widespread attitudes within the social work profession that typically ascribe blame to the victim of the assault and not the assailant. Rowett (1986) discovered that most social workers believed that colleagues who had suffered a violent attack were more 'provocative, incompetent, authoritarian or inexperienced' than themselves and thought that their assaulted colleagues had unnecessarily challenged service-users and failed to accurately assess risk. The study completed by Rowett (1986) also found that social workers who had been attacked held similar beliefs about themselves. When Rowett (1986) tested out this negative stereotype of victims by requesting both assaulted and non-assaulted social workers to complete self-assessments, no significant differences were found between the two groups. This suggests that there are no relevant distinctions between the attributes, knowledge or skills of those professionals who were assaulted and those who were not. Corroborating evidence emerges from Pahl's (1999, p 99) regression analysis of a nationwide survey of social care workers asked about their experiences of violence from service-users. This found no significant statistical differences in terms of age, ethnicity or length of service in current employment affecting the risk of being physically attacked.

Rowett's (1986) findings illustrate a well-recognised psychological phenomenon known as the Just World Hypothesis, by means of which individuals differentiate themselves from victims of violence by believing that the victim in some way caused or contributed to being attacked. Holding the conviction that others are more vulnerable to attack than oneself because of their personal characteristics is a form of psychological defence, which reduces anxiety and inflates a sense of security, albeit a false one. It operates to deny that much interpersonal violence is unpredictable, uncontrollable and can happen to anyone. Colleagues and managers may be oblivious to their adoption of the erroneous Just World Hypothesis; nevertheless, its pervasiveness in the professional culture of social work can compound the self-blame and guilt of assaulted practitioners. This can culminate in a loss of professional confidence for the assaulted social worker, engendering doubts about competence, fear of caregivers or children, and heightened anxiety during practice.

What research does reveal is that both male and female social care workers are more likely to be assaulted by male service-users, while most studies show that male workers experience more violence and threats of violence from service-users than do their female counterparts (Pahl, 1999, p 98; Braithwaite, 2001, p 143). Despite this general pattern, studies indicate that fieldworkers are, in fact, much more likely to be assaulted by a female service-user than are residential social care workers, who are more likely to be attacked by a male resident (Breakwell, 1997, p 41). Concerning this finding, it is important to bear in mind that child protection social workers predominantly interact with mothers and other female carers of children. Assaults rarely occur during a first encounter between a caregiver or child and a practitioner, as up to 85% of violent incidents take place within the context of an ongoing working relationship. Generally, physical attacks are perpetrated as repeated assaults by the same service-user (Breakwell, 1997, p 41). They are most likely to occur in the family's home, where caregivers or children are on their own territory. In a residential home, the attack is more likely to happen in places where the child feels a greater sense of control over the space.

To summarise, Rowett (1986) found that social workers who had been assaulted were as competent as their non-assaulted colleagues. Despite the research evidence from this and other studies, there remain entrenched negative stereotypes of practitioners who have been attacked within social care agencies. It is victim-blaming that often dissuades front-line social workers from reporting violent incidents, or finding that when they do request assistance, managers fail to provide effective support (Breakwell, 1997, p 62; Brockman and McLean, 2005, p 5; *Community Care*, 2011a, pp 4–5). Denial by both educators and employers that assault or the threat of assault is a serious problem for child protection social workers deprives them of the skills they need to successfully deal with it. Acknowledgement by employers that practitioners sometimes have to work with caregivers, their partners or children who are physically aggressive is the first step to: creating a supportive environment for practitioners; ensuring accurate risk assessments are undertaken; ensuring the right precautions are put in place; and ensuring appropriate training is delivered.

REFLECTIVE EXERCISE ON EXPERIENCING A PHYSICAL ASSAULT

Recall an incident with a child or caregiver or their partner when you have been threatened with a physical assault or have been assaulted. Ask yourself the following questions:

- How did you react at the time?
- How did your colleagues or manager react if you disclosed this to them?
- How did the incident affect your practice with that person or with other children or caregivers?
- How might your agency, line manager or colleagues better have supported you?
- What difference do you think this support would have made to your subsequent practice with the person who made the threat or assaulted you and with other children and their caregivers who can be aggressive?
- What can you do to obtain the workplace support you need when confronted by threats of assault or actual physical attacks?

Case Study 9.2: The Pindown experience

Levy and Kahan (1991) *The Pindown Experience*

In November 1983, the approach to managing children in local authority residential homes, which came to be known as *pindown*, was first instituted at 245 Hartshill Road, Stoke-on-Trent. From here, it was adopted by a number of other residential children's homes also run by Staffordshire Social Services. The method was conceived and disseminated by Tony Latham, who was of white British descent and qualified as a social worker in 1977, rising to the level of Senior Assistant for Children and Families in Staffordshire's local authority in 1988. The approach consisted of requiring children who presented with challenging behaviour or who absconded from the home to be confined to a room on their own. This was furnished with just a bed, chair and table. During their period in *pindown*, the child was not permitted to speak to anyone else and had no access to television, books or other forms of entertainment. Throughout their period in *pindown*, the child was required to wear his or her pyjamas, go to bed at around 7.00pm and request permission of the staff member stationed outside the room to use the toilet. The period spent in *pindown* could range from one day up to several weeks or a number of months. Many children were subjected to repeated episodes of *pindown*, and a number were not permitted to attend school while in *pindown*. This regime was often accompanied by orchestrated negative attitudes and deprecating comments from residential care staff towards the children concerned.

The widespread use of the method came to light in October 1989 when one 15-year-old girl who had spent time in *pindown* absconded from a children's home in the Staffordshire area and complained to her solicitor about the use of the method. Later the same month, the High Court issued an injunction prohibiting the use of *pindown* and it was, thereafter, permanently discontinued. A number of newspapers reported on the use of *pindown*, followed by a Granada Television *World in action* documentary. Widespread disquiet as a result of this coverage led to the establishment of an independent inquiry. The inquiry discovered that children as young as nine years of age were placed in *pindown*, while a number of children were subjected to this regime within a few days of admission to the residential home. Some children in *pindown* began to retreat into themselves, while others self-harmed, stopped eating or subsequently attempted to abscond from residential care. Most were overtly distressed and frightened by their experience of *pindown*. Many children reported feeling depressed, anxious, bored and lonely. The inquiry concluded that the method was tantamount to solitary confinement in secure accommodation, which humiliated and further traumatised the children concerned.

The anger of social workers

Intermediate Treatment, or *pindown* as it became known, was originally conceived by Tony Latham as a behaviour modification programme. In evidence to the inquiry, he claimed that periods spent by a child in a mainly empty room were envisaged as a minor component of the overall process. The greater part was to consist of regularly reviewed 'individually tailored, closely supervised, well structured and controlled [care plans], with the direct participation of the young person and all significant others' (para 5.97). The method lacked either a theoretical basis or any expert input in terms of its design and implementation. As the inquiry discovered, there was virtually no variation in the methods of *pindown* used for different children, who were instead treated all alike. In the absence of a psychological underpinning or expert advice, the method developed punitively, with detrimental consequences for the children and, arguably, for the practitioners administering it. Lamentably, it seems that *pindown* became a conduit for the negativity and suppressed aggression that social workers felt towards the children in their care. A set of logs from the homes, contemporaneous with the events investigated by the inquiry, reveal the extent to which some social workers and other residential staff disliked a number of the children or acted with callousness towards them.

According to the inquiry, many of Staffordshire's children's homes were in a state of disrepair, under-resourced and overcrowded (para 3.27). They were poorly adapted for a range of children, some of whom had special needs, while privacy and recreational space was lacking. A number of children were bed-wetting and soiling, while 'bicycle stealing, fighting, defiance, shouting, crying and non-school attendance' became commonplace among others (para 4.26). The response of staff to these problems often turned castigatory and retaliatory. As Kool (2008, pp 74–5) reveals in a review of research findings, impulse control is lowered when individuals are required to exercise self-control in relation to a number of provocations simultaneously. Many practitioners were dealing with multiple sources of anger, originating from inadequate resources and children's provocative behaviour, which required restraint in their expression of aggression. The mental energy demanded for this would have been depleted over time, resulting in sudden failures of control and the release of aggression towards *looked-after* children. The combination of pent up frustration and stress meant that some of the resultant aggression was probably *displaced* onto the children in residential care as well as other workers.

Children who absconded from the home were subjected to more intensive forms of *pindown* and for longer periods of time. Indeed, this became a standard response in an effort to discourage residents from further absconding. The opposite was achieved, however, as many children forced to remain on their own for long periods of time in *pindown* ran away from the home periodically (para 4.32). *Pindown* also became the routine means to deal with just about any infraction of the rules laid down by staff, any defiance of them or, indeed, any form of difficult behaviour for residential social workers to cope with. In one instance, a 10-year-old boy was admitted to the Hartshill Road home by the Emergency Duty Team in a highly distressed state. He is recorded as trying to abscond several times and then 'tried to bite himself to death, made himself sick and finally tried to open his tummy up with his finger nails' (para 8.15). The next day, a worker noted in the log that he was not permitted to see his mother, watch television or play (para 8.15). For residents subjected to *pindown*, the most basic entitlements such as a telephone call to a parent, speaking to other children, attending school, interacting with residential staff, access to recreation or pocket money became reformulated as privileges to be earned (para 12.4). Not only did *pindown* include the withdrawal of such entitlements, but many residential workers adopted attitudes and engaged in behaviour designed to demoralise particular children, for example, one staff member instructed others in relation to a 13-year-old girl in *pindown* to 'be nasty to her' (para 6.50).

Residential social workers found themselves with insufficient experience, training, supervision or staff numbers to manage the challenging behaviour of distressed and sometimes aggressive children in an overcrowded and grossly under-resourced setting. Their working conditions were stressful and made constructive work with the children exceptionally difficult. In such circumstances, the originally well-intentioned introduction of Intermediate Treatment to assist *looked-after* children to work through their own destructive behaviours deteriorated into a punitive form of control. Disparaging remarks, unsympathetic attitudes and *pindown* were justified as a means to re-establish control over the children. Often, these also functioned to channel the negative feelings of the social workers towards the children.

The approach known as *pindown* may have become an opportune, if subconscious, conduit for *displaced aggression*, as social care workers struggled to cater for children, many with challenging behaviour, in a grossly under-resourced residential environment. This predominant approach to maintaining discipline would of itself have precipitated aggressive responses from the children. The deprivation of companionship, recreation and freedom are all sources of frustration, while also constituting threats to the well-being of the individual and, therefore, acting as stressors. The frustration of the children's desired goals, such as wanting to communicate with other residents or watching television, would inevitably provoke aggressive reactions. Likewise, the stress caused by being in *pindown* would induce irritability and, hence, increase a child's argumentativeness or antagonism towards social care workers. Fear of retaliation by staff and further periods in *pindown* might have resulted in children engaging in *safety-value aggression* against other children in the home. This would partially account for the bullying found to be common among residents by the public inquiry.

Anger management

Although events reported by the Levy and Kahan (1991) *The Pindown Experience* inquiry took place in residential children's homes, the potential for stress, anxiety and frustration to engender anger and aggression in social workers can also occur in the community settings where most child protection practice takes place. In a survey of predominantly community-based social workers in the US, Ringstad (2005) discovered that out of 1,000 respondents, 62% had experienced some form of psychological aggression from a service-user, but around 12% had perpetrated some form of psychological aggression against a service-user. Such behaviours included insulting or shouting at the user and acting out of spite. In the same survey, 15% of social workers revealed they had been the victim of some form of physical assault by a service-user, but 4% admitted to perpetrating assaults, such as pushing or grabbing a service-user. While Ringstad's (2005) research did not explore the interdependence of social work and service-user aggression, it is likely that some social workers responded with psychological or physical aggression to the challenging behaviour of service-users. As Ringstad's (2005) research and

Case Study 9.2 illustrate, practitioners need to effectively manage their own anger in order to prevent it from being expressed as forms of direct or *displaced aggression* against children, their parents and other family members. Successful management relies on identifying the first indicators of anger early on, which are physical and behavioural, such as moving closer to physically intimidate a child, as well as emotional.

Anger is a legitimate and essential emotion, which should always be brought into full awareness and not repressed. It conveys vital information as to how a social worker is feeling about the caregiver, child or colleague who is evoking feelings of irritation in the social worker. It may be an important feeling to share with a child or caregiver through the use of the therapeutic communication skill of *immediacy*. This requires the social worker to share his moment-to-moment experiencing of a service-user to assist her to become aware of the effect she is having on others and to then use this information to promote beneficial changes. The voicing of anger by a social worker may also form part of an assertive statement requesting a young person, caregiver or colleague to desist from aggressive behaviours. Such a statement is predicated on the belief that practitioners have the right to express their anger safely and assertively and to encourage others to do the same.

Professionals unable to find direct, safe, verbal expressions of anger are liable to displace it onto others or to articulate it indirectly through *passive-aggressive* modes. Repressed or unexpressed anger may also be conveyed to children, young people and caregivers through leakage. In these situations, the practitioner, while not verbally articulating anger, nevertheless leaks this emotion through, for example, rapid speech, folded arms or abruptness. Consequently, the other person is left feeling uneasy, but without knowing why; a state of affairs that plainly hinders partnership-working and inter-professional relationships. For all these reasons, the recognition and expression of anger is important. To do this successfully, practitioners need to be attentive to their own early warning signs of anger, which are signalled by altered states. These altered states are reproduced from Williams (2010, pp 146–7) as follows:

- *Altered thinking* – For example, thinking something is not fair, that you are being got at, mocked, humiliated or ignored.
- *Altered emotions* – For example, of rising irritation, shame, anxiety, panic or anger.
- *Altered physical symptoms* – For example, getting hot, sweaty, fidgety, noticing more rapid breathing or an increased heart rate, or tension.
- *Altered behaviour or activity levels* – For example, pacing, gripping your hands, facing away from the person, drinking more, raising your voice and become sarcastic, dismissive or rude.

On detecting any of these altered states, social workers should take immediate action to prevent further escalation of their anger and the impulsive or poorly considered responses liable to arise out of it. Experiencing any or a number of these altered states should be treated as an early warning signal to stop in mid-action, wrestle for self-control and then exercise choice over the next response. O'Neill (1999) identifies cognitive, arousal and behavioural components to anger, which must be dealt with concurrently if an individual is to prevent escalation of their feelings into impulsive and aggressive behaviour. The *arousal component* refers to the physiological changes in the body, such as an elevated heart and respiratory rate, sweating, and muscle tension. The *cognitive component* comprises an individual's focus on events or people's behaviour and remarks that trigger anger, his or her appraisal of the situation or others as a threat, or self-appraisals of inadequacy alongside thoughts that increase irritation. The *behavioural component* concerns the spontaneous and aggressive expression of anger, but can refer to passive forms of acting out annoyance. Practitioners aware that they become angered during interactions with children, parents, their partners or, indeed, colleagues and managers should consider taking the time to read one of the many self-help guides on anger management.

REFLECTIVE EXERCISE ON FEELINGS OF ANGER

Recall interactions with children, young people and caregivers that have caused you to feel angry. Ask yourself the following questions:

- How do you tend to react when angry, what are your typical thoughts and behaviours?
- What kinds of behaviour by children, young people or caregivers trigger your anger?
- How do annoyances connected with your personal life or concerning work-related matters play into vexation with particular children or caregivers?
- How do you normally manage your anger and what are the strengths and weaknesses of this approach?
- Read a self-help guide on anger management (see the Appendix) and consider how you might improve the management of your anger in the future.

The aggression of social workers

Pindown was not the only cause of children's aggression in a number of Staffordshire's residential homes during the 1980s. It was also related to their treatment by practitioners. In July 1983, one social worker describes an altercation with a child at The Birches:

> after telling him several times to turn down the record player I ended up taking the record off and breaking it in half. He was extremely annoyed by this and I had to escort him upstairs until he calmed down and we were able to discuss the matter. (para 4.25)

A month later, the same social worker mentions another confrontation when he informed one resident that she would have to move from a single into a shared bedroom. She refused to leave her bedroom and began to throw furniture, at which point the social worker intervened to physically remove her. He described in the log how 'she became physically and verbally abusive. I had to restrain her (by the back of her hair) for some 10 to 15 minutes' (para 4.28). The police were called at this juncture and the girl spent the night at the police station. In yet another incident, the same social worker records an attempt to discuss with a boy how to improve himself and is in the process of agreeing a contract with him when the worker discovers that the boy has been sniffing glue. The practitioner's reaction is to insist that the boy immediately hands him the glue, which the boy refuses to do. The result is another forced removal of a child from a room, in the course of which the boy's necklace is broken (para 4.35).

The reactions of a number of residential social workers to disputes with the children created *conflict spirals* that quickly escalated into violent confrontations. In the examples just cited, a male member of staff records his interactions with several different children that all culminate in aggression by the social worker and the physical restraint of the child. In the first instance, the social worker reacts to a young person's defiance by destroying his property, provoking a retaliatory aggressive response from the young person. Isenhart and Spangle (2000, pp 14–15) contend that sources of conflict include not only disagreement over material goods, but also over interests, procedures, relationships and communication. The young person's annoyance will have been provoked not only by the breaking of his record, but also by the summary and unjustified nature of the destruction of his property. He may also have felt angered by the disrespectful behaviour of the social worker, which paid no attention to his interests and violated his right to listen to music, albeit not at a volume that disturbed everyone else. The conflict became one involving the differing interests of the worker and young person, compounded by disagreement over the nature of their relationship and mutual expectations within it.

In the second instance, the same practitioner informs a girl that she has to move out of her single bedroom. There is no indication that the reasons for this were fully explained or that the young person was properly prepared for the necessity of the move to a shared room. The ensuing conflict was not just over being required to change bedroom, but also over the manner in which it was communicated. In the third incident, the social worker precipitates a physical confrontation with a young person, resulting in damage to his property; a cause of yet more anger for the young person. It is salient that the social worker involved in these violent altercations was male, as this raises questions about the impact of gender on approaches to handling conflict. Research reveals that men tend to express their aggression in more direct and physical ways than women (Wright and Craig, 2010). Moreover, as the performance of hegemonic masculinity is bound up with the suppression of a range of emotions, including fear and anxiety, this can make it more difficult for some male practitioners to acknowledge their own apprehension, leading in turn to aggressive defensive responses. Social learning through family and peer interactions regarding the correct performance of masculinity may have influenced how this male social worker responded to provocation from young people. Social workers unwilling to admit to their fears and given to macho face-offs with children or parents in perceived win–lose contests are liable to stoke tensions and provoke the very aggression they seek to avoid. These are admittedly extreme examples of poor practice. Nevertheless, they illustrate the extent to which frustrated and stressed social workers are liable to react to conflicts in aggressive ways, which elicit retaliatory aggressive responses from others. They also suggest that social workers, whether male or female, need to be alert to the ways in which their gender may channel expressions of anger, stress and frustration.

Even when the behaviour of social workers is not overtly aggressive, children and young people may feel angry and aggrieved by their decisions and actions. Children may regard social workers as the rule-breakers when they appear to contravene social norms or behave in a manner that creates a perceived injustice. Within this social interactionist reading of children's responses, they will first attribute responsibility for the transgression to the social worker and then make a claim for redress by articulating their viewpoint. If this is ignored or their claim is denied by the practitioner, they may then seek to punish him or her through retaliatory action, often involving aggressive behaviour. A proportion of children who feel aggrieved by social workers may decide to do nothing against them for fear of reprisal. In such cases, their irritation and aggression may be *displaced* onto other children or less powerful adults. For other social workers astute to the offence they have caused, a swift apology and some compensatory action is sufficient to resolve the grievance.

For children and young people in the care system, the sources and intensity of their grievance can be amplified by a *hostile attribution bias* originating in their childhood experiences of abuse or neglect. Skills deficiencies in terms of information processing and problem-solving may also lead children to quickly resort to verbal and physical aggression when frustrated by the actions of a social worker. Practitioners also have pasts that can leave them harbouring *hostile attribution biases* derived from their own adverse childhood experiences. Like the children they are called upon to safeguard, they too can exhibit skills deficiencies in managing their own behaviour alongside that of the young people they work with. Such skills deficits result in the swift resort to verbal or physical aggression as social workers find their own repertoire of behaviours limited by social learning from their own parental figures. As a consequence of skills deficits among both practitioners and children in some of Staffordshire's children's homes, legitimate boundary-setting by residential social workers quickly deteriorated into angry altercations and physical confrontations with the children in their care. Aggression came to characterise the behaviour of many practitioners as well as that of numerous children.

The contribution of social workers to aggressive interactions

The events captured in Case Study 9.2 occurred in residential homes and while some of the specific incidents are difficult to envisage outside of that setting, the social dynamics that precipitated them are not. Social workers intervening with families during a home visit, office interview or interaction at a family centre are equally likely to encounter challenging behaviour, whether from caregivers or children. Therefore, community-based social workers also need to reflect upon their own experiences of aggression and whether they are hobbled by a *hostile attribution bias*, which makes them susceptible to attributing hostile intentions to the behaviour of children or caregivers when none exists. They also need to examine their sources of stress, their levels of irritability and the extent to which they are able to draw on a repertoire of anger management strategies and problem-solving approaches to defuse their own aggressive impulses. In addition, Davies and Frude (2004, pp 35, 37) identify a set of high-risk beliefs that social workers may hold towards themselves or service-users, which are likely to fuel anger and aggression while increasing the chance of a violent incident. These are listed in Table 9.3.

Table 9.3: Beliefs that contribute to anger and aggression

High-risk belief	Implication for practice
Some clients need to be taught a lesson	Leads to an authoritarian approach, with the use of excessive threats or penalties.
I always know best	Denies that the service-user may sometimes be in the right and their anger justified.
I must have the last word	Creates unnecessary antagonism and plays into the conflict spiral.
I can deal with everyone	Failure to recognise own limits and the appropriateness of another colleague undertaking work with a service-user.
Give them an inch and they take a yard	Reduces flexibility and willingness to concede small but important points to the service-user during a negotiation.
Humour is out of place in my interactions with clients	Easily takes offence at teasing and unable to use humour to relieve emotional tension.
Verbal attack towards clients is permissible	Erroneous belief that verbal put-downs are not aggression, further angering service-user.
I must never run away	Remaining in an unsafe situation instead of escaping to preserve personal safety.
I must never show that I'm afraid	This is not realistic and can prevent the practitioner from obtaining agency support.
I must always remain calm	Appearing completely calm can convey disinterest, inciting increased anger.
I must always stand up to them	Can create face-offs with service-users that feed into the conflict spiral.

Aside from holding high-risk beliefs, child protection social workers can contribute to *reactive aggression* from young people and caregivers by: not listening to them; ignoring their viewpoint; being unclear about what is being asked of them; making contradictory demands upon them; failing to justify the demands being made; acting in ways that appear arbitrary; or withholding information. This is not to deny that despite listening to caregivers or children, their viewpoints sometimes imperil safety and cannot be incorporated into a child protection plan. Nevertheless, there may be some scope for negotiation and accommodation of different interests. Practitioners can sometimes engage in behaviours that evidence a lack of respect, such as lateness to a pre-arranged appointment or a rushed meeting with a child or caregiver. These are likely to provoke an angry and possibly aggressive response from a child or caregiver in turn. The fact that social workers can sometimes contribute to the *reactive aggression* of parents and young people must not be permitted to obscure the reality that a number of service-users engage in *proactive aggression* to manipulate social workers in ways that increase the risk of harm to children, as demonstrated by the two foster carers in Case Study 6.1. Such deliberative and intentional behaviour is unlikely to be moderated by social workers and it would be a mistake for practitioners to blame their practice for the actions of caregivers and children who are determined to achieve their own desired ends regardless of the cost to others. Similarly, social workers may be confronted by service-users given to disproportionately angry or violent expressions of *reactive aggression* rooted in personal histories, which reflect generalised interpersonal patterns of behaviour, such as by the mothers in Case Studies 7.1 and 7.2. The unreasonableness, impulsiveness and intensity of caregivers' and young people's aggression may convey important information about the risks posed to a child. Attributing it to poor practice and blaming social workers would be a grave misreading of the evidence.

REFLECTIVE EXERCISE ON BELIEFS CONTRIBUTING TO AGGRESSIVE BEHAVIOUR

Read through the list of high-risk beliefs. Ask yourself the following questions:

- Do you think any of these beliefs influence some of your own behaviour when experiencing aggressiveness from young people or their caregivers?
- What alternative beliefs might improve your practice with service-users when they express aggression towards you?

Points for practice

- Children who develop aggression scripts due to their family background are likely to exhibit aggressive and anti-social behaviour, which will place additional demands on practitioners and may require specialist advice.

- Social workers may be reluctant to recognise their limitations when working with children who are highly aggressive and to request specialist inputs for fear of appearing incompetent. Such feelings need to be explored with a supervisor.
- Familiarity with the assault cycle and skills in de-escalation techniques can assist child protection social workers to avert or escape from physical assaults by children or adults.
- If an assault does occur, social workers have a tendency to blame themselves; however, research indicates that all practitioners, regardless of their age or experience, can be the victims of a physical assault.
- Practitioners can become angered by aspects of their work with children and families. It is important to develop anger management strategies in order to reduce feelings of anger and the potential for these to be acted out through aggressive responses to children or parents.
- Expressions of anger and aggression by social workers may be mediated by their gender and it is essential for both male and female practitioners to examine how their own social learning regarding the performance of femininity and masculinity has influenced them.

CHAPTER TEN

Concluding remarks

Conflict in child protection work

Conflict involving colleagues, between agencies, among multidisciplinary professionals and between practitioners and the families they intervene with are occupational hazards of child protection social work. Often, such conflicts can be productive, leading to new approaches to old problems. More commonly, they are anxiety-provoking and, sometimes, frightening. This book has sought to explore the nature of conflict in child protection, the thoughts and emotions it evokes in social workers, and how these impact on their practice in situations of dispute. In doing so, it has relied on theories of conflict and aggression largely propounded by social psychologists. Remarkably little research, or theory-building based on it, has been undertaken by social work scholars in the UK. While much consideration in the literature has been given to the impact of stress on practitioners, far less has been devoted to the effects of conflict and aggression.

Surveys of child protection social workers, discussed in Chapter One, revealed the extent to which they are exposed to conflict and often aggression in their employment. These surveys also pointed out the gaps in training and support systems to assist practitioners confronted by uncooperative and hostile parents or their partners. More qualitative evidence produced from public and independent inquiries, alongside a string of serious case reviews, draws attention to insufficient skills among a proportion of front-line workers and inadequate comprehension of the aggressive behaviour of family members by some line managers. Ultimately, improving the capabilities of both practitioners and their managers rests not only on better training, but also on an acknowledgement that aggression can characterise interactions with a small, yet substantial, proportion of families. Among other families, who are both frightened and frustrated by social work interventions, verbally aggressive outbursts or the prospect of physical attack can intimidate and frighten practitioners in turn. The case studies used in this book are admittedly extreme examples of conflict and aggression. Nevertheless, they foreground the dynamics of conflict, the inhibitions of social workers, denial among management and the factors that contribute to aggression.

Social workers in Britain inhabit a professional culture shaped by the expectation that they should absorb the stress caused by under-resourced and over-proceduralised work environments, while aggressive incidents with families are commonly perceived to be part of the job or blamed on the practitioner. Workplace conflict, and the stress emanating from it, increases irritability and makes it more difficult for social workers to exercise self-control and avoid aggressiveness towards colleagues and caregivers alike. Treating aggression by family members towards social workers as routine, or faulting practitioners for most incidents, ignores the evidence from social psychology about the nature of aggression and its sources in childhood experiences, substance misuse and mental health problems. This is not to deny, as Case Study 9.2 clearly illustrated, that social workers can contribute to, or provoke, aggressive behaviour from parents, their partners or children. The important point is to recognise when the aggression of family members is conveying vital information about the increased risk to a child or is endangering the health and safety of a social worker.

Case Studies 3.1 and 3.2, based on reports of events surrounding the deaths of Victoria Climbié and Baby Peter, analysed how under-resourcing and organisational arrangements can increase workplace conflict and, concomitantly, the stress, frustration and irritability of practitioners. This analysis also suggested that organisation-wide problems are often acted out as interpersonal conflicts between front-line staff. Munro (2010, 2011), who examined the child protection system in England after the serious case review into Baby Peter's death, revealed many inadequacies and made a number of recommendations for improvement. These included: removing statutory timescales for the completion of assessments on families; reducing the amount of data collected for performance management purposes; and removing prescriptive national guidelines for forms and information technology (IT) systems. These were to be accompanied by better supervision and caseload monitoring. While some progress has been made on these recommendations, the improvements they should bring to front-line child protection practice are being stalled by cutbacks to administrative posts, the freezing of social work positions, reductions in preventive services; persistently high caseloads; and ongoing difficulties in obtaining quality supervision (*Community Care Online*, 2012a, 2012b; BASW, 2012). Although the Munro reforms promise much, the financial crisis of 2008 and the colossal budgetary constraints that the government has imposed upon the public sector mean that practitioners will operate in working environments characterised by relatively high caseloads for the foreseeable future. For this reason, and despite the passage of time since the events surrounding the deaths of Victoria Climbié and Peter Connelly, the insights into conflict between professionals revealed by subsequent investigations remain salient.

Integrative negotiation, which is predicated on the search for and recognition of shared goals, is promoted to address workplace disputes. Many such issues will need to be resolved through discussion with management. Case Study 4.1, which returned to the Victoria Climbié inquiry, and Case Study 4.2, which explored events surrounding the abuse of children in a residential home, examined communication between staff and management. Dispute with a more powerful individual adds further complexity to conflicts for many front-line social workers. Negative beliefs about managers and worries concerning retaliatory responses can inhibit practitioners from open and constructive negotiation with team leaders or supervisors. But social workers can also be inhibited by aspects of their own socialisation in relation to asserting rights and articulating opinions. These inhibitions also have implications for their practice with professionals from other teams or agencies.

Case Studies 5.1 and 5.2, based on the Climbié inquiry report and the independent inquiry into the sexual abuse of children by two foster carers, respectively, explored the factors that can impede social workers from articulating their standpoints and the consequences of this for child protection practice. The case studies illustrated the power dynamics that often operate between individuals and how these contribute to non-assertive or aggressive interactions between colleagues and within the multidisciplinary team. The importance of integrative negotiation as a means of resolving disputes is again demonstrated. Case Studies 5.2 and 6.1, in particular, demonstrated how uncooperative and aggressive caregivers can play upon the inhibitions and vulnerabilities of some social workers to demoralise them and frustrate their interventions. The need for practitioners to develop their self-confidence and capability for self-assertion was highlighted.

Case Studies 6.2, 7.1 and 7.2 focused on work with resistant and reluctant caregivers. They explored the nature of non-cooperation, the employment of diversions and the use of aggression to distract or deter social workers from pursuing lines of enquiry, completing assessments or gaining access to children. These case studies also examined the sources of caregivers' aggression and the skills social workers need to develop to successfully challenge those who engage in these tactics. Case Study 8.1, drawing on events leading up to the death of Richard Fraser, and Case Study 8.2, which describes the behaviour of parents who eventually killed their infant daughter Ainlee Labonte, are concerned with how the threat of physical violence by caregivers affects social workers and influences their practice. These case studies described the cycles that underpin anger and physical assault and explored how social workers can reduce their anxiety and improve risk management with support from their agency.

The conflicts between social workers and parents or their partners in Case Studies 6.2, 7.1 and 7.2 are mediated by the fundamental principle, enshrined in British and international law, that children's welfare is best met by being brought up within their own families, if necessary with support from the state. Although this injunction protects the human rights of both child and parent, the requirement for partnership-working with caregivers that flows from it creates profound stresses for social workers confronted by persistent aggressive behaviour from parents, their partners or other family members. Emotional exhaustion and reluctance to challenge caregivers for fear of provoking yet another aggressive altercation can diminish the persistence and capacity of social workers to make appropriate *demands for work* upon parents and to insist on meaningful engagement with their children.

Finally, Case Studies 9.1 and 9.2 centred on practice with children. The first study identified the challenges that confront practitioners working with children who are highly aggressive, but also in need of care and protection. It investigated approaches to dealing with violence and the impact that experiencing an assault can have on social workers. By contrast, Case Study 9.2, set in a children's home, focused on the capacity of social workers to feel anger towards service-users and how this can be aggressively acted out. It investigated how practitioners can themselves contribute to aggressive altercations with children and, by inference, with caregivers as well. Links were made between beliefs that some practitioners may harbour and aggressive responses to the reasonable concerns and points of dispute voiced by children, young people or caregivers. Anger reduction techniques, which can assist social workers to stay in control of themselves and, hence, the situation, were recommended. These offer potential for de-escalating an angry dispute and averting a conflict spiral between worker and child.

Separate case studies have been used to illustrate and explore different practice issues and to identify a range of essential theories, strategies and skills for working with conflict and aggression. However, these do not comprise discrete packages of knowledge or abilities to be deployed in specific circumstances. Assertiveness, integrative negotiation and anger de-escalation techniques are each as relevant to working with colleagues and managers as they are to working with parents, their partners, substitute carers or children. Many of the case studies have demonstrated how agency context can increase the potential for conflict with colleagues and diminish the ability of social workers to make effective *demands for work* upon caregivers or to effectively address the aggressive behaviour of some parents, partners or children. Child protection practice is one of the most challenging areas of social work, requiring courage, compassion, self-awareness and a tremendous degree of self-control. This book endeavours to instil these vital qualities and to build the capacity of social workers to protect children at risk of significant harm.

Appendix

Williams, C. (2010) *Overcoming anxiety, stress and panic: a five areas approach*, **London: Hodder Arnold.**
This is a self-help guide to address stress and anxiety, which can induce anger and precipitate aggressive behaviours. It takes readers through a number of exercises, both written and practical, to try and reduce stressful and anxious feelings while also suggesting ways of managing these more constructively.

Dryden, W. (2000) *Overcoming anxiety*, **London: Sheldon Press.**
This self-help guide is written from a cognitive behavioural perspective and offers insights into how thoughts and beliefs can contribute to feelings of anxiety and panic. The author presents a range of exercises to increase self-awareness and describes a number of techniques to successfully manage anxiety.

Back, K. and Back, K. (2005) *Assertiveness at work*, **Maindenhead: McGraw-Hill.**
This is a generic self-help guide written for any worker in any employment situation. It explores a range of typical workplace problems, including excessive workloads and conflicts with colleagues and managers. It assists the reader to develop assertiveness skills by demonstrating the linkages between beliefs and actions through a number of workplace examples.

Dryden, W. (2004) *Assertiveness step by step*, **London: Sheldon Press.**
This self-help guide is written from a cognitive behavioural perspective and explores how beliefs about oneself, people and situations can impair self-assertion. The book explains blocks to assertiveness and presents worked examples to illustrate how assertiveness can be developed and put into practice.

Lindenfield, G. (2000) *Managing anger: simple steps to dealing with frustration and threat*, **London: Thorsons.**
This self-help guide to managing one's own anger commences with a set of exercises to improve self-awareness of anger and resentment. It then suggests a number of techniques for reducing feelings of anger and for responding assertively, rather than aggressively, in situations that cause annoyance and frustration.

References

Ahmadi, F. (2006) 'Islamic feminism in Iran', *Journal of Feminist Studies in Religion*, vol 22, no 2, pp 33–53.

American Psychiatric Association (2000) *Diagnostic and statistical manual of mental disorders IV*, Washington, DC: American Psychiatric Association.

Anderson, C.A. and Anderson, K.B. (1984) 'Ambient temperature and violent crime: tests of the linear and curvilinear hypotheses', *Journal of Personality and Social Psychology*, vol 46, pp 91–7.

Anderson, C.A. and Anderson, K.B. (1996) 'Violent crime rate studies in philosophical context: a destructive testing approach to heat and Southern culture of violence effects', *Journal of Personality and Social Psychology*, vol 70, pp 740–56.

Anderson, C.A., Deuser, W.E. and DeNeve, K.M. (1995) 'Hot temperatures, hostile affect, hostile cognition, and arousal: tests of a general model of affective aggression', *Personality and Social Psychology Bulletin*, vol 21, pp 434–48.

Anderson, C.A., Anderson, K.B. and Deuser, W.E. (1996) 'Examining an affective aggression framework: weapon and temperature effects on aggressive thoughts, affect, and attitudes', *Personality and Social Psychology Bulletin*, vol 22, pp 366–76.

Anderson, C.A., Bushman, B.J. and Groom R.W. (1997) 'Hot years and serious and deadly assault: empirical tests of the heat hypothesis', *Journal of Personality and Social Psychology*, vol 73, pp 1213–23.

Argyle, M. (1994) *The Psychology of Social Class*, London: Routledge.

Back, K. and Back, K. (2005) *Assertiveness at Work*, Maindenhead: McGraw-Hill.

Bácskai, E., Czobor, P. and Gerevich, J. (2011) 'Gender differences in trait aggression in young adults with drug and alcohol dependence compared to the general population', *Progress in Neuro-Psychopharmacology & Biological Psychiatry*, vol 35, pp 1333–40.

Baldwin, N. and Carruthers, L. (1998) *Developing neighbourhood support and child protection strategies: The Henley Safe Children Project*, London: Ashgate.

Baldwin, N. and Spencer, N. (1993) 'Deprivation and child abuse: implications for strategic planning in Children's Services', *Children and Society*, vol 7, no 4, pp 357–75.

Balloch, S. and McLean, J. (1999) 'The changing nature of work', in S. Balloch, J. McLean and M. Fisher (eds) *Social services – working under pressure*, Bristol: The Policy Press, pp 43–60.

Bandura, A. (1983) 'Psychological mechanisms of aggression', in R.G. Geen and E.I. Donnerstein (eds) *Aggression: theoretical and empirical reviews: volume 1*, New York, NY: Academic Press, pp 1–40.

Bandura, A., Ross, D. and Ross, S.A. (1963) 'Imitation of film-mediated aggressive models', *Journal of Abnormal and Social Psychology*, vol 66, pp 3–11.

Barking and Dagenham Safeguarding Children Board (2010) *Serious case review: services provided for Child T and Child R August 1997–February 2010*, London: Barking and Dagenham Safeguarding Children Board

Barnett, O.W. and LaViolette, A.D. (1993) *It could happen to anyone: why battered women stay*, Newbury Park, CA: Sage.

BASW (British Association of Social Workers) (2012) *The state of social work 2012*, Birmingham: The British Association of Social Workers.

Baumeister, R.F. (1999) *Evil: Inside human violence and cruelty*, New York: Freedman.

BBC News (2009a) 'Mother's anger after boy attacks', 4 September. Available at: http://news.bbc.co.uk/1/hi/england/south_yorkshire/8237710.stm (accessed 30 July 2011).

BBC News (2009b) 'Boys' mother "fed them cannabis"', 3 September. Available at: http://news.bbc.co.uk/1/hi/england/south_yorkshire/8235661.stm (accessed 30 July 2011).

BBC News (2010a) 'Spending review: cuts are "child protection challenge"', 21 October. Available at: http://www.bbc.co.uk/news/education-11598317 (accessed 11 April 2012).

BBC News (2010b) 'Boys' brutal attack "preventable"', 18 January. Available at: http://news.bbc.co.uk/1/hi/programmes/newsnight/8459938.stm (accessed 30 July 2011).

BBC News Birmingham and Black Country (2011) 'Ryan Lovell-Hancox murder: lessons learned "are not new"', 23 June. Available at: http://www.bbc.co.uk/news/uk-england-birmingham-13892076?print=true (accessed 13 July 2011).

Bell, M. (1999) 'Working in partnership in chid protection: the conflicts', *British Journal of Social Work*, vol 2, no 93 pp 437–55.

Benjamin, L.S. (1993) *Interpersonal diagnosis and treatment of personality disorders*, New York, NY: Guilford.

Berne, E. (1968) *Games people play*, London: Penguin.

Bettencourt, B.A. and Miller, N. (1996) 'Sex differences in aggression as a function of provocation: a meta-analysis', *Psychological Bulletin*, vol 119, pp 422–47.

Bower, S. and Bower, G.A. (2004) *Asserting yourself: a practical guide for positive change*, Stanford, CA: Perseus Books.

Braithwaite, R. (2001) *Managing aggression*, London: Routledge.

Brandon, M., Bailey, S., Belderson, P., Gardner, R., Sidebotham, P., Dodsworth, J., Warren, C. and Black, J. (2009) *Understanding serious case reviews and their impact: a biennial analysis of serious case reviews 2005–07*, London: Department for Children, Schools and Families.

Breakwell, G.M. (1997) *Coping with aggressive behaviour*, Leicester: The British Psychological Society.

Broadhurst, K., Wastell, D., White, S., Hall, C., Peckover, S., Thompson, K., Pithouse, A. and Davey, D. (2010) 'Performing "Initial Assessment": identifying the latent conditions for error at the front-door of local authority children's services', *British Journal of Social Work*, vol 40, pp 352–70.

Brockman, M. and McLean, J. (2000) *Review paper for the National Task Force: violence against social care staff*, London: National Institute for Social Work Research Unit.

Brown, L., Callahan, M., Strega, S., Walmsley, C. and Dominelli, L. (2009) 'Manufacturing ghost fathers: the paradox of father presence and absence in child welfare', *Child and Family Social Work*, vol 14, no 1, pp 25–34.

Budd, T. (1999) *Violence at work: findings from the British Crime Survey*, London: Home Office.

Bushman, B.J. (1995) 'Moderating the role of trait aggressiveness in the effects of violent media on aggression', *Journal of Personality and Social Psychology*, vol 69, pp 950–60.

Butler, P. (2010) 'Intimidated staff were left cowed and confused', *The Guardian*, 28 July.

Carpenter, S. and Kennedy, W.J.D. (1988) *Managing public disputes*, San Francisco, CA: Jossey-Bass.

Catalano, R., Dooley, D., Novaco, R.W., Wilson, G. and Hough, R. (1993) 'Using ECA survey data to examine the effect of job layoffs on violent behaviour', *Hospital and Community Psychiatry*, vol 44, pp 874–9.

Chermack, S.T., Murray, R.L., Walton, M.A., Booth, B.A., Wryobeck, J. and Blow, F.C. (2008) 'Partner aggression among men and women in substance use disorder treatment: correlates of psychological and physical aggression and injury', *Drug and Alcohol Dependence*, vol 98, pp 35–44.

Community Care (2011a) 'Two out of three social workers threatened by aggressive parents', 17 November, pp 4–5, Sutton: Community Care.

Community Care (2011b) 'Blog: bullying rife', 23 June, p 13, Sutton: Community Care.

Community Care (2011c) 'Paperwork is not social work', edited by Daniel Lombard, 19 May, pp 30–1, Sutton: Community Care.

Community Care Online (2010) 'What can social workers do when the workload gets too much?', 23 September. Available at: http://www.comunitycare.co.uk/blogs/social-work-front-line-focus/2010/09/what-can-social-workers-do-when-the-workload-gets-too-much (accessed 6 June 2011).

Community Care Online (2011) 'Alarm as children are endangered by child protection cuts', 13 April. Available at: http://www.communitycare.co.uk/Articles/13/4/2011/116655/alarm-as-children-are-endangered-by-child-protection-cuts.htm (accessed 11 April 2012).

Community Care Online (2012a) 'What difference has Munro made to frontline social work?', 28 May. Available at: http://www.communitycare.co.uk/Articles/28/05/2012/118250/What-difference-has-Munro-made-to-frontline-social-work.htm (accessed 13 July 2012).

Community Care Online (2012b) 'Munro urges government to speed up social work reforms', 22 May. Available at: http://www.communitycare.co.uk/Articles/22/05/2012/118230/Munro-urges-government-to-speed-up-social-work-reforms.htm (accessed 22 May 2012).

Community Care Online (2012c) 'Child protection plans up 60% since 2006', 16 April. Available at: http://www.communitycare.co.uk/Articles/16/04/2012/118142/research-reveals-60-rise-in-child-protection-plans.htm (accessed 24 April 2012).

Community Care Online (2012d) 'Annual care applications to CAFCASS hit all-time high', 11 April. Available at: http://www.communitycare.co.uk/Articles/11/04/2012/118138/care-applications-to-CAFCASS-hit-all-time-high.htm (accessed 11 April 2012).

Community Care Online (2012e) 'Record child referrals push social workers to breaking point', 9 February. Available at: http://www.communitycare.co.uk/Articles/09/02/2012/117972/record-child-referrals-push-social-workers-to-breaking-point.htm (accessed 18 February 2012).

Davey, B. (1999) 'Discrimination at work', in S. Balloch, J. McLean and M. Fisher (eds) *Social services – working under pressure*, Bristol: The Policy Press, pp 107–28.

Davies, W. and Frude, N. (2004) *Preventing face-to-face violence: dealing with anger and aggression at work*, Leicester: The APT Press.

Department of Health (2000) *Framework for the assessment of children in need and their families*, London: Stationery Office.

Dollard, J., Doob, L.W., Miller, N.E., Mowrer, O.H. and Sears, R.R. (1939) *Frustration and aggression*, New Haven, CT: Yale University Press.

Dominelli, L. (1997) *Anti-racist social work*, Basingstoke: Macmillan.

Dominelli, L. (2002a) *Anti-oppressive social work theory and practice*, Houndmills: Palgrave Macmillian.

Dominelli, L. (2002b) *Feminist social work theory and practice*, Basingstoke: Palgrave.

Doncaster Local Safeguarding Board (2009) *Serious case review 'J' Children: overview report*, Doncaster: Doncaster Local Safeguarding Board.

Doncaster Local Safeguarding Board (2010) *Serious case review 'J' Children: the executive summary*, Doncaster: Doncaster Local Safeguarding Board.

Dowson, J.H. and Blackwell, A.D. (2010) 'Impulsive aggression in adults with attention-deficit/hyperactivity disorder', *Acta Psychiatrica Scandinavica*, vol 121, pp 103–110.

Dumas, J.E., Blechman, E.A. and Prinz, R.J. (1994) 'Aggressive children and effective communication', *Aggressive Behaviour*, vol 20, pp 347–58.

Egan, G. (1990) *The skilled helper: a systematic approach to effective helping*, Belmont, CA: Wadsworth.

Faupel, A., Herrick, E. and Sharp, P. (2011) *Anger management: a practical guide*, London: Routledge.

Featherstone, B. (2003) 'Taking fathers seriously', *British Journal of Social Work*, vol 33, no 2, pp 239–54.

Featherstone, B. (2009) *Contemporary fathering*, Bristol: The Policy Press.

Felson, R.B. and Tedeschi, J.T. (1993) 'Social interactionist perspectives on aggression and violence: an introduction', in R.B. Felson and J.T. Tedeschi (eds) *Aggression and violence: social interactionist perspectives*, Washington, DC: American Psychological Association, pp 1–10.

Ferguson, H. (2011) *Child protection practice*, Basingstoke: Palgrave Macmillian.

Frost, N. and Parton, N. (2009) *Understanding children's social care: politics, policy and practice*, London: Sage.

Furness, S. and Gilligan, P. (2010) *Religion, belief and social work*, Bristol: The Policy Press.

Gantner, A.B. and Taylor, S.P. (1992) 'Human physical aggression as a function of alcohol and threat of harm', *Aggressive Behaviour*, vol 18, pp 29–36.

Garno, J.L., Gunawardane, N. and Goldberg, J.F. (2008) 'Predictors of trait aggression in bipolar disorder', *Bipolar Disorders*, vol 10, pp 285–92.

Geen, R.G. (2001) *Human aggression*, Buckingham: Open University.

Gibbons, J., Conroy, S. and Bell, C. (1995) *Operating the child protection system*, London: HMSO.

Goldstein, P.J. (1995) 'The drugs/violence nexus: a tripartite conceptual framework', *Drug Issues*, vol 15, pp 493–506.

Greenberg, J.S. (2008) *Comprehensive stress management*, New York, NY: McGraw-Hill.

Guardian Online (2010) 'Council at centre of Edlington torture case to face investigation', 25 January. Available at: http://www.guardian.co.uk/society/2010/jan/25/edlington-torture-doncaster-council-investigation (accessed 30 July 2011).

Haringey Local Safeguarding Children Board (2009) *Serious case review: Baby Peter: executive summary*, Haringey: Local Safeguarding Children Board.

Haringey Local Safeguarding Children Board (2010) *Serious case review 'Child A'*, London: Department for Education.

Hawkins, P. and Shohet, R. (2006) *Supervision in the helping professions*, Maidenhead: Open University Press McGraw-Hill Education.

HCPC (Health & Care Professions Council) (2012) *Standards of proficiency – social workers in England*, London: Health & Care Professions Council.

Health and Safety Executive (2000) 'Management of health and safety at work. Management of health and safety at work regulations 1999. Approved code of practice and guidance L21'. Available at: www.hse.gov.uk (accessed 20 February 2011).

Health and Safety Executive (2006) *Essentials of health and safety at work*, Caerphilly: Health and Safety Executive.

Health and Safety Executive (2011) 'The health and safety executive statistics 2009/10'. Available at: http://www.hse.gov.uk/statistics/overall/hssh0910.pdf (accessed 20 February 2011).

HM Government (2010) *Working together to safeguard children: a guide to inter-agency working to safeguard and promote the welfare of children*, London: Department for Children, Schools and Families.

HM Treasury and Department for Education and Skills (2007) *Policy review of children and young people – a discussion paper*, London: The Stationery Office.

Hogben, M. (1998) 'Factors moderating the effect of televised aggression on viewer behavior', *Communication Research*, vol 25, pp 220–47.

Hopwood, C.J., Morey, L.C., Markowitz, J.C., Pinto, A., Skodol, A.E., Gunderson, J.G., Zanarini, M.C., Shea, M.T., Yen, S., McGlashan, T.H., Ansell, E.B., Grilo, C.M. and Sanislow, C.A. (2009) 'The construct validity of passive-aggressive personality disorder', *Psychiatry*, vol 72, no 3, pp 256–67.

Horejsi, C., Garthwait, C. and Rolando, J. (1994) 'A survey of threats and violence directed against child protection social workers in a rural state', *Child Welfare*, vol 73, no 2, pp 173–9.

Isenhart, M.W. and Spangle, M. (2000) *Collaborative approaches to resolving conflict*, Thousand Oaks, CA: Sage.

Ito, T.A., Miller, N. and Pollock, V.E. (1996) 'Alcohol and aggression: a meta-analysis on the moderating effects of inhibitory cues, triggering events, and self-focused attention', *Psychological Bulletin*, vol 120, pp 60–82.

Kaplan, S.G. and Wheeler, E.G. (1983) 'Survival skills for working with potentially violent clients', *Social Casework*, vol 64, June, pp 339–46.

King, U. (1993) *Women and spirituality: voices of protest and promise*, London: Jessica Kingsley.

Kool, V.K. (2008) *Psychology of nonviolence and aggression*, Houndmills: Palgrave Macmillan.

Koritsas, S., Coles, J. and Boyle, M. (2010) 'Workplace violence towards social workers: the Australian experience', *British Journal of Social Work*, vol 40, pp 247–71.

Krahé, B. (2001) *The social psychology of aggression*, Hove: Psychology Press.

Laird, S.E. (2008) *Anti-oppressive social work: a guide for developing cultural competence*, London: Sage.

Laird, S.E. (2011) 'Complaints are a form of intimidation too', *Community Care*, 6 October, p 17.

Laming, H. (2003) *The Victoria Climbié inquiry: report of an inquiry by Lord Laming*, Cmnd. 5730, London: HMSO.

Látalová, K. (2009) 'Bipolar disorder and aggression', *International Journal of Clinical Practice*, vol 63, no 6, pp 889–99.

Látalová, K. and Praško, J. (2010) 'Aggression in borderline personality disorder', *Psychiatric Quarterly*, vol 81, pp 239–51.

Lazarus, R.S. and Folkman, S. (1984) *Stress, appraisal and coping*, New York, NY: Springer.

Levy, A. and Kahan, B. (1991) *The Pindown Experience and the Protection of Children: The Report of the Staffordshire Child Care Inquiry 1990*, Stafford: Staffordshire County Council.

Lewicki, R.J., Barry, B. and Saunders, D.M. (2010) *Negotiation*, New York, NY: McGraw-Hill.

Lindenfield, G. (2000) *Managing anger*, London: Thorsons.

Linsley, P. (2006) *Violence and aggression in the workplace*, Oxford: Radcliffe Publishing.

Linszen, D.H., Dingemans, P.M.A.J., Nugter, M.A., Van der Does, A.J.W., Scholte, W.F. and Lenior, M.A. (1997) 'Patient attributes and expressed emotion as risk factors for psychosis relapse', *Schizophrenia Bulletin*, vol 23, pp 119–30.

Littlechild, B. (2005a) 'The stresses arising from violence, threats and aggression against child protection social workers', *Journal of Social Work*, vol 5, no 1, pp 61–82.

Littlechild, B. (2005b) 'The nature and effects of violence against child-protection social workers: providing effective support', *British Journal of Social Work*, vol 35, pp 387–401.

Littlechild, B. (2008) 'Child protection social work: risks of fears and fears of risks – impossible tasks from impossible goals?', *Social Policy & Administration*, vol 42, no 6, pp 662–75.

Lloyd, C., King, R. and Chenoweth, L. (2002) 'Social work, stress and burnout: a review', *Journal of Mental Health*, vol 11, no 3, pp 255–65.

London Borough of Greenwich (1987) *A child in mind: the report of the commission of inquiry into the circumstances surrounding the death of Kimberly Carlile*, London: London Borough of Greenwich.

London Borough of Lambeth (1982) *Richard Fraser: 1972–1977. The report of the independent inquiry*, London: London Borough of Lambeth.

Lovallo, W.R. (2005) *Stress and health: biological and psychological interactions*, London: Sage.

Lytle, A.L., Brett, J.M. and Shapiro, D.L. (1999) 'The strategic use of interests, rights, and power to resolve disputes', *Negotiation Journal*, vol 15, no 1, pp 31–51.

Macdonald, G. and Sirotich, F. (2001) 'Reporting client violence', *Social Work*, vol 46, no 2, pp 107–14.

McBride, P. (1998) *The assertive social worker*, Aldershot: Arena.

McNabb, D.E. (2010) *Case research in public management* Armonk, NY: M.E. Sharpe.

MIND (2005) *Stress and mental health in the workplace*, London: MIND.

Munro, E.M. (2010) *The Munro review of child protection. Part one: a systems analysis*, London: The Stationery Office.

Munro, E.M. (2011) *Munro review of child protection: final report: a child-centred system*, Cm 8062, London: The Stationery Office.

National Task Force on Violence against Social Care Staff (2001) *Report and National Action Plan*. Available at: www.dh.gov.uk/en/Publicationsandstatistics/Publications/PublicationsPolicyAndGuidance/DH_4010625 (accessed 4 October 2010).

Nelson-Jones, R. (2008) *Basic counselling skills: a helper's manual*, Los Angeles, CA: Sage.

Newham Area Child Protection Committee (2002) *Ainlee Labonte: Chapter 8 Review*, London: Newham Area Child Protection Committee.

Newhill, C.E. (2003) *Client violence in social work practice: Prevention, intervention and research*, New York: Guilford.

Nicotera, A.M. and Robinson, N.M. (2010) 'Culture and aggressive communication', in T.A. Avtgis and A.S. Rancer (eds) *Arguments, aggression, and conflict: new directions in theory and research*, London: Routledge, pp 100–23.

NSPCC (2008) *Poverty and child maltreatment*, London: NSPCC.

Ofsted (Office for Standards in Education, Children's Services and Skills) (2010) *Learning lessons from serious case reviews 2009–2010*, London: Office for Standards in Education, Children's Services and Skills.

Ofsted, Healthcare Commission and HM Inspectorate of Constabulary (2008) *Joint area review: Haringey children's services authority area*, London: Office for Standards in Education, Children's Services and Skills, Healthcare Commission and HM Inspectorate of Constabulary.

O'Neill, H. (1999) *Managing anger*, London: Whurr.

Ostrov, J.M. and Houston, R.J. (2008) 'The utility of forms and functions of aggression in emerging adulthood: association with personality disorder symptomology', *Journal of Youth Adolescence*, vol 37, pp 1147–58.

Pahl, J. (1999) 'Coping with physical violence and verbal abuse', in S. Balloch, J. McLean and M. Fisher (eds) *Social services: working under pressure*, Bristol: The Policy Press, pp 87–105.

Paik, H. and Comstock, G. (1994) 'The effects of television violence on antisocial behavior: a meta-analysis', *Communication Research*, vol 21, pp 516–46.

Paterson, B. and Leadbetter, D. (1999) 'De-escalation in the management of aggression and violence: towards evidenced based practice', in J. Turnbull and B. Paterson (eds) *Aggression and violence: approaches to effective management*, Basingstoke: Macmillan.

Ringstad, R. (2005) 'Conflict in the workplace: social workers as victims and perpetrators', *Social Work*, vol 50, no 4, pp 305–13.

Ross, J.M. and Babcock, J.C. (2009) 'Proactive and reactive violence among intimate partner violent men diagnosed with antisocial and borderline personality disorder', *Journal of Family Violence*, vol 24, pp 607–17.

Rowett, C. (1986) *Violence in social work*, Institute of Criminology Occasional Paper No 14, Cambridge: Cambridge University.

Seligman, M.E.P (1975) *Helplessness*, San Francisco, CA: W.H. Freeman & Co.

Sell, A. (2011) 'Applying adaptationism to human anger: the recalibration theory', in P.R. Shaver and M. Mikulincer (eds) *Human aggression and violence: causes, manifestations and consequences*, Washington, DC: American Psychological Association, pp 53–70.

Shelton, N. and Burton, S. (1995) *Assertiveness skills*, West Des Moines, IA: American Media Publishing.

Shepherd, E. (2007) *Investigative interviewing*, Oxford: Oxford University Press.

Shulman, L. (1992) *The skills of helping: individuals, families and groups*, Itasca, IS: Peacock.

Sinclair, I. and Gibbs, I. (1998) *Children's homes: a study in diversity*, Chichester: Wiley & Son.

Smith, M. and Nursten, J. (1998) 'Social workers' experience of distress: moving towards change?', *British Journal of Social Work*, vol 28, pp 351–68.

Social Work Task Force (2009) *Building a safe, confident future: the final report*, London: Department for Children, Schools and Families.

Soskis, D.A. and Ochberg, F.M. (1982) 'Concepts of terrorist victimization', in F.M. Ochberg and A.D. Soskis (eds) *Victims of terrorism*, Boulder, CO: Westview Press, pp 105–36.

Spidel, A., Lecomte, T., Greaves, C., Sahlstrom, K. and Yuille, J.C. (2010) 'Early psychosis and aggression: predictors and prevalence of violent behaviour amongst individuals with early onset psychosis', *International Journal of Law and Psychiatry*, vol 33, pp 171–6.

Stanley, J. and Goddard, C. (1995) 'The abused child as a hostage: insights from the hostage theory on pathological attachment and some developmental implications', *Children Australia*, vol 20, no 1, pp 24–9.

Stanley, J. and Goddard, C. (2002) *In the firing line: violence and power in child protection work*, Chichester: Wiley.

Steiner, C. (1990) *Scripts people live*, New York, NY: Grove Press.

Stopes-Roe, M. and Cochrane, R. (1990) *Citizens of this country: the Asian-British*, Clevedon: Multilingual Matters.

Swartz, M.S., Swanson, J.W., Hiday, V.A., Borum, R., Wagner, H.R. and Murns, B.J. (1998) 'Violence and severe mental illness: the effects of substance abuse and nonadherence to medication', *American Journal of Psychiatry*, vol 155, pp 226–31.

SWRB (Social Work Reform Board) (2011) *Standards for employers of social workers in England and supervision framework,* London: SWRB

Tedeschi, J.T. and Felson, R.B. (1994) *Violence, aggression and coercive actions*, Washington, DC: American Psychological Association.

Tedeschi, J.T. and Nesler, M.S. (1993) 'Grievances: development and reactions', in R.B. Felson and J.T. Tedeschi (eds) *Aggression and violence: social interactionist perspectives*, Washington, DC: American Psychological Association, pp 13–45.

The Telegraph (2010) 'Mother kills autistic son by forcing him to drink bleach', 15 November. Available at: www.telegraph.co.uk/news/uknews/crime/8134315/Mother-kills-autistic-son-by-forcing-him-to-drink-bleach.html (accessed 16 September 2011).

Thompson, N. (2006) *Anti-discriminatory practice*, Houndmills: Palgrave Macmillian.

Thompson, N., Murphy, M. and Stradling, S. (1994) *Dealing with stress*, Houndmills: Macmillan.

TUC (Trades Union Congress) (2007) 'Bullying at work: guidance for safety representatives'. Available at: www.tuc.org.uk/workplace/tuc-13809-f0.cfm (accessed 27 April 2011).

TUC (2011) 'Know your rights – bullied at work'. Available at: www.tuc.co.uk/tuc/rights_bullyatwork.cfm (accessed 27 April 2011).

Underwood, M.K. (2003) *Social aggression among girls*, New York: Guilford Press.

Unison (2002**)** *Bullying at work: guidance for safety representatives*, London: Unison.

Unison (2009) *Time for a change: UNISON local government survey 2008*, London: Unison.

Upson, A. (2004) *Violence at work: findings from the 2002/03 British Crime Survey Home Office report 02/04*, London: Home Office.

Ury, W. (1991) *Getting past no: negotiating with difficult people*, New York, NY: Penguin.

Volavka, J. and Citrome, L. (2008) 'Heterogeneity of violence in schizophrenia and implications for long-term treatment', *International Journal of Clinical Practice*, vol 62, pp 1237–45.

Wakefield City Council (2007) *Independent inquiry report into the circumstances of child sexual abuse by two foster carers in Wakefield*, Wakefield: Wakefield City Council.

Walker, P. (2010) '"Toxic family life" of Edlington brothers', *Guardian Online*, 22 January. Available at: http://www.guardian.co.uk/uk/2010/jan/22/toxic-family-life-edlington-brothers/print (accessed 30 July 2011).

Walker, P. and Wainwright, M. (2010) 'Edlington brothers jailed for torture of two boys', *Guardian Online*, 22 January. Available at: www.guardian.co.uk/uk/2010/jan/22/edlington-brothers-jailed-torture-boys (accessed 30 July 2011).

Walsh, E., Gilvarry, C., Samele, C., Harvey, K., Manley, C., Creed, F., Murry, R. and Fahy, T. (2001) 'Reducing violence in severe mental illness: randomised controlled trail of intensive case management compared with standard care', *British Medical Journal*, vol 323, pp 1093–6.

Wardlaw, G. (1982) *Political terrorism theory, tactics and counter-measures*, Cambridge: Cambridge University Press.

Waterhouse, R. (2000) *Lost in care: report of the tribunal of inquiry into the abuse of children in care in the former county council areas of Gwynedd and Clwyd*, London: The Stationery Office.

Wheeler, M. (1999) 'First let's kill all the agents', in R.H. Mnookin and L.E. Susskind (eds) *Negotiating on behalf of others*, Thousand Oaks, CA: Sage, pp 235–62.

White, S., Wastell, D., Broadhurst, K. and Hall, C. (2010) 'When policy o'erleaps itself: the "tragic tale" of the Integrated Children's System', *Critical Social Policy*, vol 30, no 3, pp 405–29.

Wiehe, V.R. (1998) *Understanding family violence*, Thousand Oaks, CA: Sage.

Wilmot, C. (1998) 'Public pressure: private stress', in R. Davies (ed) *Stress in social work*, London: Jessica Kingsley, pp 21–32.

Williams, C. (2010) *Overcoming anxiety, stress and panic*, London: Hodder Arnold.

Wolverhampton Safeguarding Children Board (2011) *Executive summary Child J*, Wolverhampton: Wolverhampton Safeguarding Children Service.

Wood, W., Wong, F.Y. and Chachere, J.G. (1991) 'Effects of media violence on viewers' aggression in unconstrained social interaction', *Psychological Bulletin*, vol 109, pp 371–83.

Wright, K.B. and Craig, E.A. (2010) 'Aggressive communication: a life span perspective', in T.A. Avtgis and A.S. Rancer (eds) *Arguments, aggression, and conflict*, London: Routledge, pp 44–66.

Yin, R.K. (1994) *Case study research: design and methods*, London: Sage.

Index

Page numbers in *italics* refer to tables and boxes. Page numbers ending in *App* refer to the appendix